S   Hatton

The Complete
Book of
Cockatiels

The Complete Book of Cockatiels

DIANE GRINDOL

WITH PHOTOGRAPHS
BY THE AUTHOR

HOWELL BOOK HOUSE
NEW YORK

Howell Book House
A Simon & Schuster Macmillan Company
1633 Broadway
New York, NY 10019

Macmillan Publishing books may be purchased for business or sales
promotional use. For information please write: Special Markets
Department, Macmillan Publishing USA, 1633 Broadway, New York,
NY 10019.

Library of Congress Cataloging-in-Publication Data:
Grindol, Diane.
    The complete book of cockatiels/by Diane Grindol; with photos by
the author.
    p. cm.
    ISBN 0-87605-178-6
    1. Cockatiel.   I. Title.
SF473.C6G75   1998
636.6'8656—dc21   97-53094
                                                   CIP

Manufactured in the United States of America
10 9 8 7 6 5 4 3 2 1

Book Design: Scott Meola
Cover Design: George Berrian

Dedication

This book is dedicated to Dacey, among cockatiels. This book is also dedicated to Marilyn and Fred Grindol, as thanks for instilling in me a sense of wonder and the freedom to pursue my dreams.

Dacey, the gray hen cockatiel to whom this book is dedicated. She has had seventy chicks in her lifetime and has been a companion, mother and patient sojourner in my life. This photo was taken when she was eight years old. As I write this, she is sixteen years old.

Contents

Acknowledgments

I always used to wonder how acknowledgments in books got to be so long. I have a much better idea now! This book really represents the last fifteen years of my life, my love for cockatiels during that time and the many ways they have been a part of my life. It is with the support and guidance of many people that I have been able to grow in cockatiel companionship. It is for their contributions over this time, as well as during the actual writing of this book, that I wish to acknowledge the following people and their contributions to my life and my life's work. I stress, however, that the ideas in this book, and any responsibility for the actual words printed here, are mine. I have chronicled my actions, techniques and opinions, but do not assume any liability for the outcome when you use this advice.

Thank you, Jennifer Hubbard of the Pet Bird XPress—this book wouldn't be if it weren't for her! Beth Adelman has been an extraordinary champion of this book at Howell Book House. She has made the dream and vision a reality. Thank you Virginia (Ginny) Tata-Phillips, for proofreading, offering frank comments and friendship throughout this and many previous works.

Other contributors to *The Complete Book of Cockatiels* deserve accolades. Thank you, thank you Thomas E. Roudybush, MS, for contributing a large section to the book. Thanks also for your contributions to aviculture, and for moral support as we explore the paths in life both more and less traveled.

Thank you Catherine Toft, PhD, for being a silly aviculturist sometimes, one of those cockatiel owners who loves every feather of every bird in their care. Thank you, Cathy, for your professional contribution of a chapter on genetics.

Thanks to James Millam, PhD, for carrying on the work of the Psittacine Research Project, and for his contribution to this work.

Both Elsie and Herschel Burgin have contributed an enormous amount to raising quality mutation cockatiels, and Herschel has graciously captured their beauties on film for this book.

David Wrobel introduced me to cockatiel photography, and his work is included in this book as well. Several people have contributed their stories, so that you might know what it's *really* like to live with a cockatiel!

I appreciate the support of my friends in birds over the years. They have contributed, at least indirectly, to this work: Roberta Hawks for bird sitting and rescuing me when I was in need; Doris Wilmoth for being a traveling companion; Dorothy Clarke for being a friend and bird lover; Karen Gilbert for the extraordinary care she takes of her birds; Jo Miller-Cole for her dedication to aviculture; Mary Wittekind and Kathi Flood for helping me learn how to successfully show cockatiels; Stephen Fowler for listening; Al McNabney, Laurella Desborough, Joanne Abramson and Brent Andrus for their enthusiasm and diligence; Alan and BettyAnn Hedegard for friendship, guidance and understanding; Diana Guerrero for a place to light and friendship; Eb Cravens for his gentle, enlightened view of aviculture.

I appreciate the professional and technical support supplied by Thomas Roudybush, MS, Catherine Toft, PhD, Ann Brice, PhD, Michael Murray, DVM, Branson Ritchie, DVM, Blake Hawley, DVM and Kaytee, Inc., James Millam, PhD, and Thomas Tully, Jr., DVM.

Thanks for their ongoing work in being responsible for companion birds in our society, those dedicated souls who have taken on parrot rescue and adoption work, including: Bonnie Kenk, Judy Sacconago, Mary De Mattei, Jean Sangster, Mickaboo and Vivian Daoust.

I also want to acknowledge the contributions of editors at Fancy Publications. Over the years they have provided a forum for my writing, inspiration and support. These include Angela Davids, Amy Taylor, Kathleen Etchepare, Melissa Kauffman and publisher Norman Ridker.

Thanks for "being" with me and being powerful: Cookie Boudreau, Gretchen Leavitt, Robin Nelson, Randy McNamara, Sheri Lewis, Bob Muson and Genevieve Muson at Landmark Education Corp.

Stories and interviews contributed by:

Dorothy Clarke	John Kastenholz
Jo Miller-Cole	Roberta Malmgren
Christine Conneau	Billie Peck
Elisa DeSimone	Glenn Stallard
Karen Gilbert	Garry Walberg
Janet Golden-Motto	

Paintings contributed by:

Carol Cottone-Kolthoff	Nancy Kasten

Introduction

COCKATIEL
NYMPHICUS HOLLANDICUS (KERR)

Kingdom: Anmalia

Phylum: Chordata

Class: Aves

Order: Psittaciformes

Family: Cacatuidae

Genus: *Nymphicus*

Species: *hollandicus*

To go way back in the cockatiel's family tree, we're pretty sure that birds in general have somehow descended from dinosaurs. Exactly which dinosaurs might have evolved into modern birds is actually a hot topic in that discipline. But the basic fact is widely accepted, and if you've ever observed a nest of baby cockatiels before they get their feathers, you would be even more sure that this is truly their evolutionary past. Birds still retain reptilian or dinosaur-like scales on their legs. Babies have huge, scaled feet and make prehistoric noises when confronted by intruders in their nest.

Ornithologists have debated about where to place the cockatiel in the bird world. Does the cockatiel belong with the parrots or cockatoos? Anatomically, cockatiels share some characteristics with other cockatoos, such as an erectile crest, a gall bladder and powder down patches.

Research in the 1980s and '90s has supported the theory that the cockatiel should indeed be placed in the cockatoo family. And DNA research at the University of California–Davis in 1997 (conducted by David M. Brown and Catherine A. Toft) shows that the cockatiel probably belongs to a branch of the cockatoo family that includes the red-tailed black cockatoo (*Calyptorhynchus banksii*) and gang-gang cockatoo (*Callocephalon fimbriatum*) as well as the cockatiel (*Nymphicus hollandicus*). So, you own a little cockatoo.

(Nancy Kasten)

Unlike our canine and feline pets, which are each one species, companion birds can be any one of hundreds of species. Different species of birds are adapted to different environments in the wild. It is therefore useful as an aviculturist (keeper or breeder of birds) to know something about a bird's native habitat and natural behavior. That makes it all the more likely you can provide similar conditions in captivity, and so have birds that thrive.

The success of the cockatiel as an aviary bird is probably due, in large part, to the fact that it is adapted to very harsh conditions. Instead of a rainforest species adapted to the abundance of a lush tropical environment, the cockatiel is adapted to the desert of dry, inland Australia. Food is neither plentiful, varied nor rich. Temperatures in this environment range from about 40°F up to 110°F. It's no wonder our favorite feathered wonders have proven to be so adaptable and so hearty, even when kept in less-than-ideal conditions. (I feel strongly that there's a difference between surviving and thriving, so I can't recommend only minimal care for your companion.)

This is Davis, a normal gray male cockatiel. Recent DNA research shows that cockatiels are little cockatoos. They are most closely related to the red-tailed and yellow-tailed black cockatoos, and gang-gang cockatoos.

It's not difficult to believe that birds are descended from dinosaurs when you see cockatiel chicks. They have scaly feet, feathers just erupting in a regular pattern, and they hiss like reptiles if threatened. These two would be out of sight in a nest hole, nest box or brooder if they weren't posing. Cockatiels have babies only a mother could love! (*David Wrobel*)

A cockatiel is one of the few companion birds that have been kept for several generations in captivity. We are starting to produce birds that are adapted to the captive environment, which means we're on the way to having a truly domesticated species of companion bird. There are many color mutations available, they breed readily and their history in captivity in the United States is quite long. My challenge to bird breeders is to recognize this and purposefully breed good companion cockatiels. Encouraging the qualities of tameness, personableness and a quiet companion that is not stressed by life with humans is important.

Let's examine some of the history of the cockatiel as it lives in the wild and in captivity. Although this is a book based largely on personal experience, I am relying heavily in this chapter on cockatiel enthusiasts who have written down available history and who have seen cockatiels in the wild in Australia.

Cockatiels in the Wild

Wild cockatiels are gray birds and are generally smaller than our captive cockatiels. Their coloration blends in well with the Australian grasslands. On the wing, cockatiels are described as "conspicuous and noisy." Why am I not surprised? Everyone who sees wild cockatiels remarks on their swift, sure flight, with whole flocks of cockatiels whirring about.

According to Matthew M. Vriends, PhD, the cockatiel is common in Australia. Joseph Forshaw, in *Parrots of the World*, shows that cockatiels live in most of inland Australia and are found all the way to the coast in the northwest. He has sighted them in pairs in parks near Adelaide. Forshaw reports that cockatiels are found in open country, especially near water. In the north, they congregate in large flocks and are nomadic, while in southern Australia they're more migratory.

Cockatiels are reportedly not timid and are curious about humans. Wild gray cockatiels are, of course, dimorphic (the sexes are colored differently), as are their pet cousins. A male gray cockatiel, after his first molt at about six months old, acquires a bright yellow head. Both females and juveniles have gray heads with only a hint of yellow above the nostrils and along the jowls. The underside of a male's tail becomes solid black, instead of the barred yellow and black of female and juvenile cockatiels.

In Australia, cockatiels eat more grain than Australian farmers would like. They're something of a pest. Their natural diet consists of food grasses and plants, grain, fruits and berries. They reportedly are fond of acacia seeds, and have been seen eating mistletoe berries as well as raiding crops such as sorghum. I've always understood that our American mistletoe was poisonous, so don't run out and try offering it as a delicacy.

Sunshine, a pied cockatiel, and Mathilda, a pearl hen, are two of the many companion cockatiels in the United States. Cockatiels are the second most popular pet bird. (*David Wrobel*)

Breeding season in Australia depends on rainfall. Cockatiels nest between August and December, but may start as early as April. Cockatiels are opportunistic breeders. When there is an abundance of what they require to raise chicks—water and new grasses growing seeds with which to feed young—they will go to nest. Cockatiels nest in hollow limbs or a hole in a tree, usually a large hollow in a eucalyptus standing near water. They lay four to seven eggs on a bed of decayed wood dust in the bottom of the hollow. Incubation takes twenty-one to twenty-three days.

Young birds leave the nest four to five weeks after hatching. Reports I can find leave me wondering how long chicks stay with their parents, and what they are taught. How do they learn to fly, bathe and forage for food? When do they strike out on their own? Are flocks composed of family members? There is still much to be learned.

Cockatiels in Captivity

To the best of our knowledge, a team of natural science researchers, Bank and Solander, visited Australia

A BIRD BY ANY OTHER NAME

Throughout its history, the cockatiel has been known by a variety of names, both common and scientific. The cockatiel in *The Naturalist Library* had the interesting name of *Nymphious novae hollandiae,* and one of the common names that became widely used when naturalists John and Elisabeth Gould were doing their research is *corella.* The present use of cockatiel, spelled that way, with the scientific name *Nymphicus hollandicus,* was popularized by a Mr. E.J. Boosey in 1956, and the nomenclature has stuck with us to this day.

According to literature on the subject, there are numerous names by which the cockatiel has been, and still is, known. In history, the cockatiel has been dubbed the crested ground parakeet, gray parrot, yellow-top-knotted parrot, cockatoo parrot and even cockateel.

In Australia today it might be a quarrion or top-knot parrakeet. Aborigines know the cockatiel as a weero, or by one of many other names. Reportedly, the cockatiel goes by weelarra, wamba, bula-doota, toorir and woo-raling in western Australia.

in 1770 on the *Endeavour* with the explorer Captain James Cook. Their observations of bird life included what was probably the first sightings by Europeans of the cockatiel. It is surmised that they saw cockatiels in what is now New South Wales.

Naturalist John Gould and his wife Elisabeth explored Australia between 1838 and 1840, and created a great number of beautiful illustrations of Australian birds, which were published in a series of bird books. There is a painting of a cockatiel the Goulds made in 1840 in Volume X of *The Naturalist Library.*

In 1846 there were cockatiels displayed in the famous Jardin des Plantes in Paris. In 1850 the cockatiel was successfully bred in Germany, and in 1863 the birds were bred in the London Zoo. In 1865 the first successful breeding was reported in the Netherlands, 1870 in Belgium, 1881 in Switzerland, 1900 in India and 1920 in Japan.

By 1884 the cockatiel, by that name, was a well-known aviary bird in Britain. By 1902 authors hardly felt the need to describe the species, once they mentioned it, because it was so well known. In 1910 cockatiels were first bred in the United States, and they have since become a well-known companion and aviary bird here.

In most surveys, the cockatiel is the second most frequently kept pet bird in the United States, second only to the parakeet (which is properly called a budgerigar). There are reasons for this popularity, which we will explore in depth in this book.

CHAPTER 1

Choosing a Companion Cockatiel

Are you aware that a companion cockatiel will scream, bite and poop? You may be reading this book because you are trying to learn more about the cockatiel you already own, in which case I'm not telling you anything you don't know. Your companion cockatiel screams, bites and poops. In this book, I'll try to help you make all of those habits easier to deal with. But if you don't have a cockatiel of your own yet, be aware that this is true, so you know what you are getting into.

Your cockatiel might also return affection, whistle lovely tunes or nestle against your cheek. It will probably live for quite a long time and entertain you with its antics.

I believe people often give up their pets to rescue organizations and other homes because the pets didn't meet their expectations. So I advise some realistic ones for you!

The Costs of Care

The cost of a cockatiel companion is relatively minor, especially compared with the cost of other parrots. The cost of owning any bird is more than its initial price, however, and you should be aware of all the expenses involved. These include an initial "well bird" exam by an avian veterinarian within the first few days after you acquire the bird, then regular, periodic checkups to monitor your cockatiel's weight and health.

The cost of a cockatiel also includes the cost of its living quarters. These may range from a cage that fits on a table top to a flight cage or aviary enclosure. The cost of housing might exceed the cost of your bird. In that housing there will be food and water bowls, food, a calcium source, perches and toys. You might decide to have a

1

cover for the cage and must provide shelter of some kind for cockatiels who live outside.

After considering all of the apparent costs of keeping a cockatiel, think about the surprise costs. What will you do with your bird when you are on vacation? You may be able to find a friend, neighbor or family member to take care of your companion, but you may also need to hire a pet sitter or take your cockatiel to a boarding facility.

There could be unexpected veterinary expenses, as well. Cockatiels are exceedingly curious, and companion cockatiels are often out

and about in our homes. This can lead to disastrous encounters with other creatures or with doors, or to cockatiels eating objects that should never be eaten by a bird. Later in this book you'll find some tips on avoiding these types of emergencies, but of course they still could happen. That's the nature of an emergency. Cockatiels are made to prove Murphy's Law. If there's a way for a cage or a toy to become unsafe, there's usually a cockatiel willing to attack the problem.

Why a Cockatiel?

Not the least important of your considerations are your reasons for wanting a cockatiel. Will a cockatiel please you as a companion? If you are thinking of a pet bird in general, it's helpful to look at what qualities in a bird are the most appealing to you. Some of these qualities include appearance, speech ability, noise level, song, status, cuddliness, sex and care requirements. Look at each of these qualities in turn when considering a pet bird, so that you are matched with a bird who fits into your lifestyle. Ask yourself how a cockatiel will fit in with your preferences.

Realistically, your companion cockatiel will scream and poop, and it may bite, as even this lovely cinnamon hen, Carmelita, does. Are you ready? (David Wrobel)

The cost of a cockatiel, such as this pearl-pied hen, exceeds the cost of the bird. Don't forget about a cage, veterinary care, food and toys.

APPEARANCE

In appearance, the cockatiel is very elegant. There are many mutation colors available for different tastes, and the color doesn't affect health or personality. All cockatiel color mutations are in the gray, white, cream, yellow and brown range.

If you must have a bright scarlet bird, then the cockatiel is not for you—unless you can settle for that endearing orange cheek patch.

In size, the cockatiel is a small parrot. There are smaller parrots, but the cockatiel is definitely in that category. That can be a plus if you have limited space or are looking for a parrot with a smallish beak. You might have your windowsills, door frames and antiques around for a while longer.

The cockatiel also comes with a smaller price tag than some of the larger parrots, and can live as long as or longer than many dogs—probably fifteen to twenty years or more.

SPEECH AND NOISE

If what you are absolutely looking for in a companion bird is speech ability, a cockatiel may not measure up. A male cockatiel may learn to say some words or phrases, but it can't be guaranteed. In my experience, young birds who were placed in households where they were talked to a lot, and where they were the only bird, learned to talk most successfully. It seemed to help if they were from parent birds that were vocal or talked, as well.

Bozo, a male pied cockatiel, has a pleasant appearance with his bright cheek patches. Cockatiels don't come in the flashy, brilliant hues of some tropical parrots, but they do come in a variety of color mutations. Any color cockatiel makes a good pet. *(David Wrobel)*

Will you be happy with a cockatiel companion? This albino cockatiel has certainly found a good home! Cockatiels are usually cuddly companions and are elegant in appearance, but they can't be expected to talk.

If talking ability is a nice extra for you—something you're willing to try to elicit and risk failing—then you can still consider a cockatiel. You might be one of the lucky ones who has success. Most male cockatiels can learn to whistle, and most cockatiels learn to communicate, even if they are not using human-type speech.

A cockatiel has many qualities to offer in compensation for limited speech ability. After experiencing some bird vocalization, you might also come to appreciate the more reserved nature of a female cockatiel.

Speech ability and noise level can be related. The parrots who vocalize the most are the ones most apt to try vocalizing in a different language (including our language). That means the noisier your bird, the more likely it is to speak. And parrots who live with vocal people—people who talk to them—have a leg up on speech ability.

Even if you enjoy the noise, it can be a concern to your neighbors. I know a woman who bred parrots in a condominium without any complaints from her deaf neighbor. How tolerant are your neighbors? Do you plan to keep your cockatiel

Two male cockatiels, a cinnamon and a normal gray. Males are more likely to talk, and usually learn to whistle.

STATUS

Status is one reason people buy exotic birds. Cockatiels can't compete with the larger parrots for status. If you want to look cool and impress your friends, a big, colorful, macho bird is probably what you are aiming for. If you really want status, however, I would also suggest getting a post office box at an impressive address and a hot red convertible.

The point is, status and pets just don't mix. All birds are sensitive creatures with special needs and more intelligence than our other

inside or out? Can you consider a loud bird, or do you need to keep to the lower decibel range? Can you or your neighbors live with a cockatoo's screams that greet the day and proclaim their love of life? Cockatiels are quieter than most cockatoos, and as far as noise level is concerned, they are usually a good choice. But they are not silent.

Bird vocalization ranges in pitch as well as loudness. Listen to the bird species you are considering. Can you tolerate high-pitched calls? Some people really don't like a cockatiel's natural call. Cockatiels use it when they are calling to another cockatiel, or calling to you when you come home or if you're in another room. It's obnoxious right in your ear, but can be nice

from a distance. Make sure you think so before you buy a cockatiel.

Considering the range of volume and pitch offered by the various denizens of the bird world, cockatiel calls are usually well tolerated by neighbors and often accepted even in apartments.

If you prefer song to noise, cockatiels are not your best bet. While some male cockatiels learn to whistle lovely tunes, they can't ever compete with the melodies of canaries or the calls of some softbilled birds. I have had cockatiels who learned to imitate canaries when they were both housed in the same room. The rolling notes came out in cockatiel—about an octave lower than the original version—and were very interesting!

LESSONS FROM CLEMENT

I might never have shared my life with a cockatiel were it not for a friend's bird who showed me how sweet, affectionate and personable a bird can be. I once thought pet birds looked pretty and stayed in a cage. I thought care consisted of picking up a box of seed with a picture of a cockatiel on it from the grocery store.

My understanding changed when I met Clement. He came out of his cage. He liked having his head scratched. He ate a variety of foods. And there is no question that both Carole (his owner and my college roommate) and Clement had better lives as a result of their interactions.

typical companion animals. They deserve to be in homes where their social and intellectual needs are met, rather than to be displayed as status symbols.

CUTE AND CUDDLY

In the cuddliness category, cockatiels are right up there on the list. If you want a companion bird you can touch and who likes to be with you, a cockatiel is a good choice.

A companion cockatiel that has established a trusting relationship with its owners is not unlike a dog. It loves to be with its people, interacts with them, entertains them and exhibits affection. If you aren't looking for a cuddly bird, consider a more independent species, or consider providing your cockatiel with a companion cockatiel or parakeet. Cockatiels are social birds who appreciate company and interaction.

WHICH SEX?

I know of households who have adopted a "same-sex" rule for their avian companions: Their birds are all the same sex, even if they are of different species, because they don't want the birds to breed. Sex may also be a factor in your choice.

Either a male or female cockatiel can make a good pet. If you're getting a baby bird, it's just as well that both sexes are friendly, since with

Cockatiels do not make good surprise gifts. They can be a fifteen- to twenty-year responsibility. Give a cage, a book or a photo instead of a bird, and let your loved ones pick out their own birds—once they're sure they want to take on the responsibility. Ashley, a cinnamon-pied cockatiel, is pictured here. *(David Wrobel)*

most cockatiel color mutations young cockatiels look like females, then molt into their adult coloring at about six months of age. There are more than a few cockatiels with unisex names and, of course, the boys named Sue and the Henrys that became Henriettas.

Some of the color mutations are sex-linked (more on that later), and some clutches are thus color-coded: Males are one color, females another. Or a certain color bird, especially a cinnamon, pearl or lutino, from certain parents can only be a female. A knowledgeable breeder just might be able to tell you if your baby is a girl or a boy—but not always.

Does it matter? If you're just getting one cockatiel companion, it doesn't matter much. Both sexes are good companions and usually stay tame. If you want to try to teach your bird to talk, a male is more likely to do so. He's also

likely to be more verbal overall. Females tend to be more cuddly, males more aggressive and generalizations not to be true.

The truth is that cockatiel personality varies more from individual to individual than it does by sex. There's nothing more important than loving your own bird and appreciating its personality.

CARE CONSIDERATIONS

It's a good idea to read about cockatiel care requirements before getting one. If you are considering another bird species, do the same. Are you willing to commit to meeting all the needs of the bird companion you choose? Cockatiels can survive poor conditions very well, since they are native to harsh desert terrain. But surviving is not the same as thriving. They thrive with exercise, baths, a good diet and social time. Compare their requirements to a rain forest native or a songbird, if you're looking at many species.

Sources of Birds

Once you've decided you want a cockatiel, or another cockatiel, it's time to find a source. Cockatiels are common companion birds. There are local cockatiel breeders in many areas and a network of national breeders. Cockatiels are often found for sale in pet stores and newspaper want ads, and sometimes friends or co-workers will be looking for a home to place their cockatiels. This should make it easy for you to be selective about choosing your own companion cockatiel. But you will need to know what to look for and what questions to ask.

How can you find a good source from which to adopt a life companion? You will want to look for important qualities in both the bird and its seller. It is important that you get a healthy bird, a health guarantee and answers to questions about your new companion. I suggest getting a referral to a responsible bird breeder or pet store. Other bird owners, bird club members and avian veterinarians should all be able to help you find such a source.

Your needs will depend on your plans for your bird. Do you plan to keep a single bird as a pet, or will you be breeding cockatiels? Will

you be breeding show cockatiels to exhibition standards, or will you be breeding pet cockatiels? These are all valid considerations that should guide your search.

If you are breeding birds, health is paramount and information on genetics will be important. You might be glad to obtain an older bird that is ready for breeding or even a proven breeder. Tameness will be of less importance, though it can be an asset.

Many people in the national bird societies are involved in exhibition and breeding to show standards. You will want to attend some shows and get to know more about breeders and judges who are involved in this fancy, in order to invest in the right cockatiels. If you want to get involved in exhibiting your cockatiel, it is also wise to attend a few shows and get to know the exhibitors as well as the judges. Volunteering to help at a show is one way to do so. And this will really help you get to know the people you need to ask for referrals.

I strongly believe there are many cockatiels out there who would do well in shows. To recognize them, you will want to learn the standards and see some show winners. Then look at the quality of birds in the aviaries and stores near you. Such things as color mutation, lack of genetic baldness, length of crest, evenness and distribution of color are important in

If you plan to exhibit cockatiels in shows, look for offspring from proven winners. Mathilda, a pearl hen, is a champion cockatiel. Her regal bearing proved to be an asset at shows.

show birds, and you need to know what you are looking for.

If you are looking for a companion bird, you want a healthy bird of a pleasing color. A handicapped bird is not out of the question, or one missing a toenail or a toe, if it is healthy in other ways. You want a tame bird, and customer support from the pet shop, breeder or rescue organization where you obtain the cockatiel.

Though it can never be guaranteed that your new cockatiel will become the companion you dream of, you'll have a better chance if you obtain a young cockatiel that has been hand fed or handled extensively as a youngster. It is important that the cockatiel be already weaned, so that it is eating and drinking on its own. It is not necessary to hand feed a baby cockatiel for it to bond to you. Hand feeding and weaning are best performed by experienced people who know what to do. (There are so many things that can go wrong, and specialized equipment is required.)

Preferably, your young cockatiel should be from seven to eight weeks up to about four months old. It should be weaned to a pelleted diet and should accept a variety of foods. If possible, your bird should be socialized and know how to get onto your finger. Some cock-

atiels are shyer than others about strangers, so a baby won't necessarily come right up to you. You should be prepared to continue socializing and training your young bird.

Second-Hand Pets

I encourage you to consider a second-hand pet as a companion cockatiel or for breeding cockatiels as a hobby. Cockatiels are common birds, and there are often birds that need homes because of changes in people's lifestyles, health or situation. There are numerous bird placement organizations and club programs that specialize in finding homes for birds in need, as well.

I like to promote responsibility among cockatiel owners, and it seems to me that one of those responsibilities is attending to finding homes for our birds throughout their lives. There is a network of dog and cat rescue facilities throughout the United States that serve as centers for adopting those companion animals, and a similar network for birds is starting to form.

It is very possible that you can find an adult pet bird who is tame. Some of the advantages of a previously owned cockatiel are that you already know the bird is (or is not!) tame. You know its sex and some of its habits. Either it is quiet, noisy, a talker or shy. If you adopt an adult bird for breeding, you don't have to wait for it to grow up.

There are disadvantages to adopting adult companion birds, as well. If you are dealing with private owners through newspaper ads, or with friends, they might not stand behind the quality of their animal. You might not get a health guarantee, all the information you need or background material on a cockatiel's genetics or lineage.

If you adopt from a placement organization, you should be prepared to fill out a rather long questionnaire and promise to return the bird to the organization if you can no longer care for it. Remember that the goal of these organizations is to make sure the birds in their care are placed in loving, responsible, permanent homes. Most organizations will ask you to take your new cockatiel to see an avian veterinarian (at your expense). This is a good move for any new bird!

Sometimes the cockatiels that become available through breeders, friends and placement organizations are handicapped birds. A handicapped bird will be a happy companion and will accept its lot.

You have the best chance of realizing your dreams of a loving companion cockatiel if you purchase a young, hand-fed or tame baby cockatiel. You can see this gray cockatiel is young because it has a short, erect crest, female coloring and pale beak. It has a wide-eyed innocence about it, too.

WHY MICKABOO?

The Mickaboo Cockatiel Rescue operates out of the San Francisco Bay area. The name comes from founders Tammy and Ellen's own first birds: Mickey and Aboo. Their love for these birds was their inspiration for starting a bird adoption center.

They rescued Dylan (a normal gray cockatiel) in 1996. His previous owners had kept him in a tiny cage in a dark corner his whole life. He never came out of his cage, and he was given seed and water whenever they remembered.

His beak was so overgrown from malnutrition that both the upper and lower beak had grown completely together and Dylan had been unable to eat for about a week. He had feces sticking to his rear end, and he could not preen because of his overgrown beak. So he could neither eat nor eliminate.

Dylan was taken to a veterinarian immediately, where his beak was trimmed. He received vitamins by injection once a week to counter severe vitamin deficiencies.

He required a beak trim every couple of weeks, and at first would only eat millet. After eight months, he learned to eat pellets and green leafy vegetables. He looked 100 percent better!

Dylan is really sweet, doesn't bite at all, loves to come out of his cage and play, and loves showers. He still needs an occasional beak trim, but is otherwise healthy.

Mickaboo Cockatiel Rescue has no idea how old Dylan is, but he looks like a little old man. All the same, he's quite a success story.

Unlike humans, who tend to worry about the past, future and what other people think, birds simply accept what is. A handicapped bird will not be self-conscious or full of regret.

Handicapped cockatiels offer the same love and bonding as any cockatiel, and the owner has the satisfaction of providing a home to an animal that might have been difficult to place. However, if you decide to adopt a handicapped bird, you may have to make some special arrangements for the bird to get around and to have access to food and water. For some owners with limited mobility themselves, it is an advantage to have a bird companion who cannot fly away.

Many of the birds in placement organizations are smaller feathered companions. That probably has something to do with the value of these birds, or at least the value placed on them by their owners, since birds in a placement organization are usually donated.

To me, seeing cockatiels given up by their owners is a reminder of why we must always breed with care. We have our pick of cockatiels, so we can breed cockatiels with good pet qualities and good parenting skills. We should consider breeding more cockatiels only when there are responsible owners waiting for quality birds. We don't need to see birds in shelters.

Questions to Ask

When you get ready to buy your cockatiel, these are some questions you should ask before you acquire a bird.

How old is the bird?

Once it's mature, you can't tell from looking at a bird how old it is. If the bird is banded, there will be a date on the band. You should be buying a cockatiel that is at least seven weeks old *and* weaned. Some cockatiels don't wean till ten to twelve weeks old. The bird should be able to drink and eat on its own.

What sex is the bird?

The answer may be "unknown" if the bird is an immature chick. You get to be creative with unisex names—or guess. Stanley turned into Yetta in my flock. My friend had a boy named Sue and a girl named Johnny. Her children named them, assuming the lutino was a girl and the young gray a boy. The opposite proved to be true.

The answer may be obvious if you're looking at a full-grown male with a yellow head. Do your homework, though.

Is this bird banded?

In most states there is no legal requirement to band birds. However, responsible breeders usually want to keep track of their flock's genetics and identity. Bands may come from band companies, or cockatiel breeders can obtain traceable bands from the American Cockatiel Society, American Federation of Aviculture, National Cockatiel Society or the Society of Parrot Breeders and Exhibitors. Usually a band includes the year the bird hatched, the acronym of the organization that issued the

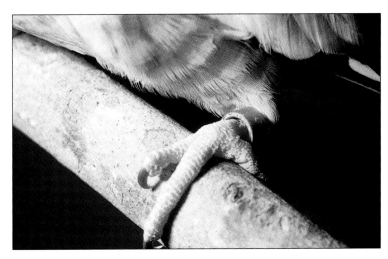

A cockatiel with a closed band that was put on the bird's leg when it was a young chick. The cockatiel's foot grew, and now the band does not come off. Write down your new cockatiel's band number; it is a means of certain identification. *(David Wrobel)*

band, a breeder's code and a number that is unique to the bird wearing the band.

Is this cockatiel tame? How do I handle it?

Even a tame cockatiel may be afraid of someone it doesn't know. The owner should show you how the bird is used to being handled. I train my cockatiels to go on my finger at a cluck, for example, and put my hand over their back to return them to their cage. Other

How old is the cockatiel you are getting? Will you be training a young chick, or has it learned behaviors at another household? Can you set the bird up for breeding, or do you need to wait? This is Lindbergh, a four-year-old lutino hen.

people may say "up" or have no verbal cue at all.

If you're a first-time owner, get suggestions from the source about working with your bird, if needed. Some tame birds love company and handling them is not a challenge at all. The challenge, then, is getting them off your shoulder!

What is this bird's diet?

I love to hear that a bird is eating a diet based on a formulated feed. It's important to keep the bird on the same diet during the stressful transition from one household to another. Often the seller will give you some of the feed when you pick up the bird, to get you started. Ask where you can obtain more.

Find out what supplemental items are being fed: vegetables, sprouts, pasta or bread, etc.?

Do you offer a health guarantee?

It's best to walk away if you don't get a health guarantee with the bird. You want to deal with responsible people. A good breeder or pet store knows there may occasionally be health problems in a flock. They want to know about and take care of any problems that may arise, and they are usually reasonably sure that you won't find anything serious. If you do, they stand behind their birds and make things right with you, the customer.

The normal health guarantee for a bird is three to five days, during which time you take the cockatiel, at your expense, to an avian veterinarian. If it is healthy, all's well. You must follow the terms of the guarantee if the bird is not healthy.

There are some things to look for in a health guarantee. Does the seller pay for medical treatment? Do you get another bird instead, or do you get your money back? It's my experience that people get very attached to their cockatiels in a short time. I've paid for a few courses of antibiotics when there were minor problems with birds I had sold, so that the buyer could keep the bird.

Can I call if I have questions?

You are going to have questions about your bird's behavior and care. A responsible bird seller or former owner will be glad to answer them.

Can you recommend an avian veterinarian in the area?

This is a resource you will need. If the seller cannot give you the name of a veterinarian, it's probably a good idea to find another seller. Your bird seller might also be able to recommend a bird club and local bird stores or bird fairs where you can buy accessories.

Do you know this cockatiel's pedigree?

You are more likely to get this information if you are buying show cockatiels. It is not as common to keep a pedigree of a bird as it is to keep one of a dog. However, if you ever breed your bird, a pedigree is helpful in knowing color genetics. If you are familiar with the birds or breeders on the pedigree, it might also tell you something about a bird's shape and appropriateness for exhibition.

If you intend to breed pet cockatiels, find out if the birds in the pedigree were good parents. Also find out if any of the ancestors were good talkers or had other special traits. If someone is breeding birds they can't tame, or birds that pick at their feathers or at other cockatiels, guess what's being passed along?

The Overview

You want a bird that is healthy, and you want to get it from responsible, caring people who will support you as you learn about cockatiels. There are a whole lot of variables that are your personal choices, but these basics should be beyond question.

Color Mutations in Cockatiels

A cockatiel is a cockatiel is a cockatiel. Although there are no subspecies or breeds of cockatiel, there are a range of color mutations. Because the cockatiel has been in captivity for a long time, breeders have had the chance to develop and establish color variations that occur naturally as mutations. In the wild this range of colors is not seen, since such a bird with an unusual color would stand out to a predator, and because closely related individuals might not choose to breed.

Color variety is part of what makes cockatiel ownership and breeding interesting. There is not much difference in personality among cockatiels of different colors, so you can choose the cockatiel you find beautiful and charming. However, with some mutations there are certain health concerns. Conscientious breeders are working on breeding out a bald spot in the lutino cockatiel, for example.

Normal Gray

This is the color of cockatiels in the wild. Genetically, many of our normal gray cockatiels carry the genes for mutation colors. It might be a wise conservation measure to develop a few flocks of pure gray cockatiels. Personally, I love gray cockatiels. I could never pick a favorite color, but I find the natural coloring of cockatiels to be beautiful.

Both sexes have gray bodies, gray beaks and feet, white wing patches and orange-red cheek patches. Mature males have solid yellow heads and black feathers on the underside of their tails. Females have gray heads with flecks of yellow, and barred yellow and black feathers on the underside of their tails. Juvenile cockatiels are marked like a female, but have pink beaks when they are young.

This is a normal gray hen. Young cockatiels have this coloring, too. *(Herschel Burgin)*

Sometimes a gray cockatiel will show its genetic heritage. A bird that is split pied (carries the recessive gene for pied coloring) may have a patch of light feathers at the nape of its neck, or may have both pink and gray pigment on its feet or beak.

Lutino

The lutino mutation first occurred in 1958 in Florida. All of our lutino cockatiels are descended from that bird. The original lutino belonged to C. Barringer and was purchased by Mrs. E.L. Moon, who is responsible for developing the lutino mutation.

Lutino is a popular color mutation. There is a lack of gray pigment

in lutinos, so their bodies are white to creamy yellow and show the striking contrast of the orange cheek patches. When babies, lutinos have yellow fuzz and red eyes, so it is apparent in the nest that a cockatiel is lutino.

Males and females still show a difference in barring under the tail feathers. This usually requires looking closely at the cockatiel in good light. The female will show faint barring, the mature male none.

Lutinos often have a bald spot behind their crest—one of the traits serious cockatiel breeders are trying to eliminate through responsible breeding.

This mutation is sex-linked. My foundation pair of gray cockatiels produced lutino, pearl and lutino-pearl offspring as well as gray chicks. I knew these were

This is a normal male gray cockatiel. *(Herschel Burgin)*

females, and that this meant the male was split to lutino and pearl. This was not evident visually, but through breeding him.

Pied

The pied pattern in cockatiels is another American mutation. It first appeared in the Southern California aviaries of R. Kersh and D. Putnam in 1949. Dale Thompson reported in an article in the *A.F.A. Watchbird* (August/September 1982) that in 1979 Mrs. Kersh was still working with the mutation.

The pied mutation results in a pattern of coloring that shows up

A lutino hen. Lutino is a sex-linked mutation.   *(Herschel Burgin)*

in many ways. There are usually blotches of color on the bird's body, and these can be any color that occurs in a solid-colored cockatiel. The bird may be predominantly white or predominantly colored. Among cockatiel fanciers, birds that are mostly white are called *heavy pied*, while colored birds are called *light pied*.

Pied cockatiels with white bodies, no blotches on their faces (called a *dirty face*) and patches of color at their shoulder are preferred for show. If the markings are symmetrical, the cockatiel is even more highly prized.Showing and breeding pied cockatiels becomes very interesting, striving for a well-proportioned and well marked bird!

A nicely marked pied cockatiel. *(Herschel Burgin)*

It is difficult to tell apart the sexes in pied cockatiels. Often behavior clues are the best way to tell. Pied birds that whistle, talk and court females are probably males. If you must know for sure, this is one color of cockatiel that you may want to have DNA sexed or surgically sexed.

Pied is a recessive mutation. Both a male and female cockatiel must show this trait or be split to pied in order to produce pied offspring. Solid color cockatiels often show that they are split pied by having a patch of light feathers on their nape, or a striped beak or light and dark pigment on their feet.

Pearl

The pearl mutation was first developed in 1967 in Germany. It has also been called the laced or opaline mutation. Pearl markings occur over the back and wings of a cockatiel. Each feather is gray with a yellow edging, or yellow and edged with gray. Heads are yellow, and tail feathers are barred black and yellow.

This mutation is dimorphic, with the male cockatiel making a striking change in color upon maturity. Starting at the first molt, at about six months old, the male pearl starts to lose its lacings and will eventually become a solid color. This transformation may take several years, and a few male pearls do

This pearl hen has yellow feathers edged with gray. *(Herschel Burgin)*

retain some pearled feathers or traces of their former coloring.

A pearl male will look like a normal gray, a cinnamon-pearl male like a cinnamon male, a silver-pearl male like a male silver, and so on. This makes records and banding important!

The pearl mutation is sexlinked, like the lutino and cinnamon mutation colors, so it can be carried by male cockatiels and show up in their female offspring. Of course, pearl offspring will be produced if a female is pearl and a male is either pearl or split pearl.

Cinnamon

The cinnamon is a solid-colored bird with dimorphic markings, just

A cinnamon male. This is also known as the Isabelle mutation in Europe. *(Herschel Burgin)*

like the normal gray cockatiel. Instead of gray, however, these birds are a warm brown cinnamon color. Sometimes cinnamons fade when housed outside or when they are genetically bred to have a marbled appearance.

The cinnamon mutation occurred in New Zealand in 1950, though our American cinnamons are from stock originating in Belgium in the late 1960s.

The cinnamon mutation is sex-linked. It can occur in combination with the other mutations, so there are cinnamon-pied cockatiels, cinnamon whiteface-pearls, and so on. A combination that does not work very well is cinnamon-lutino. The lutino masks the

cinnamon, but not always completely, so that some of these birds have a dirty tan appearance.

Whiteface

Whiteface cockatiels (originally called *charcoal*) lack yellow coloration. They have no cheek patches, either. This mutation sprang up in Europe in the late 1970s, and arrived in the United States in the mid-1980s.

Coloring is like that of normal grays, without any yellow. Males develop a white head and are quite striking. Females have small amounts of white on their face, and black-and-white barred tail feathers.

The whiteface mutation is recessive, like the pied mutation.

This is a whiteface-pearl cockatiel, a double mutation. It lacks any yellow pigment or cheek patch, but shows the pearl pattern. *(Herschel Burgin)*

A pair of whiteface cockatiels. The male has a white head. *(Herschel Burgin)*

Both parents must exhibit the mutation color or carry it in their genetic makeup to pass it on.

Albino

The albino bird has no pigmentation whatsoever. It has red eyes, a pink beak and feet, no cheek patch and pure white feathers. The albino is actually a double mutation: Albinos are lutino-whiteface cockatiels, to be exact.

Fallow

The origin of fallow cockatiels is unknown, although some appeared in either Europe or the United States in the early 1970s. Fallow cockatiels have red eyes and look like cinnamon birds with a heavy

This is a fallow male cockatiel. Fallows usually have a warm suffusion of yellow, especially on their head and chest. *(Herschel Burgin)*

This albino hen has no coloring at all. *(Herschel Burgin)*

This is a double factor dominant silver male. *(Herschel Burgin)*

suffusion of yellow. The fallow color varies from light to dark shades. This is a recessive mutation.

Recessive Silver

This silver mutation has been in existence since the late 1960s in Europe. It is a recessive mutation. Recessive silver cockatiels have red eyes, and their coloring is gray to fawn.

Dominant Silver

This is a relatively new mutation, with dark eyes, a metallic gray

Like all recessive silver cockatiels, this pair has red eyes. *(Herschel Burgin)*

body and a skull cap of darker plumage. Dominant silver is classified as single factor or double factor. (More about that in Chapter 14.)

Yellowface and Pastel

Yellowface cockatiels have an almost nonexistent yellow cheek patch. Pastel cockatiels have a light peach-colored cheek patch. These new mutations are mainly found at bird shows and in cockatiel breeders' aviaries, but they are becoming more widespread.

This normal pastel male has pale peach cheek patches. *(Herschel Burgin)*

A whiteface-dominant silver male. *(Herschel Burgin)*

This female yellowface-pearl shows a double mutation. *(Herschel Burgin)*

Double Mutations

You do not see cockatiels only in the colors and combinations described so far. That is because these colors and patterns can combine in striking ways. When a bird carries the genetic makeup to produce two mutations, for example, it can have chicks exhibiting either color, or both at the same time.

Some examples of double mutations are cinnamon-pearl, lutino-whiteface (albino), pearl-pied and whiteface-pied.

Triple Mutations —and More!

The multiple mutation phenomenon can be carried further, so that triple mutations and even more occur. This combination of traits makes breeding cockatiels *really* interesting, and makes some striking birds available to you as pets.

This probably isn't the definitive list of cockatiel mutation colors, either. The latest of these mutation colors have only appeared in the United States or Europe in the last few years. Who knows what's next?

When purchasing rare mutation cockatiels, look for breeders who are improving their lines by crossing out to large, healthy, established colors of cockatiel. This takes longer than breeding rare mutations together, but produces healthier birds with better conformation.

No matter what color your cockatiel, chances are it has a winning personality. Be sure to look beyond color and love your bird!

This lutino-pearl hen has a very subtle double mutation. The bird is white with yellow pearl lacings, and appears cream-colored from a distance. *(Herschel Burgin)*

This hen is a triple mutation: a white-face-cinnamon-pearl. *(Herschel Burgin)*

This is a quadruple mutation cockatiel: a yellowface-cinnamon-pearl-pied bird! *(Herschel Burgin)*

Routine Cockatiel Care

Keeping a companion bird is a kind of urban farming. You may find yourself rising with the sun and doing your daily chores. Of course, you may have invested in a cage cover and be in control of your avian companion's dawn! Then you'd rise with the alarm clock, but still need to attend to daily chores.

There are some other chores that you can do less frequently—weekly, or periodically. Some of these chores require attention to your bird's cage and surroundings. Others require you to attend to the grooming needs of your bird. In any case, it's important to remember cockatiels are not easy-care pets. I have friends who dress down and scrub cages every Sunday afternoon. Make sure you're ready to do the same before you acquire a cockatiel.

Daily Care

A bird cage needs to be cleaned daily. You may think you can skip a day, but it really is necessary to keep a bird's enclosure as clean as possible. I suggest changing the cage papers, food and water every day. It's also a good idea to clean the water cups or water dispensers daily, especially if you find that they get particularly slimy. They may need to be changed more than once a day, if the water gets soiled. The whole routine is up to you, but it is important to remember to keep your bird's environment really clean. Leftover food, water and droppings can grow molds and bacteria that are harmful to your bird.

There are some easy ways to accomplish daily cleaning. Some people layer paper on the bottom of the cage and just peel off the top layer each day. Keep a vacuum cleaner nearby and use it to keep your bird's area neat in

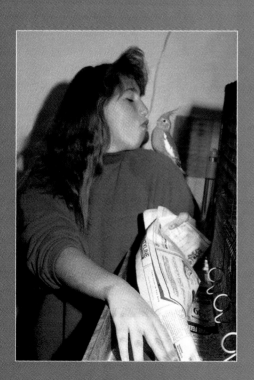

19

Davis is a mature male normal gray cockatiel. Like all cockatiels, he requires regular daily and weekly care.

the house. Clean outside enclosures with a rake or hose—whatever is appropriate. If you have an extra set of bird dishes, you can easily fill new ones and take your time about cleaning and disinfecting the old dishes.

Did I just say something about offering new food every day? Yes. For some reason I have cockatiels who like to spend their nights sitting on their food cups. I don't want to give germs a chance to grow in the cups, which usually contain a mixture of old feed, veggies and droppings. Give your cockatiel about the amount of food it will eat in a day. Don't fill the feed cup all the way to the top;

Richelle is cleaning bird cages, with help from a chick. Cage papers should be changed daily. Remember, as you clean, to watch for changes in droppings that might indicate a problem.

then you won't be wasting food by throwing the old away. At your leisure you can wash the used dishes out and leave them to dry for the next day.

During your daily routine you should also wipe off the bottom grid on the cage and remove any food residue on the bars. It will make weekly cleaning easier.

Weekly Care

I suggest routinely disinfecting bird dishes and wiping out the cage every week. There are many solutions you can use for disinfecting bird dishes. Disinfectants are used at various strengths, stay volatile for varying amounts of time and affect different germs. You may want to choose a disinfectant that does not do great damage to the environment, or that does not affect either your bird's health or your own skin. If your birds are fighting an infection or disease of any kind, follow your veterinarian's directions. You may need to use a disinfectant that will affect the particular organism you are fighting.

A standard disinfecting mixture used by aviculturists is one part bleach to nine parts water. Bleach has some special attributes to keep in mind: It acts as a disinfectant on items left to soak for about ten to fifteen minutes. It only remains active and useful for a short time, so you can't store this mixture. It is

Richelle Belanger is busy disinfecting her birds' food and water dishes.

affected by air and sunlight, and by the presence of organic matter. That means you should wash dishes before disinfecting them in bleach. Remember to use bleach in a well-ventilated area and to wear gloves. And don't ever mix bleach

Bleach does not work as well in the presence of organic matter, so you must wash dishes with soapy water before letting them soak in a bleach solution.

with ammonia products. After disinfecting them, rinse bird dishes very thoroughly with water, then wipe or air dry.

During your weekly cleanup, you can rotate toys, as well. For your cockatiel, this is like getting a whole new toy chest every week. The toys don't have to be brand new. Just take some toys out of the cage and put in others. Let each toy "rest" for a few weeks before you give it to your bird again.

Periodic Bird Chores

Periodically, there are other bird chores to do. When the cuttlebone and/or mineral blocks are either soiled or consumed, I replace them. Some cockatiels have the habit of using them as perches, and there are times of the year when cuttlebone is a favorite snack, especially for breeding birds. I also change perches a few times a year. I use natural branches, and the birds enjoy tearing off the bark from fresh branches and chewing on the softer wood. Fresh perches are a wonderful kind of natural toy for a while.

Grooming

Cockatiels need regular attention to their grooming. Usually this involves cutting some of a cockatiel's flight feathers in order to slow down or restrict its flight,

SOME FACTS ABOUT BLEACH

Bleach is essentially nontoxic and is not corrosive by any government regulatory definition. Bleach is, however, a skin and eye irritant. When it is accidentally swallowed by humans, the usual reaction is vomiting.

Bleach cannot build up in the environment. It breaks down rapidly and completely during use and disposal. Household bleach is a 5.25 percent solution of sodium hypochlorite and water. During use and disposal, 95 to 98 percent of the bleach quickly breaks down into salt. The remaining 2 to 5 percent breaks down to form byproducts that are effectively treated at municipal wastewater treatment plants or septic systems.

Bleach is designed to be mixed and used with water. It is safe for disposal down the drain, and does not need to be treated as household hazardous waste.

The Clorox Company puts out a periodic on-line newsletter. You can find it at http://www.clorox.com.

trimming nails and possibly trimming or shining its beak.

You have several options when it comes to care for your cockatiel. You can hire a professional to do this for you. Your avian veterinarian can do it for you, and at the same time he or she will be observing the outward health of your bird. Many pet stores offer bird grooming services, and bird breeders might be willing to do grooming as well. There are experienced bird owners who offer bird grooming services. Or, you can do these things yourself at home.

Often, I encourage new owners to have an experienced person show them how to groom their bird the first time or two. If they are comfortable with the procedures, they can then take over themselves. This is true for wing clipping and nail clipping. I don't think anyone but a veterinarian or experienced bird groomer should work with a bird's beak. In any case, most healthy cockatiels do not ever need their beak trimmed or groomed.

When doing your bird chores, change the cuttlebone if it is soiled, and offer new natural perches periodically.

Clipping Cockatiel Wings

Some people are really nervous about clipping their own cockatiel's wings. Usually at the root of their concern is the fact that they are afraid they will hurt their bird. Maybe we should call this procedure *clipping wing feathers* or *restricting flight*. Actually, a few of the bird's primary flight feathers are cut. Feathers that are fully grown in don't have nerves in them, and this doesn't hurt the bird. Some birds are upset by being handled or restrained. I encourage you to accustom your cockatiel to

handling so that this is not a stressful experience.

Wing clipping can be important when keeping pet cockatiels. It slows down a free-flying bird so it does not get hurt when banging into windows or mirrors. It also makes a cockatiel more dependent on its owner to get around. Sometimes wing clipping is all that is needed to tame down a sassy older bird. It also increases the chance of recovering a pet that has escaped out a window or door.

Cockatiels who live with cats, are show birds or have flight or aviary accommodations usually do not have their wings clipped. This

is a choice you can make for your companion cockatiel, as well. The danger is that a fully flighted cockatiel will fly away through an open door or window, or that it will hurt or kill itself flying into a window or mirror.

You have some control over how much you restrict your cockatiel's flight by the number of flight feathers you cut and the length of feather you leave. Cockatiels are built for speed with their long tails and slim bodies, so to ground one requires a more drastic clip than with many other species of pet birds. Usually at least ten primary flight feathers must be clipped on each wing.

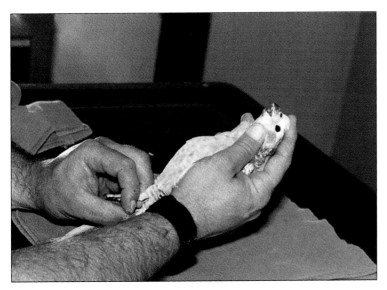

To restrain a cockatiel, hold your fingers on the cockatiel's jowls and behind its head. Hold its feet, but leave the chest free so the bird can breathe. Mathilda, a pearl hen, is modeling here, and Dr. Michael Murray is the handler.

A SENSIBLE APPROACH

I have learned of a very sensible new theory about clipping wings from Eb Cravens, a bird keeper and breeder with pet shop experience. He thinks a lot about what we can teach our parrots that their parents would teach them if they still lived in a parrot family. He suggests clipping wings slowly, one or two at a time, in order to allow a young bird to learn to be coordinated, to land properly and to develop flight muscles. I tried his approach with a clutch of cockatiels and am very pleased with the results. Those cockatiels are more agile, more sure of their control over their actions and more likely to hop onto perches instead of crawling around the cage for mobility. If you have an older cockatiel who has never learned these skills, you can use the same system the next time its wings grow out, to help it learn coordination.

To use Eb's technique, I clip one or two of the outermost flight feathers. Then I allow the bird to adjust to that level of restriction and a week or two later clip the next feather or two. At the end of several weeks the cockatiel is fully clipped. At any point along the way I could stop clipping feathers, which would allow a cockatiel to fly short distances, or to fly without gaining altitude. If I had a cat I would probably consider doing that.

RESTRAINT TECHNIQUES

To restrain a cockatiel for feather clipping, I hold it around the neck and back without compressing its breast. If you extend a cockatiel's neck slightly, so that it is straight, and position your fingers on the bird's jowls, you will very effectively immobilize it. Remember to hold its feet, too, so it feels somewhat secure, or to lay it on its back on a flat surface.

When I am clipping cockatiels alone, I hold the bird away from me to clip one side, and up against me (where it usually plays with my buttons or a towel) for the other. You may choose to use two people for this procedure: one to hold the cockatiel and one to clip. It depends on how comfortable you are and how tame or stressed the cockatiel is.

Be careful when holding a cockatiel not to press on its chest. Birds can't breathe when they are squeezed around the chest, as they have no diaphragm. If you want, you can restrain a cockatiel in a towel. A washcloth or hand towel is big enough. If you get in the habit of playing games with a towel, and rolling your bird in one for fun, wing clipping and vet visits won't be nearly as stressful for either of you.

Nature offers a guide for clipping cockatiel wing feathers. I usually clip the primary flight feathers on the outside of the

Before clipping a cockatiel's wings, check for blood feathers. These feathers are mostly grown in, but still have blood at the base.

Clip the primary flight feathers of a cockatiel, leaving the primary covert feathers as a guide. Be sure to use sharp scissors.

I use a pair of sharp sewing scissors to clip feathers, and clip them one by one. When a bird is molting, wing feathers grow in one at a time. Be attentive to the need to clip those feathers, but also watch for blood feathers. A new, growing feather has visible blood in the shaft near the bird's body. Only clip mature feathers, with no blood or nerves in their shaft. Should you cut a blood feather, the shaft of that feather will need to be pulled using pliers in order to stop bleeding. Be sure to support the cockatiel's wing if you do this yourself. Your veterinarian can do this, too, and may need to if there is not much shaft left.

With its wings entirely clipped —that is, ten primary flight feathers on each wing clipped to the level of the covert feathers—your cockatiel will still be able to fly short distances. If you've gotten to this stage gradually, it should be able to maneuver and land safely, as well.

Beak Grooming

I'll repeat here that a veterinarian or professional bird groomer should work with your cockatiel's beak if it needs trimming. Beaks are made of keratin and grow continuously. As they grow, they can look flaky. Most cockatiel beaks do not grow too long, but if yours does it is best that a veterinarian

wing, using primary covert feathers as a guide.

It is important to clip wings symmetrically; in other words, clip the same feathers on both wings. Otherwise a cockatiel is unbalanced in flight and landing. That's no way to learn coordination!

look for a medical cause for that condition. A veterinarian or groomer has the correct tools for grooming beaks, as well.

Clipping Nails

You can clip your cockatiel's nails yourself. I rarely clip my birds' nails, but I have had my birds around both young people and older people with sensitive skin who felt the sharpness of their nails. And nails feel especially sharp at some times of the year when they are growing. You might be more comfortable if your bird's nails are blunted.

Much as with wing clipping, I restrain a cockatiel around the neck and support its feet, or wrap it in a towel. Cockatiel nails are much like our fingernails. The tips are insensitive, but there are nerves at the base and it's possible to clip too far down a nail. For this reason, be ready to stop blood flow when clipping nails. This is easily accomplished with styptic powder (blood coagulant), corn starch in a pinch, or by sticking the cockatiel's nail into a small bar of soap. (There *is* a use for hotel-size soap!)

It is easy to see the growing quick on cockatiels with light-colored nails. You'll see a tiny pink or red vein. But it's not so easy on cockatiels with gray feet and dark nails. Just to be safe, I am usually conservative in clipping nails, and

A final clip, as seen from the underside of the wing. A total of nine to ten primary flight feathers were clipped on each wing.

The same clip, seen from the top of the wing. Dacey, a gray hen, is pictured.

clip only the tip. Then I clip again a few weeks later.

Most birds manage to keep their nails from growing too long simply by perching on branches. Sandpaper-covered perches are available but cannot be recommended as toenail trimmers. The

NAME THAT TUNE

Cockatiels are quite aerodynamic. Sometimes we don't notice flight feathers have grown in from clipped wings, and we risk losing a cherished pet. Occasionally there's still a happy ending. Here's the tale of a lost cockatiel that ended up with a new home.

In a daring capture witnessed by fifty or sixty students of Forest Grove Elementary School in Pacific Grove, California, Ollie the cockatiel came into teacher Christine Conneau's life. It happened in March 1989, when Christine and her friend Debbie were teaching physical education outside. Debbie thought she heard the local flock of feral parrots (that's another story). But then, "Oh, it's a cockatiel! Where did it come from?"

Despite the fact that the cockatiel was loose and on the wing, both Christine and Debbie thought it would make a good pet for their respective children. But obviously, there was only one cockatiel to go around. After the bird circled for a couple of hours, with the two friends discussing all the while whether this was daughter Leslie's or son Justin's pet cockatiel, Christine found a way to make it come closer. She started whistling *La Cucaracha*.

At last, the cockatiel lighted on the ground. But it took off again every time Christine or Debbie approached within ten feet. There were another two hours of this type of interaction. In between classes, the fourth-grade students came out to watch Mrs. Conneau try to catch a feral cockatiel. She really did, too, enticing it to her at last with her whistling.

The cockatiel was placed in a box, and Christine did the right thing, even though she felt she had earned her bird: She contacted animal control about a found bird and ran an ad in the newspaper. No one called about Ollie.

Since coming to Christine's household, Ollie has never liked anyone but Christine. He loves to preen her. He knows when she's coming home and knows the sound of her car when she's pulled up outside. In the summer he lives outside, and inside he has befriended the family cats.

Ollie's been through a lot, not the least of which was the Loma Prieta earthquake, which caused heavy damage in Northern California. His hanging cage fell down in the tremors, and for a while his family couldn't find him. Finally, it was discovered he was on the curtain rod—evidently uncharacteristically silent!

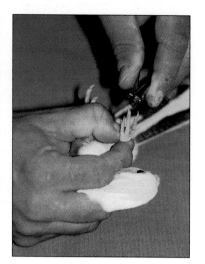

You can restrain a cockatiel yourself to clip its nails. This is Mystique, a pied female. We're lucky that her nails are light, so we can see the quick at the base of them and won't clip too far. Clip just the tip of cockatiel toenails.

sandpaper covers the entire perch, so that it rubs on sensitive feet as well as nails. It can cause sores. There are some concrete perches that are smooth on top and rough where a cockatiel's nail would touch them. You can trim nails with no effort this way.

Another possibility is to get your bird used to giving you its foot, and gently filing nails with an emery board or a small file.

CHAPTER 4

Your Avian Veterinarian Partner

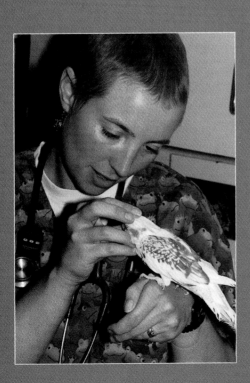

The first order of business when discussing veterinary care for your companion cockatiel is to find an avian veterinarian in your area. You've probably noticed that our pet birds are very different from our dog and cat pets. This extends to issues of health care, as well. So while your local veterinarian may be very good with all the dogs on your block, that doesn't mean he or she is the best vet for your bird. It is the veterinarians who take the time to learn more about birds on their own, or who were trained at the few universities that offer courses in avian medicine, who are best able to care for the health of your cockatiel.

There is, in fact, an Association of Avian Veterinarians (AAV) with a large network of veterinarians interested in treating birds. The AAV offers regional courses for veterinarians, holds a yearly convention and has a regular publication. A veterinarian may also earn an Avian Specialist certificate from the American Veterinary Medical Association (AVMA).

One way to find an avian veterinarian is to contact the AAV. Another way is to call local veterinarians and ask if they treat birds. If they say yes, say thank you and hang up. When someone says no, but refers you to an avian veterinarian, take that suggestion. You have found a veterinarian who is recommended by their peers.

You also may wish to contact local breeders, a bird club or a reputable pet shop to find out which veterinarian they use to care for their birds. I strongly suggest that you find an avian veterinarian you are comfortable with, who knows your birds and their history, before there is any kind of emergency need for veterinary care.

Cockatiels should have a "well bird" exam when you acquire them, and regular exams throughout their lives.

Other services offered by an avian veterinarian include wing clipping, nail trimming and boarding when you are away on vacation. A very few avian veterinary clinics offer behavior classes or access to an avian behaviorist.

In our community (and I imagine in many others), the avian veterinarian is also a center for information. We let him know when a bird is lost or stolen, and when we are looking for a good home for our companion bird.

What Makes a Good Avian Veterinarian?

My ideal avian veterinarian would be available twenty-four hours a day, would charge really low rates I

could pay over a long period of time, and would be a ten-minute drive from my house. When I got there, I would never have to wait, and the news would always be good!

He or she would also be up to date on the latest research and treatments in avian medicine, and would be an incredible customer-oriented businessperson.

But, you know, avian veterinarians are only human. They have different strengths in treating birds, in managing an office and in people skills. What you should look for in an avian veterinarian is a commitment to treating birds and to staying on top of the latest developments.

If a symptom is stumping your own avian veterinarian, he or she should be willing to call a more experienced veterinarian or an expert in a certain field. This does not mean your veterinarian doesn't know plenty—it means he or she is willing to learn more.

When a clinic or hospital cannot be open at all hours or every day of the year, is there a provision for emergency care? When your

Get to know an avian veterinarian before you have an emergency. A veterinarian will need information from you about your cockatiel's diet, housing, history and identification. Michael J. Murray, DVM, records information on a client's chart.

veterinarian is not available, who is your second choice? What do you do in an emergency? Make sure you have a plan—a plan your veterinarian should help you formulate.

You want respect for both your feelings towards your companion bird and the limits of your pocketbook. Your veterinarian should explain all of the care options and their costs, then let you decide. You both should be clear about credit, billing or other payment arrangements. If you have concerns about the birds at home that you did not bring in, he or she should be open to working out a flock treatment plan, if it is warranted.

You should expect an avian veterinarian to respect your time. He or she cannot prevent or anticipate emergencies, but appointments should be scheduled at reasonable intervals so that long waits are not the norm.

Your avian veterinarian should explain treatments and tests to you, and be willing to listen to you. You are the expert about your particular bird, and even small changes in behavior are clues to a correct and timely diagnoses. If you wish to bring up suggestions about treatments, vaccines or methods you have learned about from reliable sources, he or she should be open to finding out more. If your sources are journals, experts speaking at national seminars or other technical sources, you are a more reliable source of information than someone who merely wishes to control the situation. If you are interested in pursuing an alternative form of treatment, such as acupuncture or herbal remedies, you may need to get a referral. Many veterinarians are trained in traditional Western medicine, but only a few also incorporate alternative medicine.

The relationship between an avian veterinarian and a client is an association between an employer (you) and a hired professional. It is also a partnership between two people who are concerned about the health and welfare of your cockatiel or flock. In addition, it is a relationship between two people. You and your own veterinarian should work out your relationship on all these levels, and should be comfortable with each other.

Wendy Macias (left) is a responsible cockatiel breeder who offers health guarantees and has a good relationship with her avian veterinarian. Vet tech Linda Beard weighs the birds that are in today, and waits for fresh sample droppings.

Why Fees Are Worth It

Avian veterinarians are professionals, and their fees reflect their training and experience. I expect the first exam of a new cockatiel to cost about twice what the bird did. If the bird didn't cost anything, the exam should still cost about twice what you would have had to pay for a bird.

For some reason, people often equate the level of care they are willing to provide their companion bird with its perceived value or its original cost. I urge you, instead, to consider the commitment you have made to a living being. You took on the responsibility of caring for a life when you acquired your cockatiel.

Part of that responsibility is health, which is best maintained through a partnership between a bird owner and an avian veterinarian.

A Health Partnership

The benefits of this partnership are many, for both you and your feathered companion. The owner has the advantage of being with a bird several hours a day, every day. An owner can recognize when there is something different going on with his or her cockatiel—even when that difference is subtle. This can range from observing that a behavior has stopped (like singing or talking) to observing that a behavior is new or unsettling.

YOUR BIRD'S BEST FRIEND

by Dorothy Clarke

Perhaps the experience with our first adoptee can save you the trauma of a tragic loss. We were given an elderly gray cockatiel whose owner had to go to a nursing home. We loved the little old ladybird and hoped to compensate for her loss.

Uncovering her cage one morning, I found her on the floor with her insides outside. Later I learned this is called cloacal prolapse, and is associated with excessive straining of the sphincter muscles of the vent.

Hysterically (at least I was), my husband and I searched in the Yellow Pages for Animal Hospital. There was Rescue, Welfare, even Rehab. . . maybe we needed the Birds heading? Cages, Toys, Hand-fed Babies. . . by now I had wrapped the patient's parts in damp cloths. Pets, oh no, three pages of everything for sale except veterinary services. That's it, we need Veterinarian! I was shaking so much I could scarcely hold the crying bird and turn the pages.

My husband had started the car, and we drove to an easy-to-find address. An attendant took our bird away; I cried. The bird was back in minutes, apparently fine. What I wasn't told is that prolapse can often reoccur. The next time it was too late to get help. We had a proper burial.

We now see an avian veterinarian regularly, so we are prepared for emergencies!

I may think I know the habits of each of my avian companions, but in truth I have only observed a relative few. My avian veterinarian has examined, treated and healed thousands. There can be such a strong bond between vet, client (cockatiel) and companion person that the rapport includes a vet's reprimands, accepted in the bird's best interest.

Then there is the report of good lab results that make my day! Our vet calls personally with good or bad news after our birds are tested.

Recently we lost a magnificent young cockatiel who had checked out as healthy. A necropsy proved I hadn't "killed my bird," a heartbroken confession so frequently expressed by owners. An inhaled seed had lodged in the cockatiel's trachea, causing his death—a horrible accident that was nobody's fault. A sympathy card signed by all the clinic staff who had known precious Jonathan reinforced the concept that we are all in this together.

Sure, there is expense involved, but what price can be placed on peace of mind and spirit? Never again do I have to search the Yellow Pages for help in a crisis. My car knows the way to the Avian and Exotic Clinic.

A veterinarian brings to the partnership a knowledge of avian diseases and their symptoms, as well as a clinical way of looking at health with regard to a cockatiel's anatomy. A veterinarian also has a finger on the pulse of the avian community in your area. If a virus is prevalent or an environmental factor is affecting avian health, he or she probably knows about it.

An obvious benefit of a regular partnership with an avian veterinarian is that there is care available in an emergency. Our companions are so curious, so swift and so small that accidents do happen. Another benefit that may not be as obvious is that regular checkups can catch problems that even an owner may miss. Our cockatiels are a prey species in the wild—other animals eat them. They depend on their alert behavior and a chipper appearance for their very survival. This trait has not been lost in captivity. Even an ill bird will look bright and alert. To appear otherwise in the wild would make it an easy target.

What this means is that it is best to assess the state of your cockatiel's health through regular lab tests. Another indicator of health is weight, so a weigh-in should be part of a regular exam.

YOUR ROLE

Your role in this partnership between veterinarian and bird owner is to schedule regular check-ups, observe, listen and provide information. You should respect your avian veterinarian, as a human being and as a businessperson, which means being on time for your appointments, treating the doctor and staff courteously and paying your bills in a timely way. It is also courteous to make appointments during business hours, to find out the procedure for emergencies and to answer questions as clearly and concisely as you can.

You and your veterinarian will decide together what kind of tests should be conducted on your bird and how treatment should proceed, if any is warranted. Considerations for tests include the number and type of birds in your household, whether the population is stable or changing, whether your birds are breeding birds or pets, the birds' ages and the care they receive. Information on diet, caging and free flight time is invaluable in helping a veterinarian find the source of problems. Information on your budget might also be important. You will be making the final decision about care, based on the available options.

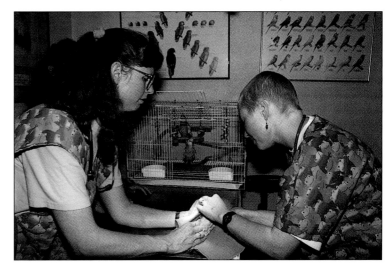

A veterinarian can make trained observations and do lab tests to ascertain the health of your cockatiel. Vet tech Linda Beard (left) and Dr. Shannon Thomas work together with a cockatiel patient.

You can help in an emergency by providing accurate information. If the bird has ingested anything suspicious, for example, bring in what's left of the substance, and if possible bring in a label or container for the product. Our cockatiels can usually be very accommodating

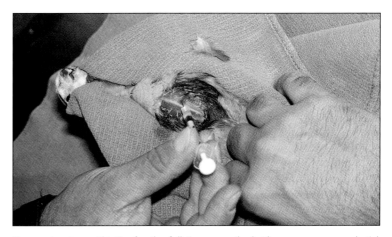

Be sure to give antibiotics for the full time prescribed. Chances are your cockatiel will feel better before then, but will need the whole dose to prevent a recurrence of its problem. You can learn to give your cockatiel injections into the breast muscle, as shown here. Audubon is a mature pearl male who no longer has pearl lacings.

BE READY FOR QUESTIONS

Your avian veterinarian will probably want to know some things about the history of your cockatiel and the reason for your visit. You should be prepared to answer questions about the following areas:

Cockatiel History

Breeder or pet store where you acquired the cockatiel.

How old is it?

How long have you had the cockatiel?

What sex is the cockatiel (if known)?

What color is it?

Are there other birds in the household?

Do you breed or show your birds?

Care History

What kind of cage do you keep your cockatiel in?

Are your birds kept together or in individual cages?

What does your bird eat?

How active is your bird?

Has its activity level changed?

What kind of socialization does your bird get?

Does it spend time out of the cage?

Symptoms and Signs

What is wrong with the bird?

Has there been a change in its droppings?

Has the bird been exposed to fumes, smoke, or nonstick cookware or surfaces?

Has the bird had access to dangerous materials it could ingest, such as plastic, fibers, medications, plants, stained glass or other lead products?

Is the cockatiel in a reproduction cycle?

Are other birds in your household ill?

Are family members ill?

Treatment

What did you do to treat the bird or make it more comfortable?

Has another veterinarian treated this bird? How long?

What were the results?

---

about providing a fresh sample of droppings for analysis. Your veterinarian may also want some blood, often drawn from the jugular vein in the bird's neck. That takes some getting used to!

The other element in your partnership is being able to follow directions regarding treatment. Don't be afraid to ask about alternatives if you're uncomfortable, either. Medication can usually be given orally or through an injection. You can learn to do either, and should ask for clarification if you're unclear about instructions

or dosage. Be aware of how to store medications. Some need to be shaken before they are administered, and some need to be kept in the refrigerator. Find out how to dispose of used syringes properly.

Be sure to follow instructions, and to give all the medication specified. Sometimes a cockatiel begins to perk up before the end of a course of antibiotics, but it's important to finish up anyway, to reduce the risk of the infection recurring. Find out what kind of results you can expect from a treatment, and if your bird will need a follow-up

exam. Will there be side effects of the medication to watch for?

Your Own Feelings

Treatment of an ill bird can be traumatic for all concerned. When your treasured friend isn't feeling well, you may have expectations about a speedy recovery or about a chronically ill bird regaining its health. Your veterinarian and staff have made careers of helping sick animals, and it is frustrating for them when their best efforts are not enough.

It will help all concerned if you deal with the facts as they happen. Can you avoid feelings caused by your own expectations and deal with what's really going on with your bird? If you can look at what *has* happened, without worrying about what should have, could have or might happen, you'll be happier and your bird will get quality care based on a realistic view of what is going on. Guilt and blame have no place in medical decisions.

Some things that happen shouldn't have. I wish I could bring back birds that have died because of my mistakes or lack of knowledge. I wish I could give Dacey a whole new life, instead of the years she spent with me during which I was learning about cockatiel care. But I can't. So life goes on, and life for my own cockatiels improves as time passes. I guarantee you I have made mistakes, and I promise I will make more—but I keep learning.

Cockatiel owners have the right to expect their avian veterinarian will handle their birds with care and sensitivity, as Dr. Shannon Thomas does.

Many years ago I held one of Dacey's chicks as it died after a veterinarian's diagnosis of calcium deficiency. The chick's keel bone was soft and its feet were soft and rubbery. This was a direct result of the diet I was feeding, and probably the greens I used as a diet supplement.

At the time my cockatiels ate seeds (this was back in the dark ages), and they were getting mostly spinach as greens. Even with a vitamin supplement, there just wasn't enough calcium. It turns out spinach has a component that binds with calcium, making it unusable to a bird. Now my cockatiels only occasionally get spinach as a treat, and all of my cockatiels eat a formulated diet. I haven't had any more problems with a calcium deficiency in babies, and I know what to look for now. My veterinarian made an important observation, and I acted on the results.

Avian illness is not always that straightforward, but we have the best chance of keeping healthy birds and constantly improving our understanding of avian medicine when we have a good partnership with a veterinarian.

by
Thomas E. Roudybush, MS

Diet and Feeding

Tom Roudybush did pioneering scientific work on the nutrient requirements of psittacines as a graduate student and an employee at University of California–Davis in the early 1980s. He co-founded the Psittacine Research Project at Davis, and went on to found his own feed company. Tom is currently president of Roudybush Inc., lectures to veterinarians and veterinary students around the world and is a popular speaker at many bird clubs and conferences.

Cockatiels, like all birds, benefit from research on their nutritional requirements. No other psittacine (parrot) has been studied as extensively, and only one or two others have been studied at all. Most of what we apply to the feeding of cockatiels and other psittacine birds is, however, still extrapolated from other types of birds, primarily poultry. The work with cockatiels begun in 1979 and continuing today at the University of California–Davis (more on that in Chapter 16) at least gives us some idea of how reliable this extrapolation is.

The proper feeding of an adult nonbreeding cockatiel is relatively easy. There are a few nutrients that must be supplied in supplements or by feeding foods rich in them. The rest are easily provided by a practical diet for birds. This practical diet usually consists of a manufactured food that needs no supplementation, a seed mix that will need supplementation, or foods from your own kitchen that you would eat yourself.

Providing your cockatiel with the proper nutrients in the proper amounts makes the difference between a bird that is surviving and one that is thriving. A relatively small effort on your part can make a major difference in the health and longevity of your bird.

Cockatiels benefit from research on their nutrient requirements. This is a juvenile pearl male anxious for lunch!

Nutrition and Balance

Nutrition is the science of balance. This being the case, there are a few bits of "common wisdom" that we need to abandon. The first is that more is better. In nutrition, more of some nutrients can be toxic, and sometimes more of one food item results in the bird eating less of something else that it really needs.

For example, vitamins A and D_3 are required in the proper amounts for normal health. A deficiency of vitamin A can result in infections, poor kidney function and eye problems, while a deficiency of vitamin D_3 can result in poor bone formation, weak bones and convulsions. An excess of vitamin A, on the other hand, can result in skin problems, eye problems, bone malformations, convulsions and, in extreme cases, death; while an excess of vitamin D_3 can result in mineralization of the kidneys or other soft tissues, muscular degeneration, anorexia and, in extreme cases, death. So, as you can see, we are not interested in giving your cockatiel the maximum or minimum amount of any nutrient, but only in giving the amount it needs.

More of one food can mean less of another in many cases. Cockatiels, like other animals, eat only the number of calories they need each day. They regulate this fairly closely and will eat just what they need under normal conditions. When you add one food to a cockatiel's diet, you simply cause the bird to eat less of something else. For example, a bird that has been eating a mix of 10 grams of cooked corn and 10 grams of cooked beans will still eat only a total of 20 grams of food when you add 10 grams of cooked wheat to the mix. It needs only the calories in 20 grams of food. So adding the wheat causes it to eat 6.7 grams of corn, 6.7 grams of beans and 6.7 grams of wheat. More wheat has caused the cockatiel to eat less corn and beans.

The common idea that a diet can be improved by adding something to it to provide missing or deficient nutrients usually causes a new set of problems. The composition of the complete diet fed to your bird is what needs to be considered.

Manufactured Diets

There are a variety of diets that can be fed to your bird, with varying results. Foremost among these are the manufactured diets. They are formulated with the idea that they supply all the required nutrients in the amounts needed. These diets vary somewhat in composition and have a few attributes that you should consider, including whether or not supplements are needed, color, fragrance, preservatives, sugar content and fat content.

All manufactured diets, both pelleted and extruded, should be fed without the addition of vitamin or mineral supplements. Properly formulated diets will supply all the nutrients your bird is known to need. The addition of supplements may add enough of some nutrients to produce toxic levels. As I mentioned before, some vitamins are toxic in excess, but it is also important to note that some trace minerals can become toxic even when their levels are just a little bit higher than a balanced diet requires. That's why you should never supplement a diet with trace minerals—even a diet in which

Selected Nutrient Requirements of Cockatiels			
Nutrient	Percent of Total Diet		
	Adult Maintenance	Adult Breeding	Growth of Chick
Calcium	0.1%	0.4%	0.9–1.0%
Protein	4–12%	10–12%	20%
Lysine	unknown	unknown	0.8%
Water	free choice	free choice	70–90%

such additions may be needed—unless you clearly understand the dangers and can measure the amount of any trace mineral added to the diet.

DYES AND FRAGRANCE

The color of some diets depends on the nature of the ingredients used in the formulation. Some other manufactured diets are colored with artificial dyes and have artificial fragrances added to enhance their acceptance by the consumer. While no systematic studies have been done to detect major problems in these products, it is worth noting that, unlike humans, who eat a varied diet and can avoid such food additives, your bird will be exposed to these chemicals with each bite it eats for as long as you feed these diets. Some cases have now been reported in which birds with behavioral problems such as feather picking have benefited from a diet that contains no artificial dyes or fragrances. Should such problems show up in your bird, changing to a diet with no dyes or fragrances might be beneficial.

Manufactured diets should be fed without vitamin or mineral supplements. Most cockatiels will eat about 15 grams of a manufactured diet each day. This is Sunshine, a male pearl-pied cockatiel. *(David Wrobel)*

PRESERVATIVES

Preservatives in foods are another matter of concern. The different types of preservatives vary in their chemical composition and in what they do. For example, vitamin C is a common food preservative that may actually enhance food value while causing no harm. Since it is produced and metabolized by most birds, it can be tolerated at levels far above what is required for a healthy diet.

Other preservatives, mainly poisons, are used to prevent mold from growing. Some of these are poisonous to birds only at high concentrations, while others are not poisons at all but are nutrients that simply change the character of the food to make it less hospitable to mold growth. An example of this is acetic acid, the active part of vinegar, which lowers the pH of the food and inhibits mold growth but is readily absorbed and metabolized by your cockatiel. Other foods are protected from molding simply by manufacturing them to be too dry for mold growth. A level of 12 percent moisture is common in these diets.

On balance, people who wish to reduce the intake of artificial ingredients in their bird's diet should first eliminate the colors and fragrances, since they do nothing to enhance the nutritional quality of the food. Preservatives should be individually evaluated. Some preservatives are

ETHOXYQUIN AND BIRDS

One antioxidant that has received much undeserved bad press is ethoxyquin. It is a chemical that prevents oxidation of food, thereby preventing loss of vitamin potency and keeping the fat in food from going rancid. It is one of the safest and most effective antioxidants available. While it has been reviled by a cult following of the uninformed, it has not been shown to cause any harm to any animal. It is still approved by the Food and Drug Administration for use in human food, and is safe and effective.

food items that can be eaten by your bird in any normal diet and are simply added to reduce oxidation or to reduce the pH of the food to prevent mold growth. All are put in the food to lengthen its storage time by preventing the loss of nutrients or to prevent the growth of mold, which can infect your bird or produce potent toxins that may harm your bird.

SUGAR

Sugar is included in some manufactured diets for cockatiels. While it may not be a problem for most cockatiels, it should be avoided in the regular diet to safeguard against yeast infection. Sugar is a good substrate for the growth of yeast, and yeast is a common infection in the mouths and gastrointestinal tracts of birds.

It is usually not a problem to give occasional sugary treats to your normal, healthy bird, but it is best to avoid feeding sugar regularly. Should your cockatiel get a yeast infection, advise your veterinarian what you are feeding and find a diet that has no sugar for the duration of treatment and for several weeks thereafter. If your bird has repeated yeast infections, eliminate sugar from the diet permanently.

FAT

Fat is necessary in the diet. Fat is usually thought of as a rich supply of energy and only secondarily as a source of essential fatty acids. But in fact, the fatty acids are much more important to a bird's diet. All animals that have had their nutritional needs tested have been found to require specific fatty acids in their diet. The reality is that this amount of fat is extremely low and is easily obtained from almost any practical diet.

The amount of fat needed in the diet of a normal cockatiel is low—about 3 percent to 8 percent of the diet. Fat is such a rich source of energy that 1 gram of fat has as many calories as 2 grams of protein or carbohydrate. In addition, fat goes directly from the blood to fat storage cells without the need for any transformation. Both protein and carbohydrate need to be transformed from their initial state into fat in a series of enzyme-mediated reactions that result in a loss of calories. This means the amount of energy available from the carbohydrate or protein is reduced by the time it is converted to fat. So a bird will store more fat from the same number of calories of fat than it will from protein or carbohydrate. This is one reason why captive birds fed a high-fat diet have a tendency to get fat, and why you should limit the amount of fat in your bird's diet.

In addition to the metabolic considerations, there is the problem of inactivity in captive birds. Cockatiels evolved in Australia as nomads; they breed when conditions are right, wherever they may be. This means that wild cockatiels fly a lot, and burn a lot of energy in the process. Since your cockatiel is captive and is often restricted in when and where it can fly, your pet is unable to burn the same amount of energy. This lack of exercise must be offset by a reduced intake of energy, or your bird will get fat. Fat cockatiels may eventually have a number of problems such as fatty tumors, reduced ability to breed, respiratory distress and low endurance.

Excess weight in birds can also have a behavioral component. Some birds may eat too much food to overcome a lack of behavioral stimuli they would normally get during exercise. If the diet is low in fat, the bird is able to eat more food to supply behavioral stimuli without gaining weight.

Other Diets

Diets other than manufactured ones are commonly fed to cockatiels, but are often difficult to characterize and recommend. Among these diets are seed mixes—both supplemented and unsupplemented—mixes containing sprouts, rice-corn-bean mixes and many other variations on one of these themes. All of these come with their own problems of nutrient adequacy that need to be overcome with supplements.

Some are difficult to supplement because the bird can choose among the foods offered, giving you less control over what nutrients it actually takes in. In most cases your bird will be fed with better nutrition and less trouble and concern if it is fed a high-quality manufactured diet.

SEED DIETS

Seed diets can have a number of nutritional deficiencies. Foremost among them is a deficiency in vitamin A. It is often assumed that birds need extra vitamin A, since it is so commonly advised that birds fed seeds be supplemented with

vitamin A. It is not that birds have an outrageously high requirement for vitamin A, but rather that seeds are outrageously low in vitamin A.

When seeds are fed without vitamin A supplements, it is likely that a sinus infection will result. There are a number of functions vitamin A serves that are important in allowing normal operation of the immune system. If vitamin A is deficient, these functions are reduced and the bird becomes more susceptible to infection. One function of vitamin A is in maintaining the lining of the sinuses and other similar areas. If the bird does not get enough vitamin A, the degraded sinus lining, combined with reduced immune function, predispose the bird to a sinus infection. These infections are painful, life-threatening and expensive to treat. And while they are often successfully eliminated, they will come back again and again if the vitamin A deficiency is not corrected.

The other organ that is commonly affected by vitamin A deficiency is the kidney. Just as the lining of the sinuses degrades, the kidney will keratinize (harden) and its function will be reduced. This can lead to gout and kidney failure.

Seed mixes should be supplemented with at least a vitamin supplement or a vitamin-mineral supplement. Extra calcium should be made available in the form of a cuttlebone or a calcium block, to

Seed diets can have a number of nutrient deficiencies, including vitamin A and calcium, and need to be supplemented. This is Sunshine as a juvenile.

overcome the potential for a long-term calcium deficiency.

An additional problem with seed mixes is that the bird is able to make food choices. Wild birds seem to forage to get the greatest amount of energy with the least amount of effort. This has carried over to pet birds as a taste for fat. Most birds offered a choice will choose seeds that are high in fat. This leads us to the problem discussed earlier of fat birds. There is no way I know of to keep birds from choosing the fatty seeds from a seed mix. There is also no way to predict the composition of the diet the bird will actually consume if it is offered a chance to make choices. Here again, the manufactured diet is a better choice.

SPROUTS

Many bird owners try to overcome the problem of deficiencies in seeds by sprouting the seeds. The benefit of feeding sprouts is that they have higher levels of some of the vitamins, which reduces the need to feed vitamin supplements. Sprouting seeds, however, does little to reduce the need for mineral supplementation, particularly calcium.

The problems of evaluating the composition of the diet the bird actually eats is even greater with sprouts than with seed mixes. When seeds sprout, the composition of the seed-sprout changes rapidly. A matter of hours can make a major difference in the nutrient profile of the sprout. This source of variation is added to the variation created by the food choices the bird makes.

The additional problem with sprouts is that they are wet. Wet foods are good places to grow bacteria, molds and fungi that can harm your bird. Since sprouts are wet for some time before they are fed, there is plenty of time for these pathogens to grow. Generally, wet food should be discarded within four to eight hours after being

SEEDS AND SUPPLEMENTS

Some seed mixes come with vitamin and mineral supplementation. But it is difficult to recommend these mixes, because the supplementation varies depending on the seed blender. Some mixes will be well supplemented, while others will be poorly supplemented or supplemented in a way that allows the bird to choose whether it will eat the supplement. You will need to evaluate these mixes yourself, but consider whether your bird can avoid the supplement and whether it supplies vitamin A. If this is not clear to you, choose another food.

made, depending on the temperature at which it is held. Sprouts are held longer than this, and therefore may be a source of infection.

RICE-CORN-BEAN MIX

Some bird owners feed a cooked mixture of rice, corn and beans. This diet is higher in protein and has a better amino acid profile than a seed mix, but otherwise it is not much better. It still suffers from deficiencies of vitamin A and some other vitamins and is low in calcium, so it should be supplemented with vitamins and a source of calcium. Depending on how well the mix is cooked and blended, there

may still be the potential for the bird to eat all of one ingredient and none of another. This reduces the effectiveness of mixing the rice, corn and beans to achieve a better amino acid profile by using complementary proteins.

This diet is also wet, which means the potential for contamination is great. It should not be held for longer than eight hours at room temperature (70°F). Fortunately, the food is cooked. This reduces the amount of bacteria, and therefore the chance that bacteria will overwhelm the bird's immune system. This diet should be supplemented with vitamins and a source of calcium.

Changing Your Bird's Diet

When a bird is used to one food, it is often difficult to get it to eat new foods. But some change is essential for birds that are habituated to a single seed, particularly a high-fat seed such as sunflower seeds. Such birds must learn to eat a healthier diet, no matter how much effort it takes.

Birds seem to resist changing diets for three reasons. The first is that the new diet may be completely unacceptable. If you try to feed a cockatiel walnuts in the shell, it is unlikely your bird will eat them. It can't. The shell is just too hard for the cockatiel. So the first thing you need to know in changing your bird's diet is that the change is possible.

The second reason birds seem to reject food is that they don't like it. These birds can usually be convinced by removing all other foods for forty-eight hours and allowing the birds to get hungry. Within that time, they constantly investigate the food dish and remove vast amounts of food by throwing it around the room in an apparent protest. But generally they will eat the new food sometime within the forty-eight hours, and quickly recover the weight they lost in their self-imposed fast.

The third reason birds seem to reject food is that they don't know what it is. We learned this at UC–Davis when we offered pellets to cockatiels that had been eating seeds. About 10 percent of our birds would not change diets even though we offered them nothing but the new diet for days at a time. We knew the diet was acceptable, because other cockatiels were eating it.

We studied the birds' behavior and discovered that these birds not only failed to eat the diet, but they also stopped examining the food dish—unlike birds that simply didn't like their diet. Birds that fail to recognize the food as food will die rather than eat something they do not recognize as food.

Curiously, reexposure to the food produces an unexpected response. Birds that did not recognize the food the first time will usually recognize it the second time and begin to eat it. The time we used between exposures was one to two weeks, though cockatiels may respond the same way with shorter times between exposures. No bird of our flock of 250 required more than four exposures to the new diet to change, even though 10 percent of the birds failed to recognize it when it was first offered. Repeated exposure is clearly one way to change a bird's diet.

OTHER THINGS TO TRY

There are a number of things you can try to get your bird to accept new food items, particularly if you are trying to get it to simply include a few more items in its diet. One of these is to induce hunger. While eliminating all familiar food items for forty-eight hours is effective for complete changes of the diet, shorter times without food may be helpful in getting a bird to sample new foods. You can lengthen the time without familiar food items to forty-eight hours as a maximum. Longer times of fasting are not helpful in getting a bird to accept new foods and simply result in more stress on your bird.

WHEN TO CHANGE?

There are a number of conditions that occur during a bird's life that require changes in its diet. Some of these include breeding, growth, sickness and extremes of weather. Other changes in a bird's life that are often assumed to require dietary changes are molting, changes of season, nail clipping and wing clipping, but there is no reason to change diet in these cases.

In some cases the bird responds when you act as if *you* like the diet. It is a common observation that birds often eat at the same time as their owners, even when the birds have food available all the time. Birds will also often take food that the owner is eating and try it. There appears to be a social context in food acceptance. The exact nature of this relationship is unknown to me, but it appears to be real and beneficial in getting the bird to accept new foods.

Some bird owners try baking needed nutrients into bread or muffins. There are some advantages to baking bread for birds that accept it. The bread is sterile from the baking, and baking can allow a variety of interesting materials to be hidden in the mix. However, baking is time-consuming and may result in the destruction of vitamins, rancidity of fat and, in extreme cases, degradation of protein quality. And while hiding little extras in a muffin may induce the bird to eat the nutrients it needs, it is not a way to get the bird to eat the variety of foods it needs.

Another method to get birds to accept novel foods is to combine the new food with an old favorite. One common form of this is to sprinkle the new food with something such as lemon juice, grated carrot, frozen juice concentrate, applesauce, etc. Some birds prefer moist foods over dry foods. The added flavor and moisture may also turn a food that has not been recognized as food into something acceptable to the bird. You can usually decrease the amount of the moist food over time, until the novel food is accepted without the moist food.

Treats can meet the need for interaction, stimulation, variety and nutritional balance when they are low-energy foods such as vegetables and fruits. This is Davey-Jones, an adult gray male cockatiel.
(David Wrobel)

Treats

Treats are often fed to birds as one way the pet and owner interact. This is enriching for both the owner and the pet, and after all, interaction is the main reason to have a pet. The problem here is that the bird's diet can be unbalanced by choosing the wrong kind of treat or feeding too many treats. In fact, some owners feed so many high-energy treats that their pet's diet ends up being composed more of treats than of the food intended

as the main source of nutrition. What we need to do is choose the type and amount of treats, so all the needs for interaction and nutrition are met.

One way to do this is to choose low-energy treats. These are usually vegetables or fruits, and must be chosen so they are low in fat and high in water. Some of the acceptable treats are broccoli, cabbage, cauliflower, lettuce, apple, pear, peach, pineapple, guava, mango, fresh corn, cottage cheese and similar foods.

Some unacceptable foods are avocado, chocolate, ice cream, cake, cookies, high-fat seeds and similar foods. Most, but not all of

the unacceptable foods can be fed in limited amounts, but we are talking about one or two sunflower seeds a day, not a handful.

Recent research on other species of birds has shown that the amount of energy one species can get out of a food may differ from what another species can get out of the same food. And in fact, young birds of the same species may get less energy out of a food than their parents. For this reason, I offer only general guidelines and not actual energy values for selected foods.

Most cockatiels will eat about 15 grams (about half an ounce) of a manufactured diet each day, but the same cockatiel fed sunflower seeds will eat only 9 grams and get the same number of calories. One pound is 454 grams, which means a cockatiel will eat about one pound of food a month. One quarter cup of pellets weighs about 40 grams and should last a cockatiel almost three days. Pellets contain about twelve times as much energy per gram as broccoli does.

With low-energy foods such as broccoli, one can feed about the same volume or weight of treat each day as one would feed of pellets. That is, a cockatiel could safely eat one quarter cup of broccoli over three days without fear of unbalancing the pelleted diet. The same rule of thumb can be used for other low-calorie foods such as most fruits and vegetables. This allows you to offer treats in small amounts each day. Treats should be consumed quickly, before they have a chance to spoil.

The above rules of thumb will allow you to choose the correct kinds of treats and to feed them in roughly the right amounts. You will, however, find that the amount of feed you buy for your bird exceeds the pound a month stated above. This is due to waste. Many birds waste far more food than they consume, particularly foods that are new to them. This should not be considered waste, but rather environmental enrichment. Many birds pick up pieces of food and carry them about their cage, chewing and manipulating the food. Frequently the food is dropped through the wire or onto the floor and lost. This is no cause for concern, as the food is filling the bird's need to chew and to interact with its environment.

Feeding is more for a bird than simply a source of nutrition. It is part of a complex set of behaviors that have evolved over time. These behaviors are social, reproductive or simply diversional, and should be allowed. In some avian species behaviors even include attempting to regurgitate food for other birds or for their owners in a show of courtship behavior. While one might not choose to participate in this behavior, it is a clear sign of bonding by the bird.

Birds usually waste less food as they become more familiar with it, although most birds will continue to use food for a variety of purposes throughout their lives.

Eating and Breeding

Breeding in birds is a multistep process, with each step imposing different nutritional stresses on the bird. The initial stage of reproduction is growth of the gonads (sex organs). The gonads of most birds sit within the body cavity in a regressed condition before the onset of breeding. When conditions are right, the gonads grow to the point where reproduction is possible. This period of gonadal growth can result in as much as a 10 percent increase in the body

Eating is more for a bird than simply a source of nutrition. It is part of a complex set of behaviors that have evolved over time.   *(David Wrobel)*

weight of some birds. During this stage of reproduction nutrients are used for growth, but the extra nutrition needed for this growth is marginal and does not usually require a change in diet.

The next nutritionally significant phase of reproduction is egg production. The hen will need higher levels of protein, vitamins, trace minerals and, especially, calcium. These additional nutrients are necessary for the production of viable eggs and to maintain the health of the hen. If the hen has vitamin or trace mineral deficiencies, her eggs may not develop normally. This can be a major cause of death in embryos.

Calcium is needed to produce egg shells. The hen stores calcium in her bones in anticipation of egg production. These stores are less than is needed for a normal clutch of eggs in cockatiels. As the hen's calcium stores are depleted, two adverse events occur. First, the hen's bones become dangerously thin and are subject to fracture. Hens in this condition are difficult to treat, because they become too fragile to handle in order to set their broken bones.

The other adverse effect is on the egg shell. With normal calcium stores but a calcium-deficient diet, a hen can lay two to four eggs with normal shells. As successive eggs are laid, they have thinner and thinner shells. These shells are less

The food we feed cockatiel parents must meet all their chicks' nutritional requirements. These are proud parents Charlie and Lacey.   *(David Wrobel)*

able to retain water within the egg, so the embryo dries out before it can develop normally. Milder cases of drying can render the embryo unable to rotate in the egg during hatching, resulting in a failure to hatch.

A hen laying eggs needs a calcium level of about 0.35 percent in her diet, compared to a maintenance minimum of about 0.1 percent. Should your pet start to lay eggs without a mate and resist your efforts to stop this laying, you should still raise the level of calcium in her diet to 0.35 percent to maintain her bone integrity.

After the eggs hatch, parents take the food they ingest and regurgitate it for their young. Since growing birds have higher nutrient

requirements than adult birds, it is necessary to feed the parent birds a diet that exceeds their needs so that they can meet the needs of the chicks they are feeding.

It is important here to understand that cockatiel parents do not enrich the diet they ingest with nutrients from their own bodies, such as happens with pigeons and doves. They simply ingest food and water and bring it to their chicks. This means that all the nutrients the chick will get are in the food the parents eat. In other words, we are feeding the parents what the growing chicks need.

For cockatiels, 20 percent protein and 0.8 percent lysine (an amino acid) are needed during growth. Most other nutritional requirements for growing cockatiels are extrapolated from poultry requirements.

HAND-FEEDING CHICKS

Occasionally, chicks may be taken from their parents for feeding by hand. In this case, your best bet is a commercial hand-feeding diet. You will have to dilute the diet with water to meet the water requirements of the chick. Water needs change with a chick's age and level of development. If hatchling chicks are hand fed, they need 10 percent solid matter mixed with 90 percent water for the first three days. After that they can be fed 30 percent solids and 70 percent water. These measurements should be determined by weight and not by volume, because while a cup of water always weighs the same, the weight of a cup of dry diet will vary depending on how firmly it is packed into the cup. Weighing the food is therefore the only precise way of measuring how much a chick is fed.

Chicks should be fed often enough so that there is food in their crops for at least sixteen hours of a twenty-four-hour day. At the last feeding of the day, the crop should be filled to capacity to take the chick as far as possible into the night before its crop empties. Generally, cockatiel chicks during the rapid phase of growth, from roughly three days to three weeks, will eat their weight in food diluted to 25 percent solids and 75 percent water. That is, a chick that weighs 25 grams in the morning will eat about 25 grams of food diluted to 25 percent solids over the course of the day. Chicks fed in this manner grow about as well as chicks fed by parent birds.

If chicks are managed and fed properly, they will be ready to wean between six and seven weeks of age. At that age, chicks should be offered the same food the adults were eating when they were feeding their chicks. Between two and four months of age, the weaned chicks can be offered the adult maintenance diet.

Sickness

The type of diet that should be fed to a sick bird is best determined by your veterinarian. Often an illness will respond to nutritional treatment, supplementation or force feeding. Many times a bird with a disease that affects a specific organ system can benefit from a diet that reduces the stress on that organ system to function. For example, there are commercially available diets that have been formulated to reduce stress on the liver, the kidney and the intestinal tract. Other diets have been formulated to be fed in emergencies to rapidly supply the nutrients needed to aid in recovery, to enhance absorption of nutrients when the gastrointestinal tract is compromised or to reduce the weight of overweight birds.

One of the advantages of regularly feeding a pelleted diet is that these special diets are also pelleted and will be easily accepted by your bird. If your bird is sick and has not been eating pellets, it is important that it eat something during recovery. Feed whatever it will eat, unless your veterinarian recommends otherwise.

Responding to Environmental Conditions

Extreme heat and cold can affect the nutritional status of your bird. In extreme heat it is important to allow your bird access to more comfortable conditions. This means it must have access to shade, a breeze and adequate clean water. High temperatures may increase its need for water, so containers that might normally supply enough water may need to be supplemented or refilled more often in the heat. They should be checked regularly.

When your bird's environment is unusually cold, it needs extra energy in its diet. This means food must always be available and an increase in the level of dietary fat may be indicated. Water must be kept clean and free of ice. As with heat, a bird in the cold must be allowed the freedom to seek an area in which it is most comfortable. Birds must be able to get out of drafts, rain or snow.

Storing Feed

The concept of feed storage is relatively simple: Keep feed cool and dry. There are, however, a few details we need to consider.

Generally, feed purchased in the pet or feed store is composed mostly of dry grains. These grains may be part of a pellet or a seed mix, but they have many attributes in common that need to be considered when it comes to storing them. First among these is that feed gets moldy if it contains more than 15 percent moisture. Usually feeds are dried to 12 percent moisture or less to prevent molding. The moisture in feed is loosely bound, which means feed can get drier or damper, depending on how much moisture is in the air around it. This is why large feed containers are usually made of paper, which allows this transfer of water between the air and the feed. Water vapor in feed moves toward cooler and dryer areas. If the feed is kept in a water-tight container, this moving vapor condenses, causing wet spots that encourage mold growth.

While small feed containers usually have too little water to

cause much condensation, you need to be aware of how the feed is stored in the place where you buy it. If 200 pounds of feed is placed in a plastic or metal can with a tight lid and the can is placed in an area where the bottom is cool, it is possible for the moisture to collect in the bottom of the can, where mold will grow. As the mold grows it will produce additional water from the feed it consumes and increase the rate of mold growth, spoiling the whole can of feed.

Even feed in paper containers should not be stored on a concrete floor, since moisture can migrate through the concrete into the feed. The feed should be stored off the floor, such as on a pallet, in a cool, dry place. Air should be allowed to circulate around the container.

Normally, keeping feed cool and dry is enough to store it for months. But sometimes it is advisable to keep feed even longer or to keep samples of feed for later reference. One way to preserve feed for the long term is to freeze it. I am often asked if freezing destroys vitamins. In fact, the opposite is true: Freezing actually *preserves* vitamins by reducing the rate at which they oxidize. Freezing any dry feed is not a problem. Wet feeds can be another matter, if physical properties such as texture or the ability to bind water are important. Freezing can change the water binding characteristics of some wet feeds,

TEMPERATURE AND SHELF LIFE

The effects of temperature on the shelf life of feed is easy to calculate. For every 18°F that the storage temperature is increased, the shelf life of the feed is cut in half. For example, feed that keeps for one year at 70°F will keep for six months at 88°F and for three months at 106°F. If the temperature is lowered, the same feed will keep for two years at 52°F, four years at 34°F, eight years at 16 F and so forth. As you can see, reducing the temperature at which feed is stored is a powerful tool in preserving its shelf life.

causing them to become mushy or slushy.

Feed that is kept dry so it will not mold and cool so that it will not oxidize is still susceptible to other problems. The main one is infestation by insects or rodents. One way to limit infestation is to keep the environment clean and free of food for these pests. This means cleaning all areas in which feed is used and stored before adding new food. This includes storage areas, feeding areas and the area around the feeder that catches spilled food.

Rodents are mainly controlled by managing the environment and by trapping and poisoning. Storing feed in areas that keep rodents out is another positive way to control rodents. This is easier for rats than mice, but can be done. It is simply a matter of finding all the possible entry sites and plugging them. If the area cannot be controlled, use rodent-proof cans.

To control insects, a number of measures are helpful, starting with obtaining feed that is free of insects when you buy it. This is often difficult, since feed can pick up insects anywhere along the path from the manufacturer to the consumer. If you find insects in your feed, they can be eliminated in a number of ways that pose no threat to your birds. Small amounts of feed can be frozen for at least three days. Most common grain insects will be killed by freezing. Either before feed is frozen or immediately after it is removed from the freezer, it should be placed in a plastic bag to protect it from any condensation that collects on the outside of the bag as it warms to room temperature. This will prevent the feed from getting moldy.

Larger amounts of feed can be fumigated using carbon dioxide. With this method, about one pound of dry ice is placed in the bottom of a plastic trash can. It should be covered with enough paper to ensure the feed placed on top of the dry ice won't freeze. Place the feed in the can, still in its bag. Close the lid and don't open it again for three days. One hundred

WATER IS ESSENTIAL

Cockatiels are native to arid areas of Australia and so have a high tolerance for hot, dry conditions. But they still drink water and must have clean water available all the time. Most water that is fit for human consumption is adequate for birds. Some bottled waters have added minerals and may not be good for your bird over long periods of time—it depends on the type and amounts of minerals in the water. Bottled water is needed for your bird only if the domestic water supply is unfit for human consumption.

pounds of feed can be treated at a time in this manner, and the feed is safe for your bird as soon as you remove it.

Moths—usually Indian meal moths or Mediterranean flour moths—are a common culprit in infested feed. Many people mistake them for worms, because the moths lay eggs that hatch into small caterpillars. The caterpillars produce a sticky silk thread as they travel, which binds pieces of feed together. This "webby feed" is a common problem in the feed industry.

The moths pose no threat to your birds, but they can be a nuisance to you. Caterpillars crawl into the corners of rooms, where they pupate. The resulting moths can fly around your house.

Moths can be controlled by the measures previously discussed, or by treating the feed with *Bacillus thuringiensis* (BT). BT kills caterpillars but is harmless to birds and mammals. To eliminate moths from the area where your birds are kept, purchase some form of BT or its toxin at your garden store. A suspension of BT can be mixed with water, and is used to control caterpillars in gardens and in commercial food production. Spray the BT mixture on all areas in which caterpillars might grow. If you need to treat feed, a heaping tablespoon of BT in the minimum amount of water it takes to make it sprayable is enough to treat fifty pounds of feed. BT need not be sprayed uniformly on the feed, since it is passed from caterpillar to caterpillar as they crawl. BT must be applied to each infested food supply, or the untreated food will be a source of reinfestation. Total control takes ten days to two weeks, because BT kills the youngest caterpillars first, leaving older caterpillars to pupate and grow into moths. If treatment does not control the moths, you have likely missed a source of moths, such as the litter under the cage.

Buying and Dispensing Feed

Buying food for your bird is a matter of considering all the factors of

Feed should make a one-way trip to your bird. Use a scoop, not a feed dish, to dispense it. The scoop should remain with the feed and should be cleaned regularly.

nutritional adequacy that have already been discussed. Once you have chosen a feed, there are several things to consider about its purchase. First is the degree of sanitation in the store where you buy the feed. It is important that the feed be kept away from livestock and that it not be stored in open bins from which you scoop feed. Feed that is exposed to birds in a store is likely to become contaminated with pathogenic bacteria. This contamination will not always result in disease, but there is no need to take the risk when a closed and sealed package is available.

Another reason to buy feed in the manufacturer's package is that the information on the package is often useful. It must include a list of ingredients, guaranteed analysis, the address of the manufacturer and perhaps instructions on the use of the feed or a customer service number. Feed that is dispensed in bulk bins may also not be covered by the manufacturer's guarantee. It is possible for feed in bulk bins to be other than what it is presented to be, or for the feed to have become contaminated or adulterated. The manufacturer is unlikely to want to guarantee the quality of

feed kept under such conditions, which are beyond the manufacturer's control.

Once you have purchased your feed it is important to store it properly, as discussed earlier. Feed should make a one-way trip to your bird. That means the feed dish should not be used to scoop the feed. If there is any health problem with your bird and you have other birds, this is one way to spread that disease. Feed should be scooped with a separate scoop that remains with the feed and is cleaned regularly.

Feed in the feeder may stay there for some time, providing it is not wet or contaminated with fecal matter or anything else that could damage the health of your bird. If feed is left in the dish for too long there is a possibility of insect infestation. Wet foods should be kept out for only a few hours, depending on the temperature. Under hot conditions, do not leave wet feed out for more than four hours. Under cool conditions, leave wet food out no more than eight hours. When wet food is changed, the feeder dish should be cleaned with soap and hot water.

Home Sweet Home

In the wild, cockatiels are keen fliers—acrobatic and fast. The hardest part for me about keeping them is the thought of caging that energy and flying ability. But there is another side: being able to keep our companion cockatiels safe from predators and giving them (and us) an interesting life. Part of my enthusiasm for sharing cockatiel care with others comes from my desire to encourage people to give their birds the things they need to be happy, and to express their love and concern for their pets. When I see the joy a cockatiel gets from being loved, and the joy people get from living with their cockatiels, I can stand the thought of keeping a caged bird.

We use the terms *cage bird, caged bird* and *captive-bred* liberally in aviculture (the keeping and breeding of birds). The thought used to horrify me, and I never thought I could keep a bird in a cage. I grew up watching birds, noting the first robin every spring and learning the names of some of our beautiful native birds so that I could recognize them when I saw them. It was a big revelation to me that "caged" birds don't always stay in their cage, but can come out and interact with their human companions. I encourage you to adopt this view of a cage as a safe place for your companion cockatiel, but not necessarily a prison.

The first time I met a cockatiel and it came out of its cage, my idea of living with a bird changed entirely. It's not far from the truth to say that my life changed, too. More later—we're talking about enclosures here.

Your bird's enclosure is for the two of you. Besides a cockatiel's physical comfort and well-being, also consider your own aesthetics and how you will keep the cage clean.

If you can think of these things as you select an enclosure, you will be much happier later.

Style and Size

Given that your bird is adapted to quite a bit of physical activity, the larger the enclosure, the better for your cockatiel. There are some nice furniture-style enclosures and inside aviaries available. There are also some fairly large aviary wire enclosures available, even though they are not as beautiful as other types of enclosures. If you get wire, be sure to ask if it was galvanized after welding. It is also a good precaution to scrub new aviary wire with a solution of vinegar and water. This reacts with any zinc on the cage and helps prevent zinc poisoning.

Some people manage to have a sleeping cage for their birds, an outdoor aviary for exercise and indoor playstands for supervised time out of the cage. This seems ideal to me, although I realize we can't all do this for our birds. Even if you don't have such an arrangement now for your cockatiel, it is something you can plan for and think about.

A cockatiel that gets out of its cage for extended periods each day and can fly throughout the house has a good life. There are risks involved with a bird that has free flight, though, so you must weigh the risk of losing your bird or having

A cockatiel enclosure is for both you and your feathered friend. It should be pleasing, practical and easy to clean. *(Courtesy of Designer Aviaries, Oroville, California)*

an accident against the health and psychological benefits of free flight.

Outdoor Risks

There is also risk involved when a bird spends time outdoors. The benefits of fresh air, sunshine and flight time are obvious. You can minimize the risks if you know the major ones. There is a risk of attack by predators, for example. You can use double wiring, small wire spacing or hot wires to keep out predators such as cats or raccoons. There is a risk of feed becoming infected by the droppings of wild birds or wild opossums. You can make sure the bowls are in a covered area.

There is a risk of parasite infection if the aviary is on natural ground. You can have the birds checked, change the earthen floor fairly frequently and treat for parasites that are a problem. There is a risk of rodent contamination of feed. If you make an outside aviary as rodent-proof as possible, and use traps (ones that won't catch your bird!), the risk will be minimized.

The Bigger, the Better

One of the most important features of an enclosure is bar spacing. There are some beautiful parrot cages out there, but many are made specifically for the larger parrots. A cockatiel could get out or stick its head through the bars and get stuck. Look for bars about half an inch apart, or for an enclosure made specifically for cockatiels.

As I said before, the size of the cage cannot be too large. I like to see cockatiels in a long cage, with a width of at least one-and-a-half to two feet. When a cage is large because it's tall, the height is really wasted space. Cockatiels will move towards the top of their enclosure, no matter how tall it is. So the space they use is an enclosure's footprint—its width and depth, not its height. It's best to look for

A cockatiel enclosure cannot be too large! Bar spacing should be small enough so that a cockatiel cannot get its head through the bars.

or build a long enclosure rather than a tall one.

If your enclosure has a grid on the bottom, both droppings and food will fall through to a tray below. This helps you keep nasty bacteria-laden substances away from your cockatiel. In the wild, these things don't accumulate because the cockatiel lives in an area much larger than a few square feet, so birds aren't adapted to living in a mess—though once your bird starts throwing things around, you might think otherwise!

Perfect Perches

Your enclosure probably comes with perches and feed cups. It's a good idea to get an extra set of feed cups, so that you can wash one while the other set is in use. Consider getting a water bottle—it keeps the water cleaner. If the perches that come with your enclosure are dowels that are all the same size, do change them. If you want to keep dowel perches, at least offer a variety of sizes.

There's a reason for offering a bird perches of various sizes: A bird is on its feet all the time. If those feet are always held in the same position, against the same surface, they have a greater chance of forming sores. I use all natural perches in my birds' enclosures. I pick up eucalyptus branches in an area that is not near a major roadway (to

A bird never kicks back and puts its feet up, so it's important to offer a cockatiel natural perches of various sizes. This is Yetta, a female whiteface cockatiel, perched on a grapevine.

avoid debris and lead from car fumes), then wash them off thoroughly with a bleach-and-water solution. When they are dry, I break them to fit the cage. Sometimes I bake the branches on a low oven for a couple of hours. *Mmmm,* the smell of fresh-baked eucalyptus! The birds have a great time tearing bark off the branches.

Some books say eucalyptus is poisonous, but my birds eat (or at least chew) the leaves and nuts, and perch on eucalyptus branches. It's a little bit of "home" I can offer to my Australian natives!

You might not live in an area where eucalyptus grows. You can use fruit tree wood (except cherry), willow, oak or maple. I understand that cherry wood can be poisonous, and we aren't too sure about pine branches and all of their gooey sap. It would be best to ask local bird keepers what kinds of branches they use safely in their aviaries and enclosures.

You can buy manzanita branches for cages. This is a very hard wood that your pet usually cannot destroy. That sounds good, until you think of the joy they are missing by not being able to chew the manzanita. A perch or two is fine, but don't ask your bird to live only with hard, indestructible manzanita.

When you have perches prepared, it's time to decorate! You do not want perches to be above food and water dishes, so that no droppings fall into them. You do want to offer a variety of roosting places and the opportunity to exercise.

A perch in front of food dishes is a good idea. I like to place the highest perches at angles across two corners of the cage. My current setup has a branch with a wingnut arrangement on the end attached at a door. The cockatiels are learning to swing out when I open the door, and swing back in again without getting flustered. A small thing, but another diversion and learning experience, as well as proof of the trust we are building.

Young chicks or handicapped birds may need special considerations. For chicks, I place perches very low in the cage, or put in a perch angled from the grate to a higher perch, so they can climb up. Handicapped cockatiels may need shelves to rest on, or low perches wrapped in abundant paper toweling to keep abrasion to a minimum.

Where to Put the Cage

Cage placement can be an important issue. You want to create a balance of safety, socialization and rest for your cockatiel. Sometimes it takes some experimentation to get it all right in your particular situation.

Cage placement is important. Locate your cockatiel's enclosure in an area that provides a combination of safety, socialization and rest.

You should consider the cockatiel's well-being. Is it safe from predatory animals in your house (cats or dogs or ferrets or . . .)? I have lived in a household with cockatiels and a cat. The cockatiels lived in the bedroom with a door closed, or visited in the living room if the cat was not inside. Dogs I have owned were taught not to jump at the cockatiels in their cages, and not to approach them when the birds were free in the room.

Is your cockatiel out of direct sunlight? A window with a view is one way to entertain a cockatiel, but your bird needs to be out of the direct path of the sunlight coming in through the window. Sunlight is beneficial to cockatiels, helping them produce vitamin D, which aids in absorbing calcium. Sunlight coming through glass or plastic does not have the same benefit, however. Meanwhile, a cockatiel can overheat if it cannot cool off in the shade or in a mist of water. It might be able to look out a window with an awning, for example, but not an unprotected window.

You may wish to provide lighting in your bird's area. In most of my cockatiel setups, I have had full-spectrum lights set on a timer, so that I could control the length of daylight hours.

The full-spectrum bulbs supposedly emit the sun's full spectrum of light, and may therefore promote the manufacture of vitamin D_3, as sunlight does. At any rate, they emit a pleasant light, and a definite benefit is that the birds' true colors show up well.

Don't forget to turn the lights off. Your cockatiel needs rest as well as stimulation. A quiet, dark nighttime repose is good for your cockatiel's health.

Is your cockatiel safe from fumes and kitchen hazards? The kitchen is a lively part of any house, but it is dangerous for our curious feathered friends. Nonstick cookware emits deadly fumes, as do many self-cleaning ovens and some drip pans and bakeware. A cockatiel out of its cage when a meal is being prepared is at risk from pots of boiling water, soapy dishwater and hot burners.

For its well-being, your cockatiel should be in a busy part of the house, where it can interact with its human flock and observe activity. Often this is the living room, but maybe in your household it's another room. Even when they aren't being held or stroked, cockatiels usually like to be out and sitting near their flock, running up and down the back of your couch, watching TV with you and generally joining in.

I offer one warning, however. Cockatiels are flock animals, and tend to be as noisy as their surroundings. I vividly remember trying to hold a Tupperware party in my house with a large, loud, deep-voiced German woman officiating. The cockatiel in the room rang his bell as hard as he could to match that volume! Needless to say, that was not a very welcome behavior.

The Bird Room

Will your companion share your living space, or have a room of its own? I don't know of too many single cockatiels with their own room, but in many multibird households there is a "bird room." I was lucky enough to have such an arrangement when I had several breeding pairs. In their room I had a seamless linoleum floor, air purifiers, full-spectrum lighting and storage for bird supplies. It made care much more convenient for this owner. Pet birds came to visit downstairs on portable perch areas, or occasionally in smaller cages.

It was really easy to have an effective quarantine, too. When I came in from a bird store or a bird mart, I left my shoes downstairs and changed clothes before I visited my own birds.

I had fun decorating my bird room, too, with appropriate posters, photos and pretty bird toys. I have a few toys I hate to give to birds, but keep them on the wall as decoration. Usually these are colorful hearts, symbolizing love and caring.

TOO MUCH TV?

I once sold a weaned cockatiel to a person who called me shortly thereafter to complain about how noisy the bird was. I knew the chick had not had enough time to develop bad habits, and knew it had not been inordinately loud when growing up at my house. I asked where the cockatiel's cage was placed. It turned out the cage was over a TV set that was going full blast most of the time. I rarely watch TV, so the chick had never been exposed to so much noise. It tried mightily to keep up the decibel level. When the owners moved the cage, they had a quiet bird after all.

An Outside Aviary

Perhaps, if the climate permits in your area, you would prefer to keep your pet outside. Outside it might be easier to provide a large enclosure, such as an aviary. The air circulates freely in an aviary, and the birds have exposure to healthy sunshine.

My own birds lived outside for a couple of years, but I found it frustrating not to have as much contact with them. They did enjoy rainstorms, though! It was a different level of interaction and enjoyment of my birds. We talked to each other, whistled back and forth, and I watched them fly and interact with each other and react to the weather.

Safety in an outside aviary is a whole different issue, too. One of my favorite birds was eaten by a predator—a raptor or a raccoon, perhaps. I'll never know.

I have limited experience with outside enclosures. There are a few points to keep in mind, however. There should be a double entrance, so there is no chance the birds can escape as you enter or leave the enclosure. Many people build fairly short doors into an outdoor enclosure, so that the birds do not fly past or over them.

Feed bowls should be easy for you to access, preferably from outside the enclosure, and should be protected from the elements and the chance of wild bird droppings being deposited in them. Water should be clean, and there should be a way to keep the enclosure clean.

There should be shelter from the wind and rain, as well as access to the weather. Some outside enclosures have an inside area. For that matter, some inside aviaries have an outside extension. I have a friend whose cockatiels can fly, through an open sliding glass door, onto a balcony overlooking the Santa Cruz mountains. Food and water are inside; the view is outside.

Keep It Clean

Whether your birds live inside or out, cleanliness is a concern. Is the cage on carpet, linoleum or tile? Is this a surface that is easy to clean? Often, plastic sheeting on walls and a plastic protector under a cage are appropriate. I'm using inexpensive shower curtains on the wall next to my cockatiel cage, with some success. They are easy and inexpensive to replace, and they wipe clean.

I also keep a vacuum cleaner near my cockatiel cage and use it daily. Our dear cockatiel companions spread seeds in the desert (thus serving their ecological niche as sowers), and they treat their modern diets the same way! Without an ambitious cleanup schedule, we could grow a lot of things underneath a cockatiel cage. Keeping your companion's area tidy will prevent the growth of mold and bacteria, and discourage rodents.

Because of the dust created by cockatiels, another device to consider in the bird area is an air filter. There are a number of designs and features available. HEPA filters are often recommended. You could consult an allergist or *Consumer Reports* to find out the air filter that is currently considered most effective. Don't forget to consider the cost of replacement filters while you're shopping.

Now that we've ventured into the hardware store, look in the mousetrap aisle. You may or may not need to worry about rodents. I have lived in locations where mice invaded aviaries and bird cages. They can be quite bold creatures, and of course they're active when both we and the birds are asleep. An outside environment should be as rodent-proof as possible. Inside, keep the area clean and consider removing feed cups overnight. Mouse droppings are not a healthy part of a cockatiel's diet.

I hesitate to use rodent poisons around my birds, and have at

This gray male cockatiel lives in an outside aviary. It has access to an inside shelter, outside sunshine and plenty of room to fly.

times used mechanical mouse-traps. There are humane traps available to catch mice alive, and an assortment of old-fashioned spring traps, sticky glue traps and whatever comes along when some-one invents a better mousetrap. I know some aviculturists who keep cats that are trained not to hurt birds.

To keep the cage bottom clean, inside you can use caging with wire grates, or have an aviary with paper on the bottom. Avoid anything resembling "nuggets," as veterinarian Fern Van Sant says—you might be tempted to clean less often, and you certainly couldn't tell as well what your bird's droppings looked like. ("Yes I can," piped up some-one at a bird club meeting. "They're on my shirt.") Monitoring droppings can be one way to assess your bird's health. Changes not associated with diet could mean there is something wrong.

When it comes to cage liners, I have seen some ingenious adaptations using paper rolls that flow through an aviary. The ends of large

ALL THE NEWS THAT'S FIT

I try to review what papers my birds look at in their cage. I don't place anything with large photos of predators such as cats or hawks on their cage bottoms, nor do I place cooked chicken or turkey ads in their cages. It might not make a difference to them, but it does to me!

commercial paper rolls can be purchased, or might even be free, where your local newspaper is printed. Other possibilities as cage liners include specially made waxy liners, paper bags or computer paper.

Newspaper is the traditional cage liner. If you call your local paper, they can tell you whether the ink they use is poisonous. Many papers have switched to safe, soy-based nontoxic ink.

There are several theories about the best design for keeping outside enclosures clean. California Breeder cages on stilts have proven easy to

keep clean. Birds are never on the ground, but on wire over it, and the mess drops through. Other substrates are cement, earth, rock and sand.

Free Flight Inside

If a cockatiel can reach curtains, wallboard or windowsills from its cage, chances are it will gnaw on them. For this reason, a cage should not be too near these deli-cacies, and time spent outside the cage should be supervised.

I like to teach a cockatiel to stay on a playstand during free flight time. One of my birds' progeny lives in a household where free flight time is just that: No playstands for these cockatiels—they are encouraged to fly repeatedly throughout the house for exercise. There is a great deal of satisfaction in watching the cockatiels wheel about and bank at the windows. There are, of course, a number of risks, as well. I'll help you learn how to clip your bird's wings in Chapter 9; you will have to decide about its lifestyle.

Safety First

A cockatiel is naturally curious. You are probably delighted with your pet's antics when it is outside of its enclosure socializing with you. You should also be aware of some hazards in the home, however. I am sure more pet cockatiels die from accidents than from old age. While accidents do happen, you can make an effort to minimize risks.

Lead

Some common items contain lead. Stained glass is made with lead, and so stained glass windows, sun catchers and lamps make poor perches for your pet. Curtain weights are often made of lead, and cockatiels just might think of chewing on them. Costume jewelry and seals on older wine bottles may also contain lead, so you should not allow your cockatiel to nibble on them.

Nonstick Surfaces

When nonstick cookware and range drip pans are overheated, they release a gas that is very toxic to birds. Entire households of birds have died within minutes because an empty pan was left on the stove or a cookie sheet sat baking in the oven. I have thrown away all my nonstick cookware and advise you to do the same. This is very important. Nonstick surfaces are also found on ironing boards and ironing board covers, in self-cleaning ovens and on some heating lamps. If you accidentally overheat a nonstick surface, you should immediately ventilate the area by opening windows.

Water Hazards

A cockatiel may accidentally or through curiosity fall into standing water in the house, including pans of dish water and open toilets. Dishwater contains soap, which may take all the oil out of a bird's feathers, leaving it shivering, unkempt and unable to keep itself warm. Please make sure all the sinks and dish pans are empty when your bird is out of its cage. And do close the toilet lid.

Tall glasses of water are a special hazard to unsupervised pets. A cockatiel may reach down for the last sip in a glass, slip in and drown because it was unable to get out. Free-flying pets should never be left unattended, and you should be observant when you are with your pet.

Fumes

Birds succumb to fumes much more easily than people. Their respiratory systems are much more complicated, and include not just two lungs, as we have, but also seven air sacs throughout their bodies and even hollow bones. Because of this, you may be using harmful products without even realizing it: hair spray, nail polish, aerosol cans, perfumed carpet fresheners, perfumed candles and bug sprays. When fogging your house for pests or laying new carpeting,

FOOD DANGERS

Both avocado and chocolate contain substances that are poisonous to birds. Do not feed items containing these foods, and make sure these foods are not out in the open when your bird is out of its cage.

for example, you would be wise to move your birds to a friend's house for a few days.

Plants

Some houseplants are poisonous, while others are quite safe for a curious cockatiel to nibble on— but are certainly in danger of being nibbled! Many plants, with no other defenses, produce chemicals

to deter predators from eating them. Philodendron and diffenbachia are two especially poisonous house plants.

Most palms and ferns are safe. Many of the traditional holiday trimmings—holly, poinsettia and mistletoe—are poisonous. I suggest decorating with fruit, nuts and pine branches.

If you are curious about the plants in your home, consult your avian veterinarian or local poison control centers. We are not absolutely certain which plants cause symptoms of poisoning in birds, but your veterinarian has some experience in this matter and a poison center knows about plants that have proven poisonous to people. Birds may tolerate them, but you would be safer not to have

Some houseplants are poisonous. Be wary of letting your cockatiel eat greenery in your home. This is a lutino hen, Lindbergh.   (David Wrobel)

ANIMAL POISON CONTROL CENTER

If you or your veterinarian need help with a case of poisoning, there is a hotline for animal poison control. You may contact the ASPCA/National Animal Poison Control Center. Be prepared to describe what happened and any symptoms you have noticed. Relay as much as you know about age, sex and weight of the cockatiel. If it swallowed a substance, have the label available.

There is a fee charged per case. Call the Center at (800) 548-2423 and the fee will be charge, to your credit card. You may also be charged per minute by dialing (900) 680-0000.

them around. As more data are collected on birds, we should be able to collect a list of plants known to be poisonous to them.

Other Pets

The other pets people commonly keep, including dogs and cats, are natural predators. Either may think of a resident bird more as a next meal than a buddy. Dogs should be trained not to attack birds. But even the most trustworthy and bird-friendly dog should be supervised when cockatiels are out of their cages. Although my cockatiels lived in relative safety

Other pets are natural predators. Dogs can be trained not to hurt a family pet, but should not be left unsupervised with a companion bird. Here, Bonnie Blue coexists peacefully with Lindbergh. *(David Wrobel)*

from a dog who lived to be ten years old, two of them lost tails when she strayed from good behavior and I was less than vigilant.

Cats and birds should be kept in separate locations. Again, supervise your pets when they are together. If a cat ever scratches or bites your cockatiel, take the bird to the veterinarian immediately. There is a bacteria in a cat's saliva that multiplies rapidly in birds and could cause death within as little as twenty-four hours if the bird does not receive antibiotics.

Flight Obstacles

Cockatiels are affectionate pets and may fly after their favorite person. You should watch carefully for

Cat bites can be fatal to a bird. Bites or scratches require immediate veterinary care.

approaching cockatiels when closing doors. Cockatiels also delight in exploring. They are ground-feeding birds in their native

Australia, and may unexpectedly explore the terrain in your home. Watch your step around your bird, and watch where you sit!

Cockatiels also enjoy looking at themselves in the mirror. Great! However, a large mirror in a room with a free-flying cockatiel may be deceptive. The bird probably will see the image in the mirror as empty space to fly into. It could be seriously hurt, or break its neck. Before allowing your pet cockatiel out into a room, it is a good idea to cover any large mirrors to prevent tragedy.

The same applies to windows. Before getting your cockatiel out of its enclosure, close the curtains or pull the shades in a room. Covering mirrors and windows are very simple procedures that may ensure a much longer life span for your bird.

Illness and Emergencies

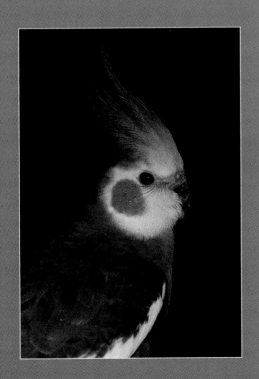

Cockatiels are fairly long-lived pets, so chances are at some point in their lives they will have an illness or a health condition that needs to be treated by an avian veterinarian. In Chapter 4 I talked about why a partnership with a veterinarian is so important, and as I go through the various illnesses that may affect a cockatiel, I hope that point will become even more evident.

Rather than viewing this as a boring chapter or one you skip, read about each illness with an eye to prevention. Also, it's important to know what to look for when you check your little friend every day. Your observations are very valuable assets in your cockatiel's health care. When you note changes in behavior and your bird's physical presentation, it's a signal that some process is taking place. That process may be disease, or it may be something as benign as a hormonal change in the spring, a rocky adolescence or a normal response to molting. As an educated owner, you can learn to distinguish these changes and take appropriate actions. However, you will see that symptoms of many diseases, from the commonplace ones to the very serious, are similar. Diagnostic tests will tell the real story.

There are also some preventive actions you can take to avoid disease in your cockatiels. If you look at how many diseases are spread through fecal matter and feather dust, for example, the importance of cleanliness becomes a lot clearer.

Illnesses and conditions you are most likely to encounter include bacterial or fungal infections, parasites, toxins, nutritional problems and metabolic disorders. I recommend keeping a good avian health-care book—one that explores bird disease and illness in depth—on hand for reference.

VETERINARY REFERENCE BOOKS

The Complete Bird Owner's Handbook
by Gary A. Gallerstein, DVM
Howell Book House, New York, 1994

The Parrot in Health and Illness
by Bonnie Munro Doane
Howell Book House, New York, 1991

Avian Medicine: Principles and Application
by Branson W. Ritchie, DVM, PhD, Greg J. Harrison, DVM, and Linda R. Harrison, BS
Wingers Publishing, Inc., Lake Worth, Florida, 1994

Prevention Pointers

You can diminish the likelihood of cockatiel illness by scheduling yearly veterinary checks and by learning your bird's weight and checking it regularly. Sometimes birds do not exhibit outward signs of illness, but weight loss or lab tests will show a medical condition.

Your bird's chances of getting a transmissible disease, such as a virus, can be lessened by taking precautions against exposure. For example, if you visit a pet store or bird event, take off your shoes and clothes as soon as you get home, and shower before you visit with your own bird. This is because some diseases are airborne and are also found in feather dust. You can also avoid exposure to disease by limiting trips with your bird to places where there are no other birds. There is no reason to take your companion cockatiel to a bird fair, for example. In our local bird club, we have a "one bird" rule—only one bird-owning household has a bird at the meeting per month.

LIMITING STRESS

Limiting stress can help prevent illness, as well. Obviously, not all stress can be eliminated, and stress needs to be balanced with conditioning your bird to some change, such as accepting veterinary visits, traveling during the holidays, pet sitters and new toys.

Stress to a bird may be different from your stress, too. Being sensitive to a bird's-eye view of the world may include not allowing the family cat to sit on a bird cage, providing roomy conditions for your feathered friends, providing a separate food bowl for each cockatiel if one is a bully, and watching out for objects that loom over a cockatiel cage. Balloons usually set off an alarm in my flock, for example. I usually attribute that to instinctive behavior on the part of a species that would be hawk food in the wild. Since I can't get inside the cockatiels' brains, of course, I may not be correct. It might just be the size and color of balloons that are alarming, along with their erratic movements.

An obvious stress is moving to a new home. I am not going to stop placing young cockatiels, but I do notice that in a new home they exhibit such symptoms as watery droppings for a few days, or they

WHAT CAUSES COCKATIEL STRESS?

New home

New owners

Change in location of cage

Change in diet

Malnutrition

Loss of mate

Predators in household (other pets such as dogs and cats)

Puberty

Temperature extremes

Objects located above them

Sudden movements and lights

Car lights at night

Crowded conditions

Cage too small

Molting

Breeding

Egg laying

Lack of sleep

Loud noise

Disease

TIPS FOR
PREVENTING ILLNESS

Observe your cockatiels daily.

Schedule a yearly veterinary exam.

Shower after attending a bird event or visiting a pet store.

Quarantine new birds coming into your household.

Quarantine show birds.

Limit stress (take the bird's-eye view of what is stressful).

Refrain from taking your pet to bird fairs, pet shops or bird shows.

Vaccinate (if appropriate).

revert to begging behavior even though they have learned to eat and drink on their own before leaving home.

While it is inevitable that any cockatiel you acquire will experience some stress simply because it has moved into a new home, there are things you can do to limit the stress. Keep the bird on the same diet. Provide a roomy cage, make sure it gets enough rest and don't subject your new cockatiel to an unusual amount of noise or activity. The key is to be aware!

VACCINATIONS

We are all familiar with the use of vaccinations to prevent serious disease. We inoculate human children and give rabies shots to our dogs and cats. It is only in the last decade that there have been advances made in identifying, testing for and developing vaccines for some of the major bird diseases.

You may want to discuss with your avian veterinarian whether it is appropriate to vaccinate your bird. This may depend on your habits or on developments in avian medicine that are not known as I am writing this. You can aid in the advancement of developments by financially supporting avian research and programs that train avian veterinarians.

Another preventive measure is quarantining new birds in your household. For thirty to forty-five days, keep a new bird in a separate room, care for it after you have seen to the other birds and take it in for a "well bird" check during that time. If you exhibit cockatiels at bird shows, your birds are going to be exposed to many other birds. When your show birds come back into your household, they should be treated like new birds and quarantined from members of your flock that did not leave the house.

Infections

Bacterial and fungal infections seem to be fairly common in cockatiels. They are caused by microorganisms. A lab test is required to

These two albino cockatiels are new to this household, and are being caged separately and kept quarantined for thirty to forty-five days.

accurately diagnose infections, since the microorganisms involved cannot be seen with the naked eye.

To a careful observer, there are some signs that might signal an infection in your bird. However, sometimes your bird will show no signs at all. This is yet another reason why regular veterinary exams are so important.

SIGNS OF BACTERIAL
INFECTION

Listlessness

Gaping

Change in behavior

YEAST INFECTION

A common infection in cockatiels is candidiasis, or a yeast infection. In people we call a similar infection thrush. It usually involves the digestive tract, including the mouth, crop and throat, but may extend to the intestines.

A yeast infection is caused by an overgrowth of the common fungus *Candida albicans*. Even healthy birds have some *C. albicans* in their systems, but an overgrowth of the fungus occasionally occurs. This may happen in chicks, which have less highly developed immune systems; in any bird after antibiotic therapy, when there is a vitamin A deficiency in the cockatiel's diet; when a bird is fed moldy food (especially sprouts); or when there is poor sanitation, which increases exposure to the fungus. If your cockatiel is treated with antibiotics, ask your veterinarian about treatment at the same time to prevent a yeast infection.

SIGNS OF A YEAST INFECTION

White lesions in the mouth

Weight loss

Thickened crop

Frequent regurgitation

Diarrhea

Sudden death (not common)

One sign of this disease is white, cheesy mouth lesions and a sticky residue in a bird's mouth. Other signs include a thickened crop, regurgitation and diarrhea. There may also be no symptoms signaling that your companion has a yeast infection.

The success of yeast infection treatment depends on how soon the condition is diagnosed and the general health of the bird.

ASPERGILLOSIS

Aspergillosis is a fungal disease of the sinuses, lungs or air sacs. It is caused by the fungus *Aspergillus fumigatus*. This fungus is everywhere in our environment, and both we and our birds are constantly exposed to it. For example, it is found in soil, rotted wood, corncob bedding, aviary dust and stored seeds and grains.

Birds with compromised immune systems are most likely to get an aspergillus infection. Low humidity, high humidity without ventilation or high air dust in the environment also contribute to aspergillosis.

The only symptom may be sudden death, or there may be respiratory problems signaling this disease. Diagnosis is difficult, except through necropsy. Reducing stress and providing a clean environment are essential in preventing infection. Though there are some

SIGNS OF ASPERGILLOSIS

Wheezing

Increased breathing rate

Respiratory clicking

Voice changes

Weight loss

Increased urination (polyuria)

Death

treatments available, often aspergillosis results in death.

TUBERCULOSIS

In birds, tuberculosis is caused by *Mycobacterium avium, M. tuberculosis* (the TB agent that affects humans) or other TB mycobacterium species. TB can be transmitted through food or water, contaminated perches or cage wire. Ticks, mites and spiders can transmit the disease to birds, as well. It is also possible for a cockatiel to contract TB through a skin wound if the bird then comes in contact with contaminated objects.

In cockatiels, TB is typically a disease of the digestive system. (In human beings TB is usually a disease of the respiratory system.) Tuberculosis is a chronic infection in which lesions form, called tubercles. These lesions can be found in the bird's intestinal wall, liver,

SIGNS OF AVIAN TB

Weight loss

Masses under the skin

Thinness despite a good appetite

Recurrent diarrhea

Intermittent lameness

Breathing problems

Swollen joints

Bright red blood in droppings

Cloacal prolapse

Lethargy and depression

Abdominal enlargement

spleen and bone marrow, and often on the skin. At first the lesions are soft, but they harden over time.

There are few outward symptoms of this disease, and the symptoms that do appear could be characteristic of many problems.

TB in birds can be treated, though there is a health risk to the caretaker. In some cases euthanasia may be warranted. Avian TB can be transmitted to humans, and it is difficult to treat. However, this is rare, and people with low resistance to disease are most likely to be affected. These include old and young people, those with serious illnesses such as cancer that lower their resistance to infection and people with illnesses that compromise the immune system, such as AIDS.

If you have a cockatiel that tests positive for TB, discuss all options with both your veterinarian and your personal physician.

Psittacosis

Psittacosis, which is also called chlamydiosis, is caused by a bacteria called *Chlamydia psittaci*. Our favorite avian friends, cockatiels, tolerate psittacosis especially well and are often accused of infecting other birds. When a cockatiel is diagnosed with psittacosis, it can usually be treated.

The disease is spread when infected birds shed the *Chlamydia* organism in respiratory discharges, droppings and feather dust, as well as through contaminated food and water. Some birds are carriers without showing signs of infection.

This is one of the zoonotic diseases, or diseases that can affect people. It is not common, but it is possible. People who contract

SIGNS OF PSITTACOSIS

Watery yellow or lime-green droppings

Loss of appetite

Depression

Listlessness

Nasal discharge

Sudden death (not common)

This pair of cockatiels, Dacey and Buzz, have been routinely tested for psittacosis. It is a common illness in cockatiels and is treatable, but could spread to their human caretaker.

psittacosis usually experience flu-like symptoms, might have pounding headaches and weakness and can experience respiratory problems or even get pneumonia, requiring hospitalization.

Any bird kept around people with suppressed immune systems should be routinely tested for psittacosis. It is important to test and quarantine newly acquired birds. Ask your veterinarian about new developments in psittacosis diagnosis, treatment and prevention.

Parasites

Parasites are organisms that live on, feed from and are sheltered by another organism, but contribute nothing to their host. Sometimes they are innocuous, but sometimes they cause symptoms. There are many types of parasites that can infect birds. Here are the more common ones.

GIARDIA

Giardia is a protozoa that can infect dogs, cats, horses and humans as well as birds. The type that affects birds, however, does not also affect people or other mammals, to the best of our knowledge. The birds most often infected with giardia are cockatiels, budgies, lovebirds and gray-cheeked parakeets.

Cockatiels get giardia from ingesting cysts found in contaminated food or water. The cysts produce trophozoites, which attach themselves to the lining of the bird's intestine and produce more cysts. These cysts are excreted in the feces, and the cycle goes on. Cysts are resistant to drying, boiling and freezing, though some disinfectants are effective against them.

Giardiasis can affect a cockatiel's ability to absorb some nutrients. In cockatiels especially, it can also lead to severe itching. One of my most intelligent, outgoing cockatiels, Charlie, exhibited this symptom by picking off his feathers underneath his wings.

SIGNS OF GIARDIASIS

Passing whole seeds in droppings

Passing partially digested food in droppings

Dry, flaky skin

Patchy feather loss

Shifting leg lameness

Persistent feather picking (especially wings, flanks and legs)

Recurrent yeast infections

Wasting of the breast muscles

Yellow urates

No response to antibiotic therapy when bacterial gut infection is suspected

Lethargy

Loss of appetite

Weight loss

Diarrhea

Unthriftiness

Itching

Death

Giardiasis in birds seems to be a regional problem, and can be difficult to cure, although it can be treated. Cockatiels with giardiasis may have no symptoms or may have one or more of the symptoms listed in the box.

FEATHER LICE

Feather lice may look like pencil marks on a cockatiel's feathers. Some lice cause itching and excessive preening. They are easily controlled with commercially prepared powders. Lice are not common on our cockatiels or other psittacine birds.

MITES

Although you will still find commercial "mite protectors" available, these do nothing to protect your cockatiel from mites and, in fact, expose it to a chemical akin to the one in moth balls.

A crusty area around the beak may signal the presence of scaly mites. These are treatable by your avian veterinarian.

Feather Picking

Feather picking does not have a single cause. It may be a symptom of a disease process, or it may be a sign of psychological problems or boredom. It may become a habit for a cockatiel.

This is a heartbreaking syndrome for bird owners, as so much of what we appreciate about our pet birds is their beautiful feathering. Birds that pick their feathers may mutilate the feathers, pull them out, break them off or actually dig holes in their skin. With true feather picking the bird will have feathers just on its head and neck, since it cannot reach those feathers to pull them out.

CAUSES OF FEATHER PICKING

Medical	*Behavioral*
Giardiasis	Boredom
Skin infection	Nervousness
Parasites	Insecurity
Internal disease	Sexual frustration
Hormonal imbalance	Stress
Infection	Excessive courtship display
Liver disease	Rewarding picking with attention
Inadequate nutrition	

If your cockatiel plucks its feathers, you should first look for and rule out physiological causes, such as giardiasis, a malfunctioning thyroid gland or a food allergy.

If your cockatiel is feather picking but there is no physical reason, you may wish to consider an emotional reason, ranging from boredom to stress to sexual frustration. Our companion birds are intelligent, sensitive animals and may be affected by their surroundings and the environment in which they live. Stressful changes and an emotion-laden home life can affect a bird's actions.

You can offer the bird a more secure or more stimulating environment, giving it lots of treats and toys that can be shredded. These may be edible, such as rice cakes, peas in a pod or broccoli florets. They may be toys such as straws, a whisk broom, wooden craft sticks or a rope toy that can be preened. Make sure the bird has entertainment when you aren't home, with a mirror or a radio, and that it is getting enough sleep.

Viruses

PSITTACINE BEAK AND FEATHER DISEASE

This highly contagious disease, often known simply as PBFD, primarily affects young birds. It may be spread by ingesting contaminated feather dust or droppings. The virus is long lived outside the body and resistant to many common disinfectants. PBFD can be diagnosed with a blood test.

If a cockatiel does contract PBFD, it is fatal. There is work being done to develop a vaccine to prevent this disease. Check with your avian veterinarian about the status of the research.

PACHECO'S DISEASE VIRUS

Pacheco's Disease Virus (PDV) is induced by a herpes virus. It may last a few days or a few weeks, but is most often rapidly fatal. In many species this disease is 100 percent fatal, though a survival rate of 20 percent has been reported in cockatiels. Our hardy little birds triumph once again.

PDV affects the liver, spleen and kidneys. Many outbreaks are

SIGNS OF PBFD

Depression

Diarrhea

Crop problems

Abnormal feathers

Loss of normal powder on feathers

Beak lesions

SIGNS OF PACHECO'S DISEASE VIRUS

Regurgitation

Lethargy

Increased thirst

Diarrhea

Orange-colored urates

Sudden death

linked to a stressful event, such as environmental changes or breeding. There is a vaccine for this virus. It is mainly useful to high-risk businesses, such as pet shops.

POLYOMAVIRUS

This virus normally affects young birds just as they wean. It is usually transmitted by adult carriers. The disease results in the sudden death of what appears to be a healthy young bird. There is often abdominal enlargement and bleeding underneath the skin.

There is a way to test for this virus and there is a vaccine available, but there is no treatment for a bird with the disease.

SIGNS OF POLYOMAVIRUS

Delayed crop emptying

Weakness

Appetite loss

Abdominal enlargement

Bleeding under the skin

Tremors

Paralysis

Diarrhea

Regurgitation

Feather abnormalities (sometimes)

Sudden death

Bumps and Lumps

Tumors and lumps on your bird may or may not be cancerous. But even a benign tumor can be serious—it may press on a nerve or obstruct a vital function, such as swallowing. Feather cysts can develop at the site of feather follicles. When a cockatiel's air sac is punctured, it can create a large, air-filled bump.

Diseases of the Organs

Liver and kidney disease are fairly prevalent in cockatiels. Treatment is based upon the cause of the disease. There are special diets available for these conditions, to aid in longevity and the bird's well-being.

Night Thrashing

You probably know your pet cockatiel as a peaceful, happy bird. It is shocking, then, to wake up to a cockatiel in an obvious panic, beating itself against the bars of its cage. Yet, this experience is not at all uncommon among cockatiel owners.

When a bird lives in a home, its owner occasionally hears wild night thrashing. When a cockatiel is away from home at a show or in a classroom, at a pet store or boarded at the vet, the evidence of

NEW FRONTIERS

There's more about cockatiel health and sickness that we don't know. Cockatiels get heart disease and diabetes, they probably suffer allergies and might contract diseases we haven't even identified yet.

DNA research has been a boon to sexing parrots and identifying individual birds. Where will it lead? What is possible with holistic medicine, herbal remedies, acupuncture and physical therapy?

This is a very exciting time to be a bird owner, when new advances in avian medicine are having an impact on our ability to successfully keep and raise birds.

night thrashing is often blood splattered all over a cage and surrounding area. This is, of course, an alarming sight. But once you understand that night thrashing is peculiar to cockatiels and have ways to deal with it, you will no longer panic when your pet does!

There have been many possible causes of night thrashing proposed over the years. I believe the underlying cause is that a bird feels vulnerable and helpless in the dark. Birds see colors well, but cockatiels are essentially blind at night. This is why a cockatiel quiets down, in most cases, when its cage is covered. When startled at night, a cockatiel responds by flailing

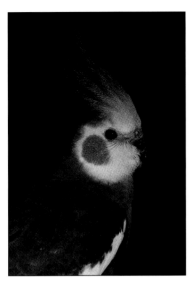

Cockatiels have a propensity to occasionally thrash around in their cages—for no apparent reason. It's not what we expect from calm pets like Crystal, a mature gray male.

wildly about its cage. If several cockatiels are in one cage or one room, the flock instinct takes over and they all start thrashing about.

Many things can trigger this behavior. Mice may be getting into your bird's cage. Mice love bird seed as much as birds do, and are even more prolific! I once found a mouse curled up in the seed cup of Dacey and Clement's cage. It refused to budge, even when it knew it had been discovered. I was alarmed, since mouse droppings may be laced with bacteria, causing sickness in a bird that ingests them. I also felt I had found the cause of my night thrashing problem.

I started to remove tempting seed cups from the cage at night, and I set traps outside the cage. Poison is not a good way to get rid of vermin, since it might be carried into seed dishes by mice. Of course, keeping a cat is an alternative—but one I tend to avoid because small birds are quarry for a hunting cat.

With the mouse problem taken care of, I was surprised to wake up to ten thrashing cockatiels one night the following spring. I calmed everyone down and read in the newspaper the next morning that we'd had an earthquake the night before. I had not even felt the slight tremor, but the birds certainly did! This might not be a concern in your area, but I live in California, and now I know I have an earthquake alarm.

Another cause of night thrashing seems to be unfamiliar surroundings. Boarders at my house tend to frighten easily for the first few days they are away from home. Unfamiliar sights and sounds (for example, my two large dogs walking into the bird room at night) trigger panic and thrashing. If you intend to travel with your pet cockatiel or to board it at someone else's home, you should consider getting into the habit of covering your bird's cage before you go. The bird will feel more secure while away from home if it has familiar nighttime scenery.

Be sure a sitter knows what the bird is used to and when bedtime is.

All cockatiel owners I know have experienced at least some night thrashing with their pet birds. Though sometimes there is no apparent reason for night thrashing, I don't think cockatiels are prone to nightmares. Rather, I believe spiders or insects may startle them, then flit away before being discovered. A bird may bump into a toy in the middle of the night or may detect an unfamiliar movement.

Prevention is fairly simple. By keeping a night light on near a cockatiel's cage, it will be able to see when it is startled, rather than floundering blindly about its cage.

When night thrashing does occur, your response should be to calmly get up and turn the light on so your bird can see again. Then start to talk softly to the cockatiel. It should begin to calm down when it hears your voice. A frightened

ANY CHANGE CAN DO IT

Night thrashing doesn't have to occur at night. Most often it does, but I had thrashing birds for a week after I changed bathrobes. They didn't recognize me after I "molted" from white terry cloth to multicolored stripes!

cockatiel will have a very erect crest and be sitting high on its perch, glancing nervously around. It may be clinging to the side bars of its cage, crest up and tail fanned out. When calming down, its crest will go down and it may start to grate its beak in preparation for going back to sleep.

You may need to administer first aid to your bird. Look at it carefully and check the cage floor for signs of blood. When molting, it is likely that a cockatiel will break blood feathers when thrashing about. The molt puts you in a sort of no-win situation when it comes to thrashing. Molting birds just don't feel well, in general. They may be quicker to panic at night, and will do more harm to their growing feathers.

I keep some common items on hand for such emergencies. Some blood coagulant (styptic powder or

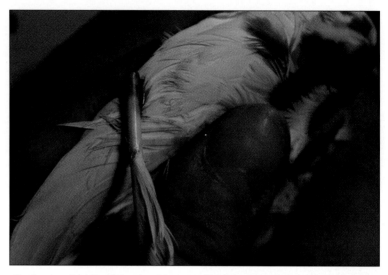

Check on cockatiels after a thrashing episode. If one of them has broken a blood feather, the shaft needs to be pulled out to stop bleeding. You may need veterinary assistance. *(David Wrobel)*

COLOR CONSIDERATIONS

The color of the cockatiel involved may make a difference in the amount of night thrashing you will have to deal with. I find my lutinos and pied cockatiels are the most likely to break blood feathers in the melee. This might be because the lighter-colored feathers are not as sturdy. There could also be a genetic reason; I don't know.

pencils, available at pet stores and pharmacies) or a box of cornstarch will help stop bleeding. In a pinch you can use flour. This should be applied to the bleeding area, along with light pressure until the bleeding stops. Broken tail feathers pull out easily and painlessly in one quick jerk, but I find I need tweezers to grasp and pull out wing feathers. If you are uncomfortable with this procedure, plan on a trip to the veterinarian, and he or she can handle the blood feathers. Tweezers may also be used to pull out a blood feather. (You'll find more information on dealing with broken feathers later in this chapter.) If a broken blood feather is left in place, it will continue to siphon

off blood. The flow will be stopped by removing the broken shaft of the blood feather. A towel completes my kit, for use in restraining a frightened cockatiel that may nip.

Most damage from thrashing is minor, and it is rarely necessary to take a thrashing cockatiel to a veterinarian. Damage may be minor but may *look* horrible. I was appalled to see that a bird I exhibited at a bird show had been startled during the night and broken a blood feather. Of course, at the show site there was no one to turn on the light for her or talk to her reassuringly. Her show cage was smeared with blood, as were the perches. Not a good impression for the day the public was invited to view the show! She was fine, but it would be hard to convince a non-cockatiel owner of that.

There is potential for serious injury to a thrashing bird, so it is a good policy for you to get up and check on your pet when you hear it thrashing. An acquaintance has a flighty hen who broke a wing one night. Bands can get caught on loose wires, and wings or heads may get caught in cage bars. It is a good idea in any case to inspect your bird's cage for safety several times a year, and repair any loose wires.

Once a thrashing bird has been calmed, you can usually leave it with only a night light. If you are having frequent incidences of night thrashing, carefully observe the room for signs of mice, bugs or alarming movement, so you know what steps to take to prevent another incident. You may need to move favorite toys to places where they do not get bumped into at night. As you pad back to bed, bleary-eyed and groggy, remember that there are cockatiel owners the world over doing the same thing. You are not alone!

First Aid

Many emergencies require veterinary care. But it's important for you to recognize the nature of the emergency and know what to do before you get your cockatiel to the vet. It's also important to establish a good relationship with a local avian vet, so you know where to take your cockatiel in the event of an emergency.

If your cockatiel seems listless or depressed, or is fluffed up on the bottom of its cage, it probably requires veterinary attention. If there has been an accident or it swallowed a dangerous substance, it obviously requires medical attention. In either case, call your avian veterinarian right away.

Until you can get an appointment (or, in the case of an emergency, until you can get to the vet's office), you should isolate the sick cockatiel and set up a hospital cage for it. Follow your veterinarian's directions once you have reached him or her. If you supply grit (which is not necessary for a cockatiel), remove it, since a sick cockatiel may eat too much and get an impacted crop.

There are specially made hospital cages you can buy, but you can place a heating pad on low under part of a box, or place a lamp at one side of a cage, and cover at least three sides of the cage to retain heat. Be careful not to allow any towel or plastic covering to touch the light bulb. If you have a thermometer, 88° to 90°F is a suitable cage temperature for an ill cockatiel and can do much to help recovery. Try to measure the temperature

FIRST AID

Until you receive veterinary care, provide these conditions for your cockatiel:

Warmth (89° to 90°F)

Dim lighting

Easy access to food and water

Favorite foods

Prevent further injury

Do not apply salves, ointments or creams to a wound

where the cockatiel is, not higher or lower in the cage or box.

The goal is to keep your cockatiel comfortable and a little warmer than usual, and not to do any more damage. If your cockatiel does not feel well enough to perch, be sure food and water is available within reach at the bottom of the cage or box. When a cockatiel is sick, don't worry about the optimum diet— feed it what it will eat, even if that's millet and sunflower seeds.

Make sure your hospital cage or box is in a quiet, dimly lit area. And make sure your cockatiel can get away from the heat source if it wants and will not injure itself. Then, get it to the vet!

BE PREPARED

I keep a few essential emergency first-aid items on hand in my bird room. A towel can be used to

FIRST AID KIT

- Blood coagulant to stop bleeding
- Towel for restraining the bird
- Scissors and nail clippers
- Hemostats or tweezers to remove broken blood feathers
- Hand-feeding formula to feed sick or injured birds
- Feeding syringes
- Pellets or seeds for a hospital stay or natural disaster
- Vet wrap for broken bones or damaged wings
- Flashlight
- Magnifying glasses to see details
- Cotton swabs to clean small wounds
- Pedialyte to rehydrate a dehydrated or sick bird

restrain an injured bird. Nail clippers are for nails, scissors for clipping wings, tweezers to pull broken blood feathers and some styptic powder or my emergency standby—cornstarch—to stop bleeding. It helps to have these items on hand at home and when traveling with your bird.

BROKEN TAIL FEATHERS

Cockatiels sometimes break tail feathers when crash landing or during a bout of night thrashing. If these bent or broken feathers are left alone, the bird's balance may be thrown off. A broken feather is not aesthetically pleasing, either. If a bent or broken feather is removed, a new one will grow in its place. If not, that tail feather will only be replaced at the next molt, perhaps several months later.

If the bird is compromised in any way, I don't pull the feather, but cut it off. If the cockatiel is healthy and looks like it can handle growing in a new feather, I go ahead and pull it.

To remove a tail feather, gently restrain a cockatiel by holding your hands over its wings. Find the base of the broken feather and give a swift tug. Tail feathers come out easily, and removing them does not seem to hurt.

BROKEN BLOOD FEATHERS

A broken blood feather *must* be removed, or else it will continue to bleed. Removing the feather cuts off the blood supply. Using tweezers, hold the blood feather at the base and yank hard. This procedure is slightly painful for the bird, especially if it's a wing feather.

Giving Medication

If you have taken your cockatiel to the vet, he or she may have prescribed medication for the bird. Some medication is administered orally and some is given by injection. Have the technician or your veterinarian show you how many cc's to administer, and how often.

A cockatiel's esophagus travels down the bird's right side, so you want to put a syringe into the bird's mouth from the left, as in hand feeding, and aim for the right side of the throat to avoid getting fluid in the cockatiel's lungs.

Often, I put a little bit of medicine in the cockatiel's mouth, wait for it to swallow, then put in a little more. Sometimes medicating orally is somewhat of a disaster, with the cockatiel shaking its head

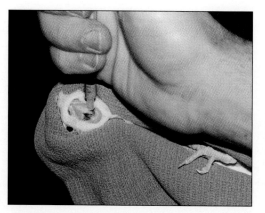

Mystique, a gray pied hen, demonstrates the proper way to administer oral medication. Hold the syringe in the cockatiel's beak on the bird's left side. A cockatiel's esophagus is on the right. Give the cockatiel a little of the medicine at a time and let it swallow.

Give a cockatiel injections into its breast muscle (wetted down with alcohol here). Your veterinarian can give you a demonstration before you try this.

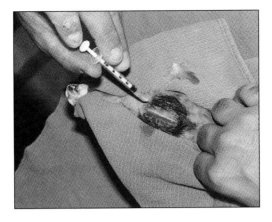

and the liquid flying all over. My veterinarian has learned to flavor the most bitter medicines, so this is not as likely.

Make sure you get thorough instructions and a live demonstration before giving your own cockatiel injections. Injections are given into the breast muscle. You can wet down the breast feathers to see more clearly. Tap any air out of the syringe before giving an injection, and dispose of needles properly.

Cockatiel Escapes

Remember that even the most tame cockatiel may take off from your shoulder for a flight. Maybe it expects you to follow? It's really important to secure all doors and windows before you take your cockatiel out of its cage; a cockatiel does not have much of a homing instinct—it is a nomadic bird in its native Australia. Besides, it probably

hasn't ever seen your house from the outside, so it doesn't have any landmarks to return to.

If your cockatiel flies away, out a door or window, there are some steps you can take to get it back. A cockatiel will attract another cockatiel. I'm not suggesting you put

another bird outside, but a prerecorded tape of your pet's whistles, or a decoy bird in a cage, may attract the escapee. Another big cockatiel attraction is food. Put some out in a familiar cage.

You should make posters and call anyone who might have heard about a found cockatiel. This includes the local animal shelter, avian veterinarian and pet stores that carry birds or bird supplies. Ask your local newspaper about a lost bird ad—many offer them free as a community service. If there are any bird rescue or adoption centers near you, they will keep a record of your loss and may have suggestions for finding your bird.

Hopefully, you have kept a record of your cockatiel's band

Most lost cockatiels have never been outside and don't know how to find your house. If you lose a cockatiel, putting a decoy bird outside might help to attract it home. Also notify pet shops, bird adoption centers, the local animal shelter and your avian veterinarian about your lost bird. *(David Wrobel)*

number and have a few photos around. In your ad, or in posters, be specific when describing your lost pet. Hard as it is to believe, not everyone knows what a cockatiel is. Say "lost cockatiel," but also say "small, gray-crested parrot with white on wings."

Major Emergencies

Are you ready for the biggest emergencies? What would you do if there were a fire in your home? It's a good idea to always have a plentiful supply of food and water for your cockatiel. If you are ever caught in an emergency, at least you can get by for a few days with these supplies.

A carrier is essential if you must rush out of the house. Do you have a carrier or small cage, and is it within easy reach? In a pinch, what would you do? One suggestion is to put a cockatiel in a pillow case if

EMERGENCY PREPAREDNESS KIT

Travel cages

Water

Feed

Feed dishes

Cage liner

ID information (band numbers, description, photos)

Plastic bags for waste disposal

Water purification kit

Medication or vitamins (if needed)

Plan arranged with others for bird care

nothing else is handy, or under a jacket if you happen to be wearing one.

Since big emergencies are generally unexpected, it's a good idea to carry with you a detailed list of whom to contact and how to place

your animals if you are ever in a car accident or are otherwise incapacitated. Make sure loved ones or animal-loving friends have a copy as well. It can bring peace of mind to know that your animals are provided for.

Give some thought to what would happen to your birds if you were suddenly unable to take care of them. What if you had to stay in the hospital overnight? What if you had to stay much longer? What if you die?

Talk this over with people you think would provide your birds with homes, and write your wishes down. Give a copy to a friend, or show that person where you keep it in your home. Keep another copy in your safe deposit box.

In many states it is possible to arrange a trust fund for your animals in a will. Check with your lawyer to find out if this is possible in your state.

CHAPTER 9

Taming, Training and Talking

I f a cockatiel learns to accept certain handling and commands from you, it makes life easier for both of you. Some hand-fed birds like people, so taming is not an issue, but they may still need some rules regarding manners, commands and their limits within a household. Once your bird trusts you, it will want to be with you and will be a pleasant companion in many household activities. Cockatiels love to do dishes, for example, and they like to do homework, too.

It's also a good idea to get your cockatiel accustomed to all kinds of handling, so that veterinary appointments are less traumatic. And show training for exhibition cockatiels is different yet again. It is easiest to hand tame very young birds, but cockatiels, in general, are tractable birds, so it is also possible to work with an older, untamed one. You just need to allow more time in that case.

Observation plays a key role in training your cockatiel. I rarely get bitten by any cockatiel, and have only been bitten a few times by my own birds. That's because I watch them closely, and don't push in some situations. Dacey bit me the first afternoon I got her. I had expected her to be like the other tame cockatiel I had met. She was scared and reacted to handling in a strange, new environment. I learned a lesson, and she hasn't bitten me again in sixteen years.

Learn to read body language. Most bites happen when a cockatiel is scared. In the language of cockatiels, extreme fright or warning is communicated by rocking back and forth and/or hissing. Not a good time to handle that bird! Use a towel, let the cockatiel simply be with you and settle down, or try another day.

This is an alert cockatiel, with a raised crest and skinny body. Watch body language to see if it's a good time to work with your cockatiel. In this case, it's not!

When your cockatiel is wary, its crest is up and its body is skinny. A relaxed cockatiel will explore its surroundings. It is normal for a cockatiel to test the sturdiness of a perch with its beak as well as its feet, so if your cockatiel reaches out beak-first to your outstretched finger, chances are it will explore a bit, then climb on. It's important for your reaction to be one of providing a steady perch, not drawing away!

Taming and Bonding

Young cockatiels have a strong instinct to bond, as pairs do later in life. Young birds buddy up, and are constantly searching for a friend until they have found one. Single

pets bond to their owners, and become wonderful companions. Cockatiels *do* have much more in common with each other than with any person (in general!), so I strongly suggest getting just one pet cockatiel in the beginning. You may add a companion later.

At five weeks to three months old, a chick's beak is still pink and soft—unable to hurt you, so it's a good time to start the taming and bonding process. Many people prefer to have a cockatiel's wings clipped before taming, as discussed in Chapter 3. It does help initial taming by making a cockatiel more dependent on you for mobility.

Key words to remember when working with your cockatiel are patience and consistency. This is sometimes a slow process, but a very rewarding one. Take things one step at a time. You are going to try to build the bird's trust in you. It will need to know that you will *never* tease or hurt it. There is no place in bird taming for physical punishment of any kind. The trust you are building is very fragile, and can be broken for long periods of time by a fit of anger.

You will find that taming sessions are conducted most easily away from a cockatiel's cage. 'Tiels tend to be very fond of their homes, and will head for them time after time if they are in sight. Cockatiels love bright, shiny objects, so it's best to take your

jewelry off before starting a training session. You will also want to make sure you handle your cockatiel with clean hands. If you have handled another bird, be sure to wash your hands before touching your pet.

To get a cockatiel away from its cage, you can either open the door and wait until it comes out, then transport it to another room, or reach into the cage and get your cockatiel out of it. You might want to wrap it in a washcloth or towel if your bird is a biter. Whether carrying your confined bird with bare hands or in a towel, be careful not to compress its breast.

This cockatiel is territorial about his cage and not so sure of hands. Taming and training sessions will be conducted away from his cage. *(David Wrobel)*

I favor allowing a bird to come out of its cage on its own, since it will be less afraid of hands in its cage later on. Some cockatiels stubbornly remain in their cages, though, even when the door is open. In that case I forcibly get them out, and have to work hard later on to teach them to perch on my finger and exit the cage quietly. You can tempt a cockatiel to leave its cage by putting a treat on the door. It should come to investigate something irresistible.

LEARNING THE LADDER

Take your cockatiel to an enclosed, fairly small area for training. A bathroom (with the toilet seat down) or a small bedroom works well. If there are windows, pull the curtains so your cockatiel does not hurt itself flying into them. Release your clipped friend near the ground. It will be fairly uncomfortable on the ground, with you towering over it, and will want to get back up to shoulder level. You will help your bird do this.

Follow the bird around, or go to where it is cowering on the ground and maybe hissing and swaying from side to side. Talk to your cockatiel in a soft, reassuring voice. Put a finger in front of the cockatiel, and press gently against its breast to make it step up on your finger. You may need to gently cup your other hand over its back and guide it from behind.

If the cockatiel is scuttling away, you may have to work on just approaching it for the first few lessons—the same if its first reaction is to bite! Especially as you are just getting to know each other, do not let a cockatiel know that it can scare you away with a bite. Most bites are warnings—nips that warn you away without actually drawing blood. Don't pull away, and chances are good you won't get hurt. A cockatiel has only its beak to communicate with, after all, and is trying to tell you many things as you get acquainted.

You will need to gauge the progress of your taming sessions. A tame, willing cockatiel can start learning things right away. A wilder or more scared cockatiel just needs to feel comfortable with you first, before graduating to training.

Once your cockatiel has gotten up on your finger, you will want to repeat this action over and over. Make an imaginary ladder with your fingers, pressing against the bird's breast with one finger while rolling back with the finger the bird is on, slowly allowing the bird to get higher and higher with each "rung" of the ladder.

I like to use a verbal signal to tell the bird what I am asking it to do. I make a certain cluck for my birds when I ask them to step up on my finger. You could also use the "up" command, in popular use among bird behaviorists. It doesn't matter what the exact command is, as long as you are consistent and your cockatiel knows what is expected of it. "Up," since it is a convention, makes it easier for people who don't know your bird to handle it.

As the bird begins to realize what the command means, you may ask it to hop or fly some distance to your finger. Eventually, you may be able to call your cockatiel from across the room this way! This is an invaluable asset to you if your cockatiel ever gets outside. I have lost a few cockatiels outside, and sometimes they returned to my house but didn't know how to come down from the trees or telephone lines.

If, at any time, the bird gets frightened and flies off, go and pick it up off the ground to start over. You are teaching your bird, through your consistent behavior, that it *will* do what you ask it. You must be able to persevere at this task longer than your little cockatiel! Longer shouldn't really be that long. Work intensely with your cockatiel for about ten minutes at a time, two or three times a day.

A SHOULDER PERCH

Once your bird gets to the level of your shoulders and face, you may talk to it calmly, and perhaps move out of your training room. If at any

This cockatiel is known to be tame, but just in case, Wendy Macias has removed any enticing jewelry.

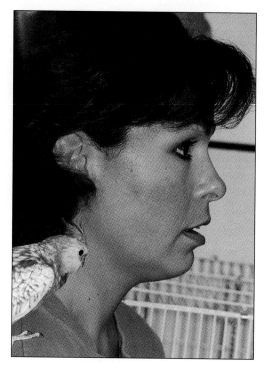

are madly rushing around and in a hurry, your cockatiel will pick up on that and be its most obstinate, flighty and difficult to catch. Creating a calm end to time-out for free flight is advantageous for both of you.

It is very nice to have a cockatiel trained to enter and exit its cage calmly. When time to come out of a cage starts turning into a frenzied chase around the cage, I slow down and start some other training. When a cockatiel has become finger tame, I start practicing going through the cage door. With a cockatiel on my finger, I calmly approach the cage, so that at first the bird gets up to the entrance, then comes back out. Later we go through the entrance and back out. Finally, we work on the cockatiel stepping onto my hand inside the cage and exiting it calmly.

Another useful everyday command for life with a cockatiel companion is "down." Whenever it is time for a cockatiel to step off your finger onto a cage, another person or a playground, you should use this command until the cockatiel learns what it means. It won't take long—cockatiels are intelligent birds. I have seen one bird (an Indian Ringneck) learn the "stay" command and stand absolutely still, stopping in its tracks when it heard the command. There's a challenge for you and your cockatiel!

time it gets startled and flies away, you will go and rescue it from the floor, walk the ladder back to shoulder level, then talk some more.

You should only allow your pet to sit on your shoulder if you are sure it will not bite. You need to protect your eyes and ears. A station on a shoulder allows a shy bird to hide, also, so I like to wait until a cockatiel is feeling pretty confident about its relationship with people before I let it ride around on my shoulder. It is also helpful for your cockatiel to know the "up" command and obey it consistently if it is allowed on your shoulder, so

you can easily remove your bird. Remember to remove any jewelry or to train your cockatiel not to peck at it. A persistent cockatiel can sever a gold necklace, tug at earrings, or may get heavy metal poisoning from costume jewelry.

BACK TO THE CAGE

A useful way to return a cockatiel to its cage is to gently place your hand over its back. This prevents the cockatiel from opening its wings to escape, but is a very quiet way to handle your bird. You want to avoid grabbing at your bird and handling it roughly if at all possible. If you

Shy Birds

What if you are having trouble picking up a cockatiel? The bird might be shy, aggressive, unsure of itself or not bonded to you in any way. There are some ways you can increase the odds of success with an intractable cockatiel. For example, Buzz came to me as an older adult, but was madly in love with Dacey, who is quite a tame pet. If I picked Dacey up from a perch first, Buzz was anxious to follow and also stepped onto my hand.

If a single bird is giving you problems, try picking the bird up from the rear, while distracting it with your other hand in front. It won't know why it is all of a sudden on your finger.

If your cockatiel is not becoming manageable and hand tame,

Sunshine, a male pearl-pied cockatiel, is demonstrating stick training. If your cockatiel will not get on your hand, this is an alternative way to work with it. *(David Wrobel)*

another technique you can use is training the bird to hop onto a stick or a ladder. This works with Charlene, who persists in her fear of hands but is otherwise willing to please and be cooperative about going back into her cage. Instead of a finger against her breast, we put a dowel up to it and use the "up" command.

NO SHARING FOOD

No matter how tame your bird gets, never let your cockatiel eat out of your mouth. Human mouths contain gram-negative bacteria that is harmful to birds. Bird bodies are populated by gram-positive bacteria. This is one of the things a veterinarian checks for in routine exams. The different bacteria show up with different colors on a gram stain.

If you want to share food with your pet, give it its own dish of your food, or hand feed pieces of popcorn, cereal or treats.

Taming an Older or Difficult Bird

The taming method I have outlined is so far a very active one. You are asking the bird to do something, then demanding that it do what you ask. For an older cockatiel, you may wish to use a gentler and more long-term approach.

Since I have several cockatiels, I am not so much in a hurry to tame every new bird. This slower method also allows me to tame a bird while doing other things, since the basic idea is to just let a

cockatiel become comfortable around people, and eventually to allow itself to be touched and handled.

In this slower method, the bird is allowed to show me when I have its trust—I am not demanding obedience. Just as with finger and ladder training, I remove the bird from its cage or allow it to come out. Then I take it to another room, or remove its cage from the room, and place the bird on a perch or stand.

There are many playgrounds and perches available for cockatiels, or you may make your own. If your pet is allowed to roam up and down the back of the sofa, this is sufficient. At this point I just allow the bird to join in evening household activities. It will spend an hour or two just staying on its perch and observing what goes on. For a week or two (or an hour or two, depending on the bird), I don't approach it. If it does fly off the perch, though, I retrieve it, and use a finger ladder to get it back to its perch.

Once the bird is comfortable being around the family, I try to approach it. I get my hand as close to the cockatiel as possible and just leave it there. I start to do this about three or four times in an hour. The next step is to practice picking the bird up off the perch and putting it back, without frenzied flight.

Finally, it will get comfortable enough for you to handle or scratch its head, or for the bird to communicate in a relaxed manner with you. Most, though not all, cockatiels like to have their head

Most, but not all, cockatiels like to have their head scratched. For an older, untamed cockatiel, start by blowing on its head, or wait till molting time, when it will appreciate being preened. *(David Wrobel)*

scratched. As I am able to move my hand closer and closer without signs of aggression, I also blow lightly against the grain of feathers on its head, just behind its crest. Eventually I am able to replace this light pressure with finger strokes. As a cockatiel becomes used to this petting, it will rotate its head so you can scratch under its chin or over its ears. Sometimes a cockatiel will purposely bend its head down to be scratched at the approach of a finger.

An older, untrained cockatiel is usually not an ideal pet, and may never be quite as tame and trusting as a hand-fed baby, but if you are patient and caring your efforts will pay off with a closer relationship. The results of taming and training increase communication and understanding across species, producing a closeness you cannot imagine without experiencing it. Both you and your bird have much to gain from some simple work on training.

Teaching Cockatiels to Talk

One of the fascinating things about birds is their ability to verbalize using words. This attribute can be one of the reasons someone chooses to buy a pet bird—because some birds can speak our language, our fascination with them is heightened. However, if you're looking for

a bird with the potential to talk, I can't recommend a cockatiel. Cockatiels *might* talk. Some do, some don't. Don't count on it. These birds, of course, have other characteristics that can make up for a lack of talking ability, such as even temperament and whistling ability.

Some cockatiels do talk, especially males. Male chicks who are members of a family where they are the only chick, and that are talked to quite a lot, turn out to be the best talkers. Until recently I would have said that in my experience females don't talk. I have a little hen now, though, who is making garbled attempts at speech. Among my cockatiels, there are families that have a propensity to talk.

A talking bird is a joy and a curse, depending on what it says and what variety there is in the bird's vocabulary. I'm sure you want to maximize your bird's potential, so I have assembled some tips from experts.

RULES OF THUMB

Sex makes a difference. Male cockatiels talk best, while female cockatiels who talk are very rare. A male bird of a species that can learn to talk and lives with a vocal person has a good chance of learning speech. Birds seem to learn speech better from high-pitched voices than from deep voices, and may learn from another bird as well.

THE LEGEND OF BURT

by Janet Golden-Motto

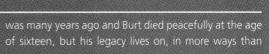

The following story was first posted on one of the many bird lists on the World Wide Web. The original story was just about Burt, but I asked Janet how involved she got with birds after knowing him. Her response shows that an older cockatiel can be tamed and can become a family pet. You'll get an idea of what it takes, too. It also shows where cockatiel ownership can lead. Her own cockatiel wasn't the last bird she acquired!

Burt, a normal gray cockatiel, belonged to one of my brothers-in-law. This bird had an incredible singing repertoire. He didn't whistle the songs, he belted out the words to all of his songs very clearly and in perfect tune. One of his favorite songs to sing was *The Worms Crawl In*. If you're not familiar with it, it goes like this: "The worms crawl in, the worms crawl out, the worms crawl in and out your mouth."

Anyway, a sister-in-law decided to have her wedding on the patio of the home in which Burt's cage just happened to overlook the festivities. Burt, being a sociable kind of 'tiel, decided it was probably just an oversight on everyone's part that he wasn't invited to join the flock, so he decided to join in, with his favorite song.

Thank God for video camcorders! Occasionally, after a particularly grueling holiday dinner with this sister-in-law, I take great enjoyment in reviewing her wedding tape. It goes something like this: "Do you Deborah take [The worms crawl in, the worms crawl out] this man David to be [The worms crawl in and out your mouth] your lawfully wedded. . . etc., etc., etc." All of this is overlaid with the sounds of much giggling and guffawing from her wedding guests (not me, of course). That

was many years ago and Burt died peacefully at the age of sixteen, but his legacy lives on, in more ways than one.

A couple of years ago while at a pet store just to buy fish food, my husband and daughter coerced me into buying a cute little gray cockatiel with promises of, "Oh, pleeeeese Mom. I *promise* I'll take care of him and he looks just like Burt" and, "Oh sure dear, I'll remind her to feed and clean up after him," along with, "Yep, he'll be one sweet little tame birdie for you in about two or three days. Yep, he's a hand-fed baby" from the pet store owner. I'll give you one guess as to how long those promises lasted.

The taming of Rocco, as he became known, turned into my project. I scoured local libraries and bookstores for information on the care and taming of cockatiels and joined every 'tiel chat line I could find for advice. My very first posting to the 'Net was "Help! my 'tiel hates me!"

After several months, a dozen Band-Aids and a couple of pounds of millet spray bribes, I had a very sweet little cockatiel who loves head scratches and does the wolf whistle. No, he may never be the singing sensation Burt was, but I love him just the same.

During the process of taming Rocco, I discovered how fascinating companion birds are and I developed the dreaded, incurable disease known as *bird fever*. So far, I've been able to control my illness by allowing a young, hand-fed (honestly hand-fed this time) blue-crowned conure to also own me. It's a long story, but you know how it is when bird people get started talking about our babies. . . .

We are fascinated by a bird's ability to talk, but not all cockatiels are talkers. You have the best chance with a verbal male.   *(David Wrobel)*

A bird picks up words that come with drama or excitement or are pronounced with enthusiasm by their owner. This is why many birds have a sailor's vocabulary—swear words are usually associated with a lot of animation in a household! Once a bird learns how to say a word, subsequent additions to its vocabulary are easier.

Some species are incredible mimics, but others really aren't. That's why recognizing speech in a bird is important. Most birds start off imitating tone and intonation before the actual words are formed. This sounds like gargling, or singsong garbled intonations. Some birds don't mimic exact sounds *per se*. I have met a few people with talking pet budgies who never realized their bird's fast, high-pitched chatter was actually words.

Patience would seem to be a virtue in teaching talking, as well. Eb Cravens (who has had years of experience with birds and customers at Feathered Friends of Santa Fe, New Mexico, and is now an author and speaker about natural methods of bird keeping) says one of his favorite yellow-crowned Amazon parrots didn't utter her first word until she was three years old, while other Amazon or African Grey chicks he has worked with were already saying at least one word at weaning time.

And finally, Cravens has a word of caution for bird customers: Anyone looking for a bird with talking ability needs to realize that other, less desirable habits come along with that ability. Talking birds are vocal birds in general, so incredible talkers may also be incredible screamers. Some people have successfully trained demanding screamers to whisper instead of scream, but it doesn't always work that way.

REPETITION

There are many ways to reach the goal of training a pet bird to talk, and they are more or less rigorous in their approach. Perhaps the simplest is repetition. If there is something you would like your cockatiel to learn to say, you should repeat the word or phrase often. It might help to keep in mind that cockatiels learn what their owners say in an excited manner, and learn best from high-pitched voices.

If there are certain phrases you would like to teach your bird, there

Mirrors work well to stimulate cockatiels to talk. Bozo is admiring himself, talking and whistling to his reflection in the mirror.   *(David Wrobel)*

COMMUNICATION AND LOVE

Many people are awestruck by a parrot's ability to talk. All of our favorite little Australian parrots have the capacity to communicate on some level. When we unlock that ability, the bond seems to grow even stronger between a person and an avian companion. Here is a story about John Kastenholtz of Wisconsin and his cockatiel companion.

John and his male cinnamon cockatiel, Koori, have established a routine in the morning. Koori rides around on John's shoulder until it's time for John to head for work at St. Norbert College in De Pere, Wisconsin. Then, John waves and Koori answers, "See you later!"

The communication between Koori and John has deepened their bond. *(John Kastenholz)*

Koori was being particularly exuberant one morning, screaming and not quieting down. In frustration, John said, "Naughty bird, Koori's a naughty bird!" and locked him in his cage. As John rounded the corner to go out the door that morning, his heart melted when Koori called out, "See you later!" John, no longer angry and frustrated but grinning ear-to-ear, wished he had a way to apologize to Koori for his actions just a moment before.

One Christmas, John got a new suitcase. He left it sitting across from Koori's cage for some time, unused. Koori didn't pay any attention to the suitcase until the morning John intended to leave for vacation. The cockatiel refused to stay on John's shoulder that morning, but flew down to the floor and headed for the suitcase. This happened repeatedly.

"Don't let anyone say birds aren't intelligent," says John. "Koori had watched me pack my suitcase the night before. I'm sure he knew I was going away, and he wanted to go along. What a sweetie-pie!"

something like a hulled sunflower seed, shelled peanut, safflower seed or other treat.

You can add appropriate associations to the idea of repetition. In other words, as you teach your bird certain words, also teach it how those words are used. Say "hi" or "hello," for example, when entering a room, "goodbye" when you leave and "night night" when the cage is covered at night. Food can be identified as "apple," "toast," "grape" or whatever, and combined with "want" or "thank you." This promotes communication between owner and bird, and the bond between them usually grows.

FLOCK INSTINCT

Another way to train cockatiels to talk is to take advantage of the fact that birds are naturally communicative with their flock. If there already is a talking bird in the household, or if friends own one, it is possible for a bird to learn to talk from the example of the other bird. I had a flock of cockatiels for a while who could all say their own version of "Jonesy's a pretty bird!" long after Jonesy had moved to a new home.

If there are no other talking birds handy, there are tapes and videos available that repeat phrases. Mirrors also work well to stimulate cockatiels to talk—they will talk to themselves.

are a variety of training aids available that repeat catchy words or phrases. Some use a woman's voice, some a parrot's voice, and some record a bird owner's own voice.

If you reward your bird in some way when it says the word, it will probably say that word more often! Food rewards should be small enough to eat fast, and usually are

ALEX

Probably the most famous talking parrot in the world is Alex, who lives at the University of Arizona in Tucson. Dr. Irene Pepperberg has been doing intelligence studies with Alex, an African Grey, for many years. Alex successfully identifies colors, shapes and materials, and he counts. He knows how to identify same and different, bigger and smaller. In standard intelligence tests, he tests at the level of a chimpanzee or dolphin. Studies with Alex have changed the way the scientific community thinks about the intelligence of birds.

It should be stressed that an owner and pet cannot expect to achieve the level of success of either Alex or a professional bird trainer. Alex has been worked with two to eight hours a day for more than twenty years. A bird trainer only trains birds; most bird owners have a life!

If you appreciate the knowledge we have acquired about parrot intelligence through Dr. Pepperberg's work with Alex, consider making a donation to the Alex Foundation, Department of Ecology and Evolutionary Biology, University of Arizona, Tucson, AZ 85721.

Dr. Irene Pepperberg (pictured) has been working on parrot intelligence studies with Alex the African Grey for more than twenty years. They have affected both the public's recognition that parrots are intelligent beings, and work with dysfunctional children.

THE MODEL–RIVAL TECHNIQUE

This is the technique used by Dr. Irene Pepperberg in intelligence studies with Alex the African Grey parrot at the University of Arizona in Tucson. Basically, two people model a behavior. One asks, "What shape?" and the other replies correctly or incorrectly and gets an appropriate response from the trainer: praise for the right answer and a sharp "no" and no reward for the wrong one. At some point the bird is asked the same question and treated the same way. One of the disadvantages of this technique is that it takes two people, but it can also be a fun way to get your family involved in training the bird.

TALKING ON CUE

For bird trainers, who usually give regular performances, it is important to be able to elicit a behavior from a bird on cue. And it is possible for us to borrow their techniques for our pets.

Most trainers establish a "bridge" that tells the bird it performed a required behavior and will be rewarded. This ranges from the sound of a clicker to the word "good." The idea is to give the bird the bridge *as* it does a desired behavior—if it gets a treat a few moments later, it has no idea what the treat is rewarding. When a bird says the word you want to establish a cue for, like "hello" or "how ya' doin'?" you say "good," and then reward it with a treat or hugs. You hope this will increase the frequency the bird says that word. Then you start presenting a cue,

THE PERFECT COMPANION

by Elisa DeSimone

A family in my area had made arrangements to acquire a cockatiel from a bird breeder whom I was visiting. I acted as a delivery person. I pulled up to a large house and rang the bell. Excited barking and yapping greeted me, and it didn't take long before I knew I was in an animal-loving household. The last dog adopted from the SPCA was known as number six. She and her compatriots were milling around the kitchen as I handed over their new pet. Three years later, Elisa DeSimone has this to say about her companion cockatiel and subsequent interest in birds:

I now have three wonderful 'tiels: three-year-old Lennie (whiteface-pearl), twenty-one-month-old Alfalfa (whiteface) and eight-month-old Harley (whiteface-pied). They're all boys, each with a very different personality.

Lennie is the most gentle and by a mile the cuddliest. He is very smart and loves having anyone give him attention. However, he is not at all clingy. When I got him, I had no expectations, really. I just wanted a cockatiel for my birthday (it was my seventeenth), to serve as a companion. He has fit the bill perfectly. He *never* disappointed me and when he lost his beautiful pearling, I thought well, now I know I have a boy bird and can teach him to whistle and talk!

I did succeed in teaching Lennie to talk, using a CD with ten different whistles and phrases. Alfalfa and Harley both learned to talk and whistle from Lennie. They are naturals at speech and have a learning rate faster than my Amazon. They are so amazing.

This is Lennie at three years old. *[Elisa DeSimone]*

Alfalfa was purchased in Los Angeles. He is the most mischievous 'tiel, and has been to the vet several times for "accidents" such as eating philodendron leaves. I am extremely careful with him now! I don't let my mother buy any poisonous plants. I keep all of the cockatiels' wings clipped and I never let any bird out of its cage unsupervised. Danger lurks everywhere, I've found out.

Alfalfa is the "personality kid" of the cockatiel flock. He has so much character it is amazing. He says "hello," "pretty bird," "I love you" and "thank you," as well as imitating more sounds than most African Greys I know. One benefit of Alfalfa's curiosity is that he eats a healthier diet as a result. Since he loves plants, I decided to stick some mustard greens in the cage. He attacked them with gusto, and the other birds followed. Whenever I introduce a new vegetable, it is gladly accepted. And I hear that cockatiels are among the pickiest of birds!

Harley is very outgoing and loves being held. He talks a blue streak in a clear voice and knows some whistles, as well. Like all my pet birds, he makes big kissing sounds when I greet him. While he is not keen on being touched, he may yet learn to trust me. He has come a long way from the terrified, hissing creature he was when I first got him.

I interact with my cockatiels in the early evening. That's when they all get to hang out on the patio with me, and each bird gets fifteen minutes of one-on-one attention. Lennie gets his head scratched, Alfalfa talks to Mackenzie and Harley talks to me during "special time."

I credit Lennie with turning me into a true bird lover. I have rescued many birds, joined organizations such as The World Parrot Trust, and thought about becoming an avian behavioral consultant. I truly respect all birds for who they are—a concept that many people unfortunately do not understand. Unconditional love.

(continued)

Every cockatiel is different, and that is what makes them special. To be a successful bird owner, you have to be patient, caring, understanding and have high self-esteem. They can be shy, nervous, intimidating and aggressive, but you can't take it personally—especially when a bird bites! You must accept that all birds are emotional, intelligent animals, prone to mood swings. If you can't accept this, you shouldn't own a bird.

Of course, cockatiels are the absolute sweetest, most gentle birds—the easiest with which to have a smooth relationship. But still, you must always love them for who they are.

which could be a hand signal or words like, "Can you say hello to the folks? Hello." The cue and response are linked. When the bird says "hello," you give the bridge and the reward. When it doesn't, you simply present the cue again. Once a bird has learned to learn this way, it is possible to teach it other behaviors quickly.

IF TRAINING FAILS

No cockatiel can be guaranteed to talk. There are even absolutely silent African Greys, and cases of birds forgetting words once they reach adolescence. The adolescent needs to be worked with and retrained. It is the norm for birds to stop learning new words after about eighteen months of training. This is not because a bird stops learning, but because it isn't offered continuing opportunities. Eb Cravens stresses the gentle approach, and always uses a verbal reward or cuddles. He advises that to produce an accomplished talking parrot, owners need to keep bringing new incentives and initiatives into the bird's life.

A bird may also move from repertoire to repertoire over time. Some birds will pick up phrases they have heard only once, especially if what was said excited their owner.

I feel that an owner who has a talking cockatiel got an added bonus. Owners should realize that even if their companion does not use human speech, it still can communicate a vast number of things. Birds show affection, ask for food, attention and baths, and express joy and anger by their actions. Birds recognize their owners and can be affectionate or playful, rowdy or in a bad mood. A close bird–owner relationship exists when each is acutely aware of the other, whether that is expressed in chirps or in human speech. When I come home late, my sixteen-year-old cockatiel hen Dacey says "clirp, clirp" to greet me, even under her cage cover in the middle of the night.

Potential owners of pet cockatiels should be aware that they should be willing to cherish their pet for the qualities it does have. Friendliness, cuddliness, beautiful coloring, beautiful flight, whistling and singing are some of the wonderful qualities of nontalking birds. As we do our human acquaintances, we need to appreciate each bird for its individuality!

Entertaining That Cockatiel

One night when I was writing, a young female cockatiel named Mystique was out of her cage and was keeping busy exploring her environs. She was quite taken with a block of wood on top of her cage—a piece that had broken off a ladder. Mystique flung the wood to the floor, then looked inquisitively over the edge. Thinking she had misjudged the edge of the cage, I returned the block to the top. Mystique then grabbed the wooden piece and pushed it off the edge again. A game of fetch ensued, in which she dropped the piece of wood off the cage eight times, and I put it back eight times. The last couple of times, she dropped it into a cup I held out. She had taught me to fetch, and I had taught her where to drop the block.

Clearly, Mystique's actions were deliberate. We interacted during the game and we each got our exercise. Play with a cockatiel isn't usually so orderly or structured, but I encourage you to invent new games and activities for your cockatiel.

Entertainment can also be called *environmental enrichment* or *socialization*, and it's vital for the well-being of our intelligent birds. It might involve an interesting food, training to learn new behaviors, play, providing a stimulating environment for a cockatiel, or it can be a new toy or some direct interaction with its owner.

Cockatiels are flock animals; they require socialization and relish play. They are naturally curious birds. If brought up with trust and a variety of experiences, they will be into everything and investigate all kinds of new items and situations. A cockatiel that receives no stimulation might well become afraid or unused to trying new toys, foods or experiences. I heartily recommend that you socialize your bird to some degree, as you would a growing child or a young puppy in your home.

New Experiences

It is surprising what a cockatiel can enjoy when it's open to new experiences. It's a good idea for your feathered companion to get used to bathing, traveling in a carrier and meeting new people. Being open to new experiences may save your pet from stress when it is time for a trip to the veterinarian's office or to accompany you on vacation.

One of the ways to train an exhibition cockatiel is to expose it to many new situations. Show cockatiels need to learn to stay calm when confronted with people who look different. They meet people who have glasses, mustaches and hats. Companion cockatiels benefit from familiarization with different parts of the house and by traveling in a carrier. I have never driven around with a cockatiel just for the experience, but over the past decade I have taken birds to fairs, libraries, club meetings, shows, schools, day care centers and senior centers.

Dacey, who has been with me through fifteen years of moving, has lived in numerous homes in numerous enclosures, from small cages inside to aviaries outside. Dacey, her progeny and I have all survived a few earthquakes, including a rather

New experiences for cockatiels range from meeting people with hats to taking part in educational exhibits. This is Doris Wilmoth and friends staffing a table for the American Cockatiel Society.

large one that left us without power for three days. Our adaptability might have something to do with our varied experiences!

Bathing

Most of my cockatiels have grown to love baths—especially now that I know enough to bathe them! My first bird bath experience was rather traumatic. Dacey was my constant companion at that point, my only cockatiel and my only pet. She had to show me the ropes.

Dacey was sitting on a hanging basket over the sink one day when I washed some parsley and put it in the basket for her as a treat. She jumped in the parsley and—to me as an uneducated cockatiel owner—she

seemed to be having some kind of seizure. I quickly rigged up a sort of hospital cage with a light bulb for warmth. I swaddled the cage in towels. When Dacey suddenly appeared normal and luxuriated in the warmth I had provided, I realized that she had been bathing in the wet parsley!

I felt silly, but I also learned to provide her with regular showers. Now I keep a spray bottle or mister near my bird enclosures at all times. The birds appreciate frequent showers in warm weather. Occasionally I roll a cage of birds outside to bathe them in spray from an outside hose (which has run for a couple minutes to flush out nasties), and then they dry in the sun. We meet a lot of the neighbors that way.

I encourage you to give your bird baths regularly, at least once or twice a week. When a cockatiel learns to love its baths, it will hold its wings open, contort its body and try to lift every feather up to catch the water. Soaked cockatiels look pathetic. As it dries, a cockatiel will preen itself industriously, spreading oil on all its feathers from a gland at the base of its tail. Encouraging preening through regular bathing is a good thing, and this little bit of housekeeping helps keep cockatiel dust to a minimum.

Bathing John (a girl) with a spray bottle. The water in the bottle is warm.

Bathing can take many forms. A cockatiel can be lightly misted or really soaked. One way to give a bath is to put warm-to-hot water in a plant spray bottle. Mist your birds, especially from above, so that a rain shower is simulated. You may also use an atomizer to do this—a hand-pumped sprayer that creates a fine mist instead of a heavy shower. For a number of birds, you could get a clean, unused weed sprayer that can also be pumped and used to shower the flock.

A cockatiel can receive the benefits of a bath just by being in the bathroom when you shower. The moist air in the bathroom is good for your cockatiel and also stimulates it to preen. There are numerous shower perches available, or your pet can have the run of the curtain rod or a towel. Obviously, supervision is the key to safety. The toilet seat should be down and your companion should not be exposed to soap or very hot water.

Most cockatiels spread their wings and lift their feathers to delight in every drop of a bath, as Lindbergh, this female lutino, does.   *(David Wrobel)*

You can teach your cockatiel to bathe in a faucet where the water is running gently, and some cockatiels even bathe in bowls of water. My own cockatiels generally prefer to be sprayed with water, although nesting females will jump into a bowl of water to wet their breast feathers and, in turn, the eggs they are incubating.

It is important to bathe a bird early enough in the day so that it can dry and to avoid showering a cockatiel when its environment is fairly cold. As I mentioned, cockatiels will especially love to be showered in hot weather. Then, two or three baths in a day would be welcome! A bath helps them cool off, especially if they are sprayed on the feet and under the wings. I never go on a summer trip with cockatiels without packing a water bottle. Spraying them regularly while traveling in hot weather is a must for their health and safety.

Home Alone

Some of us work outside our homes and have cockatiels who learn to accept that schedule. For much of the time I have shared my life with cockatiels, I have also worked full time. On those occasions when I pop home during the day, I often find my birds sleeping. They have definitely learned to adapt to my schedule!

There are a variety of ways you can enrich your cockatiel's life, even if you aren't home with it. You can leave a radio on, or a stack of beautiful CDs. You can place your cockatiel's cage near a window with a view (just make sure you avoid leaving it in direct sunlight). It

Providing music in your absence can be a good way to entertain your cockatiel. You probably want to play music when you're home, too. Charlie, a normal gray male, was a real music lover and favored classical music.
(David Wrobel)

would probably like watching wild birds at a feeder or birdbath.

Frequently providing washed branches or new perches gives a good diversion for a cockatiel, as they chew on the leaves and bark of fresh greenery. New perches offer the same kind of long-term diversion. Of course you supply toys, and you may want to rotate these so there's always something new to play with.

A mirror is entertaining to cockatiels, as they chatter or sing to their reflection. A cockatiel does seem to regard a mirror as an interesting companion. Many males will whistle to the image in a mirror and females will spend time near a mirror, so that it provides a sort of companionship.

The "Other" Pet

Perhaps you're wondering if your cockatiel would benefit from an animal companion. In general, I encourage people to get just one

cockatiel, which will bond to them, before considering whether they want to own more than one bird. You get a good idea of the care involved in bird ownership with one cockatiel. You get to know an avian veterinarian, find

Supplying a mirror is one way to enrich your cockatiel's life. This is Bozo, a normal pied male, who loves whistling and talking to his reflection.
(David Wrobel)

out how you feel about feed scattered around a cage and whether you want to provide the care and stimulation a cockatiel requires.

Even if you decide you do want another bird, your cockatiel may not want a birdie friend. Sometimes a bird with a close relationship with its human companions has no idea it is a bird and snubs any addition to the family. When my first cockatiel, Dacey, had lived with me for about a year, I added a new cockatiel, Clement, to our family. At first Dacey reacted to the new cockatiel as she would to her mirror: She pecked at Clement, who did not react as a mirror image does! Dacey caught on quickly.

Other times jealousy is fierce, usually triggered by human attention. And people often wonder whether their tame cockatiel companion will become untame when it shares its life with other birds.

A suitable companion *might* be another species of bird that more or less becomes the cockatiel's pet. Budgies usually become close cockatiel companions, without speaking exactly the same language. Often they can share the same cage, although introductions should first be in neutral territory, away from either bird's cage. And you must be sure the birds interact safely together before you let them share a cage.

Canaries are another good choice. Cockatiels can watch the antics as a canary jumps about in a separate cage. Cockatiels can also be inspired by canary song. I had a cockatiel and canary duo that sang duets. The cockatiel came in a couple of octaves below the canary, but he did try his hardest to trill those canary ballads! Of course, any living thing needs to be treated well. Canaries are a type of finch and require different care than cockatiels. If you invest in a living companion, be sure you are willing to take good, responsible care of it.

I have also known cockatiels and guinea pigs that developed some interest in each other. This should be interest from afar, as a

A budgie may be a suitable companion for a cockatiel. These are three stunning examples bred by Nancy Sondel of Soquel, California.

guinea pig pen is not a sanitary place for a cockatiel. The rodent's antics can be interesting for a cockatiel to watch, however, and they share an interest in similar treat foods.

You're the Entertainment

Of course some of the best entertainment a cockatiel can have is interaction with you, its closest companion and best friend. Cockatiel companionship varies from hands-on petting to simply being in the same room with you. Cockatiels like the morning routine, whistling

Cockatiels usually love to watch canaries flit about in their (separate) cages. In some ways, a canary can become a cockatiel's own "pet." This is Doodles, a hand-fed canary owned by Nancy Sondel.

at their image in the bathroom mirror, soaking up the shower's spray and nibbling on toast for breakfast. They can also learn to stay on a playground in a room where there is quite a bit of activity.

Later, in the evening, cockatiels might enjoy running up and down the back of the couch or sitting on your shoulder. Most behaviorists don't advise allowing parrots on shoulders, because they can become territorial about it. In general, cockatiels are pacifists and gentle, and it's okay. But remember that curious cockatiels will peck at moles, freckles and jewelry when they perch on your shoulder. If any of the above are of value to you, you should remove the item in the case of jewelry, or the cockatiel in the case of more personal markings!

If a cockatiel allowed on your shoulder is overly aggressive, you

should not allow it to be in that position. You can also start working with an avian behaviorist on a method of training. Possible suggestions are training your bird to sit on your knee or wrist and hand instead of migrating to a high perch on your shoulder. It is also wise to teach your bird "up" and "down" commands, so that you are indeed in control of the cockatiel's actions and the cockatiel will obey you.

By returning it repeatedly and consistently to a playground, your cockatiel can also learn to stay in a specific area when it is out of its cage. I took advantage of this to take a bird to work in an office for a while. It worked until Charlie grew his wings in and sailed triumphantly over the drafting department. Then he was banished.

Another type of interaction enjoyed by cockatiels is preening. I

sometimes put my hands on a cockatiel's back, so it is used to that, but it is not a bird's favorite way to be caressed. On the other hand, you have a great opportunity to do your cockatiel a real service when it is going through its molt. Pinfeathers seem to be itchy, and cockatiels will preen each other in the places they can't reach, such as their head. If your cockatiel has never enjoyed being touched before, this is a good time to start, when the interaction will be appreciated.

Cockatiels like being rubbed behind their crest. Rub the feathers against the grain or blow lightly on them. If pinfeathers are coming in, rub off the keratin sheath—but not too close to the bird's scalp if the feather is still growing in. New feathers have nerves and a blood supply.

Another favorite spot is well marked: Cockatiels love to be stroked where their cheek patches are, and around their jowls and beak. Here, too, you can help them preen if they're molting or just pet them if they're enjoying the attention. Once your cockatiel learns to enjoy this preening behavior, chances are it will ask for it!

Toys

Cockatiels are curious birds who usually spend large amounts of time in their cage. In the wild they would forage, establish territories,

Debra Wrobel packs a lunch with her friend. Any kind of interaction is entertaining to a cockatiel. It doesn't have to be anything special—cockatiels have a great time doing routine things with their people. *(David Wrobel)*

A cockatiel will enjoy being out of its enclosure in a place it can observe what's happening to the "flock." This is a lutino male named . . . Susan!

avoid predators and seek safe roosting spots. In our living rooms and bird rooms, they can be entertained by toys. It's also a good idea for a cockatiel to know how to play by itself, rather than encouraging a spoiled cockatiel to scream for your attention.

Cockatiels are attracted to color and movement. They like to chew as a diversion. It is a good thing to look for these attributes in a toy. Colorful toys are stimulating and enjoyable. Chewable toys are a diversion. These include toys made of wood or rawhide. Bells are usually a cockatiel favorite.

Good toys have parts that can be manipulated, such as beads that move or pieces that can be pushed or pulled. This means that many toys are suitable, if they are the proper size and are made of safe materials. Toys that are too small, such as plastic budgie toys, may fracture when manipulated by larger, stronger cockatiels. Toys that are too large may harm a cockatiel, or may simply be intimidating!

If a cockatiel does not accept a toy right away, don't give up on it. You can hang that toy near its cage, so that the bird gets used to the toy. Then move the toy to just outside the cage. Finally hang the toy inside the cage. Your cockatiel may step to the opposite side of the cage at first, but eventually curiosity should get the better of it. My cockatiels were originally afraid of a colorful spiral swing I bought them, but now it is a favorite perch.

It does a lot of good for both you and your bird to be conditioned to accept change. A toy manufacturer has begged me to encourage companion bird owners to help expand their friends' world, and I do agree. So often if a bird is initially afraid of or ignores a new toy, the owner lets the bird have its way. Imagine how the bird's world becomes a smaller and smaller box in this way. The big toys are ruled out, visiting the living room is ruled out, bells or acrylic or rope are ruled out. If the pattern continues, maybe the bird ends up with only its own cage and a favorite toy.

Even if they are abundant, the same toys can get boring. You can make life more interesting for your cockatiel by rotating toys. When you have a few, try putting one or two in a cage for a week, then changing toys the next week, using another set. The same toys can be "new" all over again for your companion.

Safety is always a concern when it comes to toys. Many longtime bird toy manufacturers were inspired to revise their lines or invent new toys in order to improve on the interest and safety of existing toys. However, with toys, Murphy's Law is probably most in effect: Whatever can go wrong, will go wrong. There is no absolutely safe toy around active birds.

Look for toys that allow a cockatiel to be entertained through color, movement and chewing.

Some toys, such as those with rope, should really only be used under supervision. There's too big a chance that there could be an accident with loose fibers or loops. On the other hand, a curious cockatiel can turn a seemingly safe toy into a dangerous one. Cockatiels often like to sleep or rest with their head inside a bell that is large enough. Many of my cockatiels had played with an acrylic toy in their cage. I came home from work one day, however, to find an inquisitive baby had hooked the clasp of the toy through his lower beak. I was a mess; the bird was extricated by a friend and it healed well.

Safe materials to look for in toys include indestructible plastics, bells with clappers that cannot be removed, vegetable-tanned leather and safe, untreated woods such as pine. Any dyes used should be nontoxic, preferably human food-grade dyes.

Toys are often found at your local pet supply store, but that's not the only source. You can make your own toys, or turn everyday objects into toys. My little pied gets as much enjoyment out of her block of wood as she has from expensive toys. Other "found" items that can be toys are rings cut from toilet paper rolls, empty film canisters and empty thread spools. Cockatiels play gladly with blouse or shirt buttons, and will extend that to rings, watches and earrings if you aren't observant! Audubon, in one of his roles as a sidekick for a talk I was giving, deftly removed an amethyst from someone's bracelet. Luckily, we found the stone and the owner was able to have it repaired.

Cotton rope, shoelaces strung with toasted oats and carefully crafted homemade toys with all safe materials are well accepted as playthings. Baby toys are a possibility and are sometimes available at garage sales (make sure you wash and disinfect them before giving them to your bird). Other toys for entertainment include perches and ladders. Many cockatiels learn to climb wooden or acrylic ladders, or have a favorite perch or playground. One cockatiel I know goes for rides on his ladder, allowing himself to be placed upside-down. This took some conditioning on the part of his owners, but now they have a game they play together.

Though I would have to agree that our cockatiels do not rank among the smartest parrots, I could not agree with offering

CLEANLINESS STILL COUNTS

Make sure you keep all your bird's toys clean. Some toys clean up well in the dishwasher. Others do not. Dyed wood tends to run when it's wet, and rawhide can spoil. You are better off replacing these toys when they are soiled.

them an uninteresting life. Both you and your bird will find it more exciting to play together and grow in experiences.

Entertaining Foods

Healthy foods that have pieces that can be torn apart, or foods that are light and crunchy, and again, fun to tear apart, can make interesting treats. Although a bird's main diet should be based on a formulated diet, treats can be fun for both cockatiels and their human companions—who often derive pleasure from preparing treats for their cockatiel. The birds have exposure to different tastes and textures, as well as the fun of eating them.

Because entertaining foods are meant as a treat and not as a large part of the diet, choose foods low in fat, salt and sugar, but high in entertainment value.

Travel

My birds have come to love travel. When you travel, you have the options of getting a pet sitter who will come to your home, or boarding your bird at a home, a veterinarian's office or a pet store. Or you have the option of taking your cockatiel with you. Try it some time!

Check first to make sure your cockatiel is welcome at your destination. Then plan for either car or

The rule has always been "tails out" when my cockatiels enjoy some unsalted, air-popped popcorn. These are Crystal, the gray male; Lindbergh, a lutino hen; and Mathilda, a pearl hen.   *(David Wrobel)*

air travel. Birds are not welcome on trains and buses.

It would be smart to pack at least a minimal first-aid kit when traveling, with a blood coagulant, towel and scissors. You should pack some water from home, so that your companion doesn't have to change, which would only add to the stress. Don't forget to take along your bird's food, too. You don't know if and where it's available at your destination. What else you pack depends on how you plan to travel.

By Car

First, make sure you have a water sprayer or mister with you, especially in hot weather. A good way to

cool off a cockatiel on a drive is to spray it with water.

Prepare your cockatiel's cage for travel. This includes removing hanging toys that might become dangerous flying objects during the drive. Replace water with a leafy green vegetable, or fruit if your bird likes it. These don't spill as water does. Then offer your cockatiel water along the way when you've stopped. Your travel cage should be small enough to fit in your car and be seat-belted in.

My cockatiels love tootling down the highway and looking at everything going past. Charlie used to streamline himself and "head into the wind," so to speak. If your

Recommended Fun Treats	
Food	**Preparation**
Beans	Fresh green beans, sprouted lentils or legumes
Broccoli	Seeded crowns, or peel stalk and cut in pieces
Breakfast cereals	Whole grain, no added salt or sugar
Corn on the cob	Cut in wheels; you can include the husk and silk
Eucalyptus	Wash thoroughly, offer leaves and branches
Frozen vegetables	Place in strainer, thaw under running water
Grasses	Collect when they have green seeds on top (choose an area to collect away from roadside exhaust fumes and free of pesticides)
Millet spray	Occasional treat only, as seeds have high fat content
Peas	Defrost frozen peas or open fresh pods
Popcorn	Air-popped, no salt or butter
Rice cakes	Push through bars of enclosure
Toasted oat cereal	Offer in a dish, or string on a shoestring as a toy

cockatiel is frightened, covering its cage with a light sheet should let light in but not allow your cockatiel to see the scenery.

There are many hotels and motels throughout the country that will allow you to bring pets into your room. With a little planning, you should be able to find one. I keep a copy of the Motel 6 directory in my glove box, since most do accept pets.

If you are staying at a hotel en route, remember to be courteous. Cover a dresser with a towel before putting a bird cage on it, clean up after your bird and cover it at night. Supervise your pet so it doesn't chew or poop on furniture or draperies. If we are courteous and don't abuse the privilege, we'll continue to be accepted at these locations with our pets.

BY AIR

I delight in thinking of cockatiels who fly at 30,000 feet. If only their wild cousins knew! It takes some preparation to travel by air with a companion cockatiel. There are two choices: The cockatiel can ride in the cabin with you (on some airlines) or it can be shipped air freight. In both cases, you need to call the airline ahead of time to arrange this, and the cockatiel will get its own ticket. When a cockatiel needs to travel alone, there are counter-to-counter services that can help you arrange that.

Airlines also sell approved carriers or can advise you what model to buy. Ventilation on all sides is required, as is certain labeling, and the carrier should have sloped sides so that air cannot be cut off.

There may be restrictions on the number of pets allowed in a cabin, or they may not be allowed at all. Check before you make your own reservation. Another arrangement to make is with your avian veterinarian. If you are traveling between states, you may need a health certificate.

Again, for air travel supply a cockatiel with a formulated diet and leafy greens or juicy fruit. When it is traveling under my seat, I have usually managed to slip bits of airline food to my cockatiel companion. The only peeps I get out of them are on take-off and landing, when the air pressure causes my ears to pop as well.

I sent one cockatiel chick in the baggage compartment. I'll try not to do it again. The bird was fine: Georgie hopped out of his shipping crate, was very chipper and became a wonderful pet for my

Traveling with a 'tiel can be entertaining, and you can make it safe for your bird. *(David Wrobel)*

brother. I was a nervous wreck, and winced at every bit of turbulence.

It can be quite attention-getting to travel with a feathered companion. Be prepared to talk about birds with your fellow passengers. Maybe you can pass on some useful tips!

GOING ABROAD

Do you have plans to travel abroad with your pet bird, or do you plan to purchase one when you are overseas? There are specific permits you will need to obtain from both the U.S. Fish and Wildlife Service and the U.S. Department of Agriculture in order to do so.

The U.S. Fish and Wildlife Service, in accordance with the terms of the Wild Bird Conservation Act of 1992 (WBCA), issues regulations that provide for permits to allow foreign travel with your pet bird. Most pet birds are in the Appendices to the Convention on International Trade in Endangered Species (CITES), so you will probably need to obtain a CITES export permit, which allows you to bring your bird back into the United States. When you leave the U.S., you must have this permit validated by the U.S. Fish and Wildlife Service and keep a copy to show upon returning. You may also

need to secure permits from the country you are visiting.

If you purchase or obtain a pet bird while out of the country, there are different requirements. You may only import a pet bird into the United States that was purchased or obtained abroad if you have lived outside the country continuously for at least one year. If this is so, then you may import a maximum of two birds. You must secure all permits before *shipping* the bird back home. It's too late once a bird has been shipped and is in quarantine. Quarantine, which is necessary when importing birds from countries other than Canada, can be arranged by contacting the USDA.

PERMIT, PLEASE

Permit applications and any additional information you may need for international travel or shipping are available from the U.S. Fish and Wildlife Service's Office of Management Authority. Call (800) 358-2104 or fax (703) 358-2281.

For more information about importing pet birds into the United States, you can also phone the USDA at (301) 734-5097. For information on exporting animals, phone (301) 734-8383. You may visit the USDA Animal and Plant Health Inspection Services (APHIS) web page at www.aphis.usda.gov/oa/petbird.

TRAVELING 'TIELS

Roberta and Billie lived in Britain when they acquired cockatiels. Billie is a musician and a British native. Roberta is an American. After successfully saving a baby sparrow, they acquired a gray male cockatiel. Cheeky was an adult when they got him, and probably an aviary bird. His wings remained unclipped, and he did eventually learn to fly to them to visit, but he did not seem to crave human companionship.

Roberta and Billie decided to get a companion for Cheeky, and so Annie, another normal gray male, came into their life. You can't tell the sex of a young cockatiel, so obviously there were some misconceptions about gender when Annie arrived. Annie is another aviary-raised bird and only good company for Cheeky.

Harvey, a lutino, was hand-fed as a baby and turned out to be the tame, friendly companion bird they had originally hoped for. Now there were three.

When Roberta and Billie decided to move back to the United States, they called the U.S. Embassy to find out what the procedure was for bringing their companion cockatiels. Policy changes from time to time, but they were put in touch with the U.S. Fish and Wildlife Service, and eventually the

U.S. Department of Agriculture sent them the papers they required.

The total cost, including shipping, necessary papers and vet checks, was about $800 to $900. A friend wondered if they shouldn't think, instead, about buying new birds once they had relocated to the States! Obviously she didn't understand the bond between a bird and its owner, or the lifetime commitment one makes to a companion animal. There really wasn't much question that the birds would make this move.

Roberta and Billie hired a shipping company located near Heathrow Airport to handle the arrangements. They got the appropriate shipping containers early so the birds could play in them and become accustomed to them. The birds also got their required health certificates. Billie loaded the birds into their container and watched them being taken away by strangers. It would be over a month before he saw them again, because of the thirty-day quarantine period required in the United States.

Roberta arrived in the U.S. first and made weekly phone calls to the birds. The quarantine experience did not seem to be a pleasant one for the birds. The grays shrieked, and Harvey developed a

mean streak. Quarantine personnel stayed in touch with Roberta, and things never got too serious.

The cockatiels have been joined, in ensuing years, by gray-cheeked parakeets and another cockatiel from Britain. When Jamie left to come to the United States, Roberta and Billie took him themselves directly to the counter at the airport. There were cages of penguins on the docks at the same time, so he wasn't the only avian passenger.

The birds have a huge playground arrangement along one wall of a room and free flight throughout the house when Billie is home during the day. Cheeky and Annie keep each other company. Harvey and Billie have developed a special game. Harvey likes to climb on a long ladder, and Billie gradually started moving the ladder and even flipping it over. Now Harvey flaps his wings and accepts being flipped upside-down as they play.

What is the value of a cockatiel? To Roberta and Billie, it is obviously the value of their commitment to care for another being that has become a part of their life. Health care bills or transportation costs do not decide the value of a bird for them. Neither does its initial cost or its resale value. Or its rarity. It's not the cost of replacement—it's the individual bird that counts.

CHAPTER 11

Is Your Cockatiel Being Weird?

I am always pleased to hear from owners of pet cockatiels after they have had their baby a couple of weeks. They ask the most wonderful questions. And then I know the baby I handled, fed, talked to and watched grow up is appreciated and loved—if not spoiled rotten!

Most new owner questions concern very common cockatiel behaviors, but one has to observe a few cockatiels in order to know that. For many cockatiel buyers, this is their first pet bird.

Perfectly Normal

Pet birds do have a variety of behaviors that are unique and very different from those we expect of our canine and feline pets. Is your cockatiel weird, or is it just being a cockatiel?

BEAK GRATING

When a cockatiel is relaxed and getting ready to fall asleep, it will often grate its beak, making a rasping sound. This isn't the most pleasant sound in the world, but it doesn't last all that long, either. You know you have a happy, contented bird when it does this.

GARGLING

Among cage birds, cockatiels aren't known to be the best talkers. But some males are persistent about trying. The first indication that your cockatiel is interested is when it makes gargling noises. These become inflected like human speech over time, then turn into words.

DUST

Cockatiels have down feathers that disintegrate, turning into a dusty powder. This is especially noticeable when your have several birds. For this reason, an air purifier is recommended in a bird's quarters, and it's not a good idea to keep your bird near bookshelves or sensitive electronic equipment (such as a home computer).

Dust can be kept to a minimum with frequent spray baths, which encourage preening.

Because of the dust they produce, cockatiels do sneeze occasionally. Constant sneezing, or "productive" sneezing with a discharge, are signs of illness and should be investigated.

Cockatiels spend many of their waking hours preening. No, they don't have fleas! This is Mathilda, a pearl hen. *(David Wrobel)*

Each feather is carefully preened, as oil is spread on it from a gland at the base of the cockatiel's tail. Mathilda demonstrates the technique here. *(David Wrobel)*

PREENING

Cockatiels spend many of their waking hours preening. During preening, they take oil from a gland at the base of their tail and run it over each feather. You can encourage this behavior by bathing your bird. When your bird preens often, its feathers have a lustrous quality. Because they are well kept and there's plenty of natural oil on them, the bird can shed water and stay warmer better, and natural dust will be minimized.

PLUGGED NOSTRILS

Cockatiels may look as if they have plugged nostrils, but in fact, they have a natural bony plate just inside their nostrils that belongs there. Don't try to remove it! What is *abnormal* is a discharge of any kind from the nostrils or wet feathers above the nostrils.

Cockatiels have down feathers that disintegrate and produce dust. For this reason, it a good idea to house cockatiels away from sensitive electronic equipment and bookshelves.

NIGHT THRASHING

For some reason, our calm, cheery pet cockatiels are prone to fits of thrashing about their cage at night. This behavior, and what to do about it, are discussed in greater depth in Chapter 8. The best preventive measure is to keep a night light on near a cockatiel's cage. When night thrashing occurs, the proper course of action is to turn on the lights and talk to your birds in a soothing tone of voice. Check for broken blood feathers or injuries, then turn off the lights when the birds have calmed down.

Possible causes of night thrashing include earthquakes, bugs, bumping into toys in the dark (when birds can't see), nightmares, a perch falling or. . . . We don't really know, but it happens to everyone!

DOING A BAT IMITATION

Occasionally a cockatiel will grab a curtain rod or other high perch with its feet, spread its wings and fall forward, holding that position for a few minutes. In breeding

FLAPPING

Sometimes a pet that does not have much free flight time out of its cage will exercise in place by holding on tight to its perch and flapping its wings hard. This is a normal behavior.

Males may show dominance by lifting their wings and appearing bigger to a trespasser. Here Bozo displays for Ashley. These two are male and female, but they don't like each other. *(David Wrobel)*

birds, this is a behavior used mostly by female cockatiels to claim or guard the entrance to their nest box. My nonbreeding pets have done this off the living room curtains, which I take as a sign of territoriality or dominance.

I'M BIGGER THAN YOU ARE! (OR AT LEAST MORE IMPORTANT)

One behavior you'll see in males is holding their wings high up over their head. This is a way of making themselves look bigger, and is part of establishing the pecking order in the flock.

Most often I have seen a cocky male react this way to another male. Once, however, a male that had been hand fed and coddled reacted this way when I entered his aviary. He wanted to make sure I knew who was boss! If two males in your house or aviary are displaying this dominance behavior, it is generally more of a bluff than a real threat. Just let them go ahead and work it out themselves.

CREST PLACEMENT

A cockatiel's crest makes it an attractive, elegant bird. To some extent it also indicates mood. Owners of young cockatiels will notice that their birds' crests are held erect most of the time. As they mature, cockatiels hold their crests down when at rest and relaxed.

These are two male cockatiels showing aggression. Their body feathers are tight and sleek, their crests are back and their beaks are open. Despite the show, they didn't hurt each other.

When a cockatiel is startled, the crest goes straight up. When aggressive or angry, it is held back; usually the bird's beak will also be open, or the cockatiel will be hissing if it is very angry.

MOLTING

The process of molting is interesting and confusing to first-time bird owners. Cockatiels tend to molt twice a year, in the spring and again in the fall. More frequent molts can be triggered by a warm environment or by the number of hours per day a cockatiel is awake.

Birds don't lose *all* their feathers at once. When a bird molts, it replaces its feathers systematically over a period of time—about six weeks to two months in cockatiels. Molting starts with the feathers on the head and ends with the long tail feathers. At the first molt, juveniles start getting in their adult coloring.

For females coloring does not change, but males get bright yellow heads and solid-color tail feathers. In the case of pearls, males will lose their pearl markings.

New feathers are called pin feathers and are encased in a keratin sheath that looks like plastic. The pin feathers have a blood supply and nerves, and any damage to

The juvenile male gray cockatiel on the left is molting for the first time. His adult coloring, with yellow head feathers, is coming in. The bird on the right is an albino.

CONTORTIONISTS

Cockatiels have a unique way of scratching their head: They lift their leg up and over their wing. This looks a little clumsy, but seems to be the way cockatiels are designed.

Mathilda the contortionist!
(David Wrobel)

them will cause pain and bleeding. The fastest way to stop the bleeding is to pull the feather. (Most broken blood feathers are wing or tail feathers. Use a pliers for the wing, but a quick jerk near the base will pull out a tail feather.)

A cockatiel can usually unfurl its own keratin sheaths from pin feathers, but may want you to preen its head feathers, which it can't reach. A little scratch will probably be appreciated. This is also a good time to improve your relationship with your pet, especially if you have a marginally tame bird.

Cause for Concern

By carefully observing the members of my small flock of cockatiels, I have been able to assess what is normal. But not all "weird" cockatiel behavior is innocuous. Discharge from the nostrils or vent, constant gaping, head flicking, tail bobbing or feather picking all indicate a need for veterinary attention.

Other signs of problems are detailed in Chapter 8.

If your bird is doing anything unusual and you feel concerned, there's never any harm in asking your veterinarian or the bird's breeder. Better to be safe than sorry.

Birdie Burnout

Birds tend to be addicting. We joke at bird club meetings about being bird-aholics, about how many new additions came home from the last show or fair, about the raffle prize. Each new addition is a new responsibility, however, a new cage to clean and more vet bills in order to ensure a healthy bird.

I have set personal plateaus for the number of birds I wish to own. For several years that plateau was exactly two birds. I would keep babies from a clutch or two, acquire potential mates, then tire of the cleaning chores, the noise and dust and mess. In order to truly enjoy my cockatiels, I sold the "extra" birds and went back to enjoying my original pair. One year that plateau somehow crept up to five cockatiels. I had eight birds, but sold babies or placed the poor breeders to get down to a tolerable number of feathered bodies requiring care.

The daily care and attention needed by a single pet could become monotonous or routine. And with a dozen cockatiels, not every bird gets handled every day. Sometimes chores get overwhelming and I start to feel more like a caretaker than a pet bird owner. This is birdie burnout. At each plateau of cockatiel ownership I have encountered it, and have found ways of dealing with it. It can happen with the one-bird pet owner just as easily as with a multibird breeder.

When birdie burnout sets in, special effort is required in order to put a spark back in the relationship between owner and pet. Pet bird ownership really *is* fun, and there are ways to keep it fun.

Bird ownership is a joy when it's new, but sometimes you get burned out and need a new perspective.

Watch the Birdie

Combining your bird hobby with another hobby can make both more interesting. I really enjoy taking photographs of my birds. Take a photography class to learn the basics, then practice on your feathered friend. Photographs can be made into pins, puzzles, postcards, stamps, stickers, mugs, plates and business cards. There's nothing like admiration from your friends to renew your interest in your bird and spur your interest in maintaining its beauty!

You will get the best photographs of smaller birds by using a macro lens. Other possibilities include using a wide-angle lens, or using a telephoto lens and lighting the area well. Cockatiels can also be photographed with a standard lens, or even a 110 (nonadjustable) camera.

When shooting close-ups with a flash, diffuse the bright light of the flash by putting tissue over it, or even a strip of white-out tape.

As you frame your photo, remember the basics of composition. Try to have the bird fill the frame and carefully consider the background. Prop up a towel, a piece of construction paper or another solid-color object for the background. Birds in combination with plants make good photos, too.

If you don't have photographic equipment, perhaps you can use your talents in drawing, sewing or crafts. Cockatiel needlepoint, elaborate sewn cage covers and developing recipes for cockatiel treats are all possible ways to combine your bird hobby with other interests.

Breed a Brood

Breeding your birds may be the cause of your birdie burnout, and if so it's time to take a break from breeding. But if you've never tried it, breeding can be an exciting experience. You will not need to devote so much of your time to interacting with a breeding bird (though there will be a great deal of care and feeding involved), and the bird will be occupied constructively.

You need two healthy birds of opposite sexes to start. Ask successful breeders about cage setup, dietary requirements, light requirements and type of nest box for the bird you have. If you cannot locate successful breeders, start reading and educate yourself through the avian publications and books

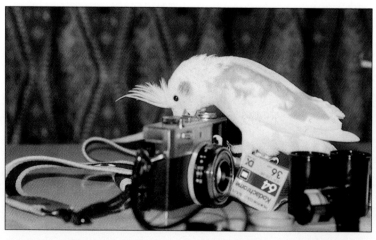

Cinnamon-pied cockatiel Ashley plays among photo equipment. Sometimes combining bird care with another hobby can make the bird chores seem less tedious.

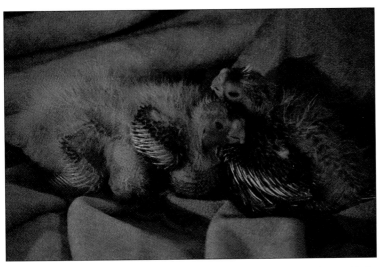

Breeding your birds may be interesting—or may be the cause of your birdie burnout! Sometimes cockatiel chicks are so ugly they're cute.

TAKE A BIRD TO WORK

This solution to birdie burnout is not for everyone. It *is* possible for those with their own office, the self-employed and those who work in relaxed offices. When the company I work for was a small family business, I took a cockatiel in daily. Lacey sparked conversations for us and led an interesting life—enhancing her existence and ours.

available. Chapter 13 in this book is a place to start, but you'll need to do more research before you actually begin breeding.

Exhibit

Maybe your bird can be more than just another pet. Maybe you have a champion! Attend a bird show to see what goes on, get an appropriate show cage and enter your cockatiel just for fun. It may not win, but *you* will win by listening to the judge's comments about the qualities of an ideal specimen. Invariably, *condition* and *training* are factors that keep coming up, as are certain facets of conformation.

If you breed your birds, what you learn at a show will give you a better idea of which qualities are desirable. Exhibiting birds offers a goal in a breeding program.

If you never win a single prize at a bird show, you can still enter and attend for the chance to network with other people who are serious about their birds and exchange ideas and experiences. Sometimes this human interaction makes the daily interaction with my birds more worthwhile!

Share

Most of us keep our cockatiels as close companions. They offer us beauty, song, close physical contact, joy and comic relief at the end of a stressful day. There are numerous ways to share these rewards with people who cannot care for their own pet. Check with the activities

director of a local nursing home or senior care center. More than likely they would welcome a visit.

Of course, it would be nice for the residents to be able to touch or feel a bird, but not all birds will accept so much handling. Does your bird do a trick? Are there other visual aids you could pass around: feathers, bands, a stuffed bird, photos? Be prepared to answer basic questions about what your pet eats, its talking ability, how old it is, how long it will live and so on.

Other possible places to share birds and bird care include libraries, grammar schools and 4-H meetings. I once took Dacey and Buzz, with two porcupine-pinfeathered babies, to the children's story hour at our local library. We got a lot of attention, spread a lot of care knowledge, and I still get a respectful greeting from the reference desk clerk when I go into the library.

A sharing activity will make you feel good, also. For a moment you are a celebrity and an expert, so you feel good about yourself.

Join a Bird Club

You are not alone in your love of birds. I highly recommend flocking together with other bird owners at club meetings, or keeping up with news about the species you favor through national societies and their publications. Most bird clubs host informative speakers, and just talking to other members can give you ideas about care or housing or ways to solve a problem you have with your own bird.

Remember to listen attentively, weigh the value of advice carefully and selectively adopt the ideas that apply to your bird in your situation. Question everything you hear. There are many ways to reach the same goal. Speakers are merely saying, "This is how I do things." You are free to try their method, improve on it or reject it.

Surf the Internet

With a computer, modem and software from an Internet service provider, you can visit Internet sites all over the world. The World Wide Web offers a good place to do research and to meet other people with your interest. Sites vary from personal home pages where you can take a look at pictures of pet cockatiels, to commercial sites where you can buy products, to informational sites with links to a host of other sites on the same topic. Many of the larger service providers also have their own chat rooms where you can visit with other bird owners.

Both the American Cockatiel Society and the National Cockatiel Society have web pages, as do many breeders and some magazines. Check them out!

Along with access to the World Wide Web, you can usually set up an e-mail account with a service provider. This allows very low-cost communication with cockatiel owners and friends all over the world.

Try New Foods

Interesting snack foods for pet birds are numerous, but I often find myself stuck in a rut. Every once in a while I flip through back issues of *Bird Talk* magazine and get inspired to try something new. Sometimes that means I bake for my birds, sometimes I discover a new vegetable at the supermarket. Sometimes I discover that the birds like vegetables I had never thought of offering them. Consider converting your pet to a high-quality pelleted food. That can be very easy or a real challenge.

Keep a Journal

Maybe you've just forgotten about all the interesting things your bird does! Start a journal of behavior, care and breeding information. If you like to write, this could be inspiration, or if you are methodical about weighing chicks and

FASCINATING FALCONS

No matter what species of bird interests you, there is something to be learned from the speakers at bird clubs. One of the most inspiring speakers we have had at the Monterey Bay Cage Bird Club was a falconer. His birds were very different from our pet parrots; in fact, his falcons preyed on birds the size of our cockatiels and Amazons.

Walt, however, made sure we knew that if we had a goal and stuck to it, we could reach it. He had been told falcons couldn't be bred in captivity, but with artificial insemination, good care, creative feeding and hours of training and hunting, he had spent thirty-five years doing the impossible!

Your goal may be raising hyacinth macaws, reintroducing an Amazon species back into the wild or training a cockatiel to do tricks. Whatever it is, don't ever let anyone tell you that you can't do it!

recording feedings, your information could really help out someone new to your species or to hand-raising chicks.

You will look back on a journal as a sort of "baby book" in fifteen or twenty years, or the bird's next owner will find the information invaluable. New owners love to learn about their chicks. Many of my customers know and remember their cockatiels' birthdays!

Learn More About Birds

There are numerous books, publications, seminars and national meetings at which one can learn about birds. At some universities there are courses in ornithology or exotic bird care and management. How I wish I lived near one of those!

There are plateaus in learning, also. Just when I feel comfortable with my knowledge of cockatiels, something else comes to light about genetics, feeding, health or management.

Plan to learn birds' Latin names, learn about the native habitats of birds that interest you, or stretch your interest in birds to include the local Audubon club to do some birding. Our pets are native species in other countries—visit those countries to admire parrots flying free.

Teach

Even though we never know everything, after a couple years of bird-keeping, reading *Bird Talk* and networking with other bird owners, we often know much more than the beginner. There are people just getting started with bird-keeping all the time. If you have good information to share, consider offering a class at a community recreation program, or a continuing education class through a local high school or junior college. In the process you will become a local expert. You could find that pet stores or the local SPCA call you for advice.

Sharing what you've learned about your pets with others can make the whole endeavor of birdkeeping exciting again.

(Carol Cottone-Kolthoff)

Help Out

There are many organizations that help birds, from medical research to parrot adoption services. All could use assistance, and most also need funds. A fund-raiser could be as small as donating a raffle item or as large as organizing a whole event. And for most organizations, your time is even more valuable than your money.

It's a great way to give back to the birds for the joy they are. You'll feel great about it and meet new friends. That's bound to put a spark back into your life. To get started, I suggest contacting an organization you would like to support and running your idea by them or asking what help they need. Have a good idea of the skills you have to offer. Chances are needs vary from staffing booths to public relations work, office work or phone work to fostering birds and building aviaries.

Count Your Cockatiels

If all else fails, maybe you have just reached a plateau. Consider putting your bird or birds into the hands of enthusiastic, caring individuals so they can reach their full potential. Maybe it's time to cut your flock back to a manageable size. Then again, maybe it's time to expand!

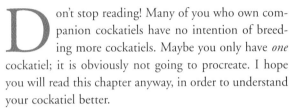

Breeding Cockatiels as a Hobby

D on't stop reading! Many of you who own companion cockatiels have no intention of breeding more cockatiels. Maybe you only have *one* cockatiel; it is obviously not going to procreate. I hope you will read this chapter anyway, in order to understand your cockatiel better.

It isn't a common or a safe practice to neuter cockatiels. That means they have behavior changes and hormone surges that you both have to deal with. Some female pets lay eggs. And a pet cockatiel bonds to a pet owner as it would to a cockatiel mate, and even goes through parts of the breeding cycle, so I hope you stay tuned. If you simply have a cockatiel companion, you can use the information to avoid stimulating your cockatiel to breed. You can be sure to provide an egg-laying female with the calcium it needs when laying eggs, even though you know those eggs won't hatch. You can be understanding and wait for a cockatiel to complete its breeding cycle and return to being your loving pet!

To Breed or Not to Breed?

If you own two or more cockatiels, you may have thought about breeding them. Maybe the cockatiels have thought more about breeding than you have, and are doing so at every opportunity! My first inclination, when talking to people who are thinking of breeding their birds, is to give them as much information as I can to discourage them. Do you have time to provide cockatiel parents with the food and housing they require? Are you prepared to hand-feed chicks if anything goes wrong? Are you prepared to pay vet bills, if needed, for the parents and the chicks? Do you have homes for the babies? Do you know that

cockatiel chicks must be marketed, sold and placed into loving homes? Not everyone is willing to take on the task of breeding cockatiels.

If your cockatiels are more interested in breeding than you are, consider the alternatives. You can reverse breeding stimuli, take their eggs before incubation, separate the birds, or go ahead and let them breed, taking responsibility for their health and the chicks' futures.

There are many reasons you may want to breed cockatiels. If you have begun to exhibit your birds, it is fun to have goals and to breed winning cockatiels yourself. Exhibition standards give you a goal in your breeding program— one that is rewarded by your peers and is personally rewarding. If you enjoy your cockatiels and have nice pets who get along with each other, breeding cockatiels is a good hobby with enough of a monetary reward to offset some of the costs.

If you are a young person in a 4-H or Future Farmers of America program, it is very possible you can raise cockatiels instead of large farm animals as a sort of condo livestock. One of my favorite bird breeders calls herself a farmer, although she lives in a suburban neighborhood of a fairly large city. I think it's wonderful to farm in an urban setting.

If you are thinking about breeding as a way to make a living from your home, consider all the costs,

There are many reasons for breeding cockatiels, but your goal should always be a happy, healthy chick like this one. *(David Wrobel)*

from setting up aviaries to purchasing stock to finding markets to caring for hundreds of cockatiels twenty-four hours a day, every day. And consider the responsibility you have to find a good home for every single bird you breed.

For whatever reason you are breeding cockatiels, please consider the health and welfare of your own cockatiels, the needs of the people to whom you will sell cockatiels, and the greater goals of aviculture and all cockatiel owners. Look at what you can do to make a difference in the quality, health and personality of cockatiels available to new pet owners. Look at what you can do to provide

cockatiel owners with good information and support as they learn about the new being in their home. Look at what you can do as a responsible aviculturist in the way of keeping records, offering health guarantees, banding your birds and supporting a research, conservation or adoption project. There's really more to breeding cockatiels than putting two birds together in an enclosure with a nest box.

Breeding fulfills the natural instincts of a pair of cockatiels. It is also entertainment for pets who may spend more time with each other than with their owner. Cockatiels raising chicks are anything but bored.

A common concern of cockatiel owners is that their birds will somehow become wild if allowed to breed. I bred cockatiels in my living room for many years and did not find that to be the case at all. When my cockatiels aren't breeding, they are my loving pets and we interact as before. This is not true of every exotic bird species, so I consider it another very special cockatiel characteristic.

So that you're prepared for it, you've never seen so much fury packed into a small package as a cockatiel defending its nest. It will hiss, sway and jump up at you. This could be an intimidating display. You can choose to be intimidated or not. I prefer to keep a very hands-on relationship with my breeding cockatiels, and reach past the hissing parent to stroke babies or clean up a nest box. Cockatiels can adjust to many situations, so you can decide how this relationship will be.

One Plus One

It may seem obvious, but the first requirement for breeding cockatiels is a pair of birds consisting of a male and a female. The bonding instinct is very strong in cockatiels, so two birds of the same sex may act like a mated pair. For most color mutations, it is easy to determine sex once the birds have molted into adult plumage at about six months of age. But the pieds are difficult to sex, and some people don't have a good knowledge of the differences between the obviously dimorphic sexes.

One day a man called to say he wanted to give his cockatiel to me. The man, who had owned his bird for two years and had told me it was a male, walked up to the house with a very obviously female gray cockatiel. It happens. Females have some yellow on them (what do books mean, anyway, when they say "yellow head?"). This particular bird was split pied, so she had a big yellow patch on her nape. Henry's named changed to Henrietta, and she was the light of her new owner's life for many years.

Sometimes you decide to breed cockatiels, and sometimes they decide. This is Chip, the little adolescent pipsqueak who fell for Treasure, a show bird.   *(David Wrobel)*

You already know you need a male and a female bird to be a successful bird breeder. These should be healthy birds. Schedule a veterinary exam if the birds have not been in for a while. Breeding is stressful for a cockatiel, and any latent infection or disease could surface.

If possible, I let young cockatiels choose their own mates by keeping a number of males and females together and watching their interactions. Quite often I pair up young birds, caging them together for several months before I expect them to breed, matching characteristics I like from color to personality to conformation. This way the birds know each other and develop a rapport before they tackle the job of parrothood. I do the same with

sexually mature cockatiels, giving them at least a couple of months to get to know each other before I expect them to breed and raise babies. I am happiest when my pairs get along, and I think they do a better job of raising their chicks, too.

Male cockatiels in my flock do a sort of woodpecker-like drumming on perches and cage bars when they want to impress the females. They are usually very vocal in the courting phase of breeding. They square their shoulders, make little stiff hops and lean right up next to a female to sing in her ear. A cute display that always makes me glad I'm not a female cockatiel—their "sweet nothings" are usually not soft, but ear-splitting.

Good signs of compatibility include pairs that match their

Imitating Nature	
Here are some of the stimuli you can use at any time of year to encourage your cockatiels to breed.	
Stimulus	**What It Simulates**
Frequent baths and mistings	Rainfall
Fresh greens and soft foods	Sprouted wild grasses
Breeding diet	Abundant food sources
Branches, wood toys	Encourages chewing
A nest box	Nest hole in a tree

behaviors. They both preen, stretch, sleep or eat at the same time. Bonded pairs sleep together on the same perch, and are usually close to each other. Very close pairs preen each other and call to each other if separated.

Sweet Inspiration

Once you've noticed key signs of compatibility and your cockatiels are one to one-and-a-half years old, you probably want to entice them to raise a family. Some of the keys to inspiring a pair of cockatiels to breed come from their natural history. Cockatiels are nomadic birds and opportunistic breeders who nest when conditions are right. Right for them is rainfall that creates an abundant food source, an available nest hole in a tree and a mate. You can make conditions right by providing frequent showers, abundant food and a nest box.

Long daylight hours may make a difference. It wouldn't hurt to provide about fifteen hours of daylight to breeding pairs, to get them in the mood.

Offer frequent baths or mistings to simulate rainfall. If your bird does not like to be misted, you can offer it bowls of water or take it into the bathroom with you when you are in the shower. Be sure there are plenty of the soft green foods needed to feed hungry chicks. I even offer breeding birds sprouted grasses I have harvested from a location that is not sprayed and is not near a road. Be sure there is a cuttlebone or calcium block available for your cockatiels, so that the hen has adequate calcium to make eggs. You might also change the pair's diet to a breeding formulation.

As the pair gets ready for parrothood, they have the instinct to chew. Provide plenty of branches they can destroy. When you put up

a nest box, you will find that the birds will customize the entrance hole. I put pine shavings in the bottom of the nest box to prevent eggs from rolling into each other and cracking. I use only pine shavings, as paper is too absorbent and might dry out the eggs, and cedar chips may be harmful.

Cockatiels develop a special repertoire of calls as they start to explore the nest box. The male usually inspects the box first, calling to his mate from inside. I imagine he's extolling the virtues of the real estate. If a pair is ready to breed but no nest box is provided, this activity will still take place. Your cockatiels will explore areas under furniture, inside cupboards and

Inspire birds to breed by giving them showers, abundant food, long daylight hours and a nest box. Notice that this pair has redecorated the entrance hole to their new home.

closets and behind shelves, looking for a suitable location in which to nest. Cockatiels have used provisional nest sites successfully, ranging from drawers to shoe boxes.

If your birds have the luxury of having a planned nest box, it can be made in a variety of shapes and sizes, from any of several materials. If you have an experienced pair, find out what they are used to. In the wild, cockatiels would choose a dark tree hole in which to nest. Many nest boxes are dark inside to make the pair more comfortable.

Cardboard boxes provide shelter for one nest of babies. I've seen plastic drums modified into nests. There are metal and polymer boxes on the market. A common, inexpensive and traditional cockatiel nest box is a twelve-inch wooden cube. Usually the lid lifts to allow inspection, though I would personally love to have a nest box that allows inspection from the side in the rear, where the chicks are.

A traditional box can either be fastened flat on the outside of a cage and opened from the back, or fit on the wall of a flight or aviary and opened from the front. Features include an entrance hole and a perch or porch on which Dad can stand guard at night when Mom is in the nest box. It's usually best to figure out if you want a box that hangs from the front or back before you go looking for one. I use rope to attach nest boxes to the door openings of my birds' cages. Wire or S-hooks may work for you. Be sure there is a way, later, to clean and inspect the nest box.

Nature Takes Its Course

As the proper stimuli are provided, the cockatiels' bodies begin to change. They form brood patches on their chests, warm places where eggs will touch their skin with no

barrier of feathers. The pair will start to do everything together. The male will display for the female, whistle, bob his head and square his shoulders. They will groom each other and will scream when separated. The pair will begin to mate.

Cockatiels are not shy. They copulate many times in a day over a period of about two weeks. The female is quite vocal, emitting a sort of rolling coo. The male stands on the female's back and grates his beak as he reaches his tail over to place his vent on hers. Or at least that's what is supposed to happen. Inexperienced pairs don't always get it right the first time. I had one pair that each sat on a perch on opposite sides of the cage, playing their respective roles in mating. Obviously, that clutch was infertile, but they did eventually work things out.

INFERTILITY

Infertility is a common problem in first clutches. Sometimes the cockatiels just need to have a clutch or two of eggs before they get things right. It helps to have sturdy perches in your cage or aviary, or even a flat board for them to stand on while mating.

Sometimes infertility is caused by incompatibility. If a pair really isn't working out, change mates, replace one of the pair or find some other arrangement. Sometimes it

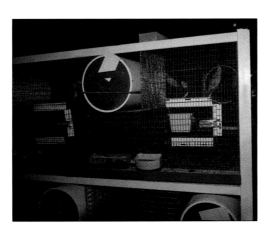

This round cockatiel nest box is used at a breeding farm in Joliet, Illinois. Many shapes and sizes of nest boxes will be accepted by a breeding pair—including a drawer or closet if nothing else is available.

sounds like there's a cockatiel soap opera going on in my flock. Dacey and Clement, her first mate, raised many chicks together but quarreled often. One or the other of them would get possessive of the nest box, and Clement had a bad habit of chewing feathers from the chicks' heads. He was eventually placed in a home to be a companion for another cockatiel, but not to breed.

Buzz chose Dacey as his lady love over several females I had at the time. He and Clement had a few aerial battles, which ended with Buzz stealing her heart. Dacey's life changed considerably. Buzz was a gentleman, always at her side, and they hardly uttered a cross word in the ten years they had together.

Dacey, in fact, is something of a Marilyn Monroe of cockatiels. Many of the males whistled at her and tried to win her affections. The only incidence of wife beating in my flock happened when one of the smitten could see Dacey but not get to her, and he attacked the female I had paired him with.

Sunshine, a gorgeous pearl-pied male, was paired up with a lutino, one of Dacey's daughters. He left her for a young chick, however. Another pair had a pearl-pied daughter that he courted from the moment he saw her. She was only three months old at the time, but he had found his life's companion.

PLAY IT AGAIN

Bob Hawkins of Sydney, Australia, sent me a copy of this article about enthusiastically sensual cockatiels owned by a local disc jockey.

Jon Harker reports that his whistling cockatiel, Bogart, is still in an amorous mood. Harker claims Bogart has been celebrating the coming spring by making love to his mate Bacall while whistling the first verse of the *Marseillaise* at the same time.

Bogart, who can also whistle *Bridge on the River Kwai* and mimic the ringing of telephones and microwave ovens, has been learning the French national anthem for the past six weeks while sitting on Harker's shoulder as he prepares scripts at his computer.

—The Sunday Telegraph, August 24, 1997

Breeding cockatiels is partly about being aware of your birds and observing interrelationships as well as physical needs.

DIET

Conditioning your pet cockatiels for breeding consists of feeding them a healthy diet all year and being sure they get enough exercise. It is thought that good muscle tone is one of the ways to prevent egg binding in hen cockatiels.

The pair should have a formulated diet. I supplement the diet with fresh greens or other low-calorie, fun foods with a variety of textures and colors. I concentrate on those high in infection-fighting vitamin A. There should be a cuttlebone available at all times for calcium. Treats should be nutritious and low in calories. Avoid fat, sugar, salt, caffeine, alcohol, chocolate and avocado. Be sure clean water is available at all times.

Tom Roudybush has covered nutrition and diet in a separate chapter—this is just a quick review. Breeding cockatiels have special dietary requirements. While she is forming eggs and shells, the hen needs extra calcium, vitamin D_3 to utilize the calcium and protein. This can be provided by switching to a breeding formulation of the brand of feed the birds normally eat.

Laying Eggs

When a female cockatiel enters the nest box and spends a long period of time in it, she is laying her first egg. That's usually somewhere around the ninth or tenth day after you put up a nest box, but again I'll remind you that your cockatiels aren't reading this book. They'll do what comes naturally.

A hen goes into labor for up to ten hours with each egg she lays. If you look in, she will often have her tail up against one wall of the box. If she emerges from the nest box at this time, she may look fluffed up and ill. This is always a hard call for me, but if you know that your hen is laying an egg and it's about that time, wait to see if the egg actually emerges. However, if your bird is fluffed up, looks ill and is on the bottom of the cage not seeming to care about anything, she is egg bound and needs immediate help.

When a hen is egg bound, the egg is obstructing the only outlet in her body for waste, and toxins start to build up. It is critical that she expel her egg. Hold her over a light bulb for warmth, or immerse her up to her neck in warm water to try to help her expel her egg. If heat does not help after an hour or two, you should seek veterinary help in order to save her life.

This problem has occurred in my flock only once in the last fifteen years. It was when Dacey and I were both new at breeding cockatiels. Honestly, she wasn't getting an optimum diet. We were both starving graduate students at that point. I learned a lot, and Dacey laid the egg off the top of a lampshade after the light bulb warmed and relaxed her enough.

It seems to take forever, but finally that first egg arrives. I mark my birds' eggs with an indelible soft-tip pen on both ends. An egg will split in two if it hatches, but the number will remain intact, so I

ARE WE ON THE SAME PAGE?

It's always been a relief and a source of amazement to me that cockatiels don't read the same books I do. Somehow they know what to do to raise a family, and I do all the worrying. Sometimes I have gotten less-than-subtle reminders that my cockatiels and I did not read the same books about breeding cockatiels.

Sunshine sang to his eggs. Priscilla, a cinnamon-pied hen, insisted on laying a whole clutch of eggs before beginning to sit on them, instead of starting to incubate the first or second egg. Her idea of a clutch was ten eggs, instead of a normal five. Dacey and Buzz usually spent a lot of time in the nest box together, when I would expect parent cockatiels to take turns caring for eggs and chicks. No one adequately described what a miracle it is to hold a peeping egg in your hand, either.

always know which egg it was. I keep records of what date an egg is laid and what date it hatches. Not every egg hatches, and sometimes an egg will be early or late, so numbering the eggs makes my records more accurate.

Usually parents do not start sitting on that first egg right away. Relax, it's normal. For reassurance, review Chapter 16 on the research

being done at UC–Davis. Cockatiel eggs stay fertile for at least three days, even if they are not incubated. The pair usually starts incubating when the second egg has been laid. In a typical clutch, the hen lays an egg every two days. A normal clutch size is five, but that can vary from four to nine eggs—or even ten.

Time to Sit and Wait

Parents usually vigorously defend their eggs, even tame pet parent cockatiels. They most often exhibit a very touching partnership in incubating eggs and caring for babies. The male usually takes on these duties during the day, the female at night. This is truly a joint effort.

A caller once asked to borrow one of my male cockatiels for a few days in order to impregnate her female. It doesn't work that way with cockatiels. In a pinch, if there is a loss or if one parent or the other is hurting the chicks, either parent can probably raise the brood alone. But they are meant to work as a team on the important work of carrying on the existence of cockatiels in this world.

While cockatiels are incubating eggs, it is a good idea to provide them with a bowl of water in which to bathe. The parents may exhibit some exceptional behavior and like to go swimming in the

Pearl hen Lacey is protecting an average clutch of five eggs. When Lacey is out of her nest box, she is the calm, friendly bird who is my pet the rest of the year. *(David Wrobel)*

bowl of water—at least, this is exceptional in my flock. Happily, this is a good thing. They go back to the nest with moist breast feathers and regulate the humidity of their eggs that way. This prevents embryos from drying up inside the egg and sticking to it, unable to hatch.

This behavior could very well differ in other parts of the country. I live on California's central coast, where it is dry and fairly cool most of the time. The extra moisture is probably needed, and somehow the parents know that.

When you think about it, it's a wonder we can ever hatch eggs mechanically. Some people do successfully incubate cockatiel eggs, however. The advantage of taking eggs to incubate is that the parents

will be stimulated to lay again. In general, production is not a big deal with cockatiels, but maybe if you had an order to meet or were breeding exceptional birds, you would want to try this.

While the parent cockatiels are sitting on their eggs, they have an endearing habit of periodically turning the eggs. If an egg happens to stray from the warmth of the brood patch, they gently roll it under them again and settle back over the whole batch. It's beautiful almost beyond description. I guess this is one of the advantages of my way of breeding my companion birds—that they are comfortable enough to let me watch this.

I am also constantly active cleaning nest boxes, handling the chicks and talking to the parents.

Obviously, I've been a hobby breeder enjoying the experience. Things would have to be different if I wanted to raise production and make money breeding cockatiels.

Time to Hatch

Cockatiel eggs hatch somewhere between eighteen to twenty-three days from when they were laid. Before an egg hatches, the chick inside starts peeping. The birds hear the peeps a couple of days before I do, responding with a loud, excited call. Not only the parents, but all cockatiels within earshot get excited about chicks hatching. In my household having chicks next door has been a trigger for some pairs to raise families of their own.

Inside the egg, the chick has a lot of work to do. It uses a special egg tooth to peck around the circumference of the egg. This takes from a few hours to two days to peck all the way around, depending on the strength of the chick and the thickness of the egg. This action is called pipping.

Once a chick has pipped most of the way around its egg, it turns violently inside the shell and suddenly bursts out of the egg. A newly hatched chick is wet and has the appearance of an embryo. Its eyes are closed and it has a yellow down (white down if it is a whiteface chick) rather than feathers. The wings are only buds.

Finally, the blessed event occurs. A chick hatches! You can still see the egg tooth on this youngster. *(David Wrobel)*

HOW LONG SHOULD YOU WAIT?

You may have eggs that do not hatch. I generally leave eggs with the parents for about a week past the date they were due to hatch. Young chicks will appreciate their warmth, and if it's just a late arrival you will know by then.

The incubation period does vary; I have had eggs that hatched at seventeen days and others at twenty-three days. This seems to depend on genetics and the weather. When it is warm out, chicks develop faster.

The first chick will often hatch on the same day as the second. Remember, the parents don't start sitting on that first egg right away. It doesn't start developing right away, either. Peeping eggs seem to talk to each other, too. Sometimes a chick will hatch a day or two early, to join its siblings.

Its main requirement during the first few hours of life is warmth. For a couple of hours it will probably feed from its yolk sac, so you don't need to worry if parent cockatiels don't feed their offspring right away.

Parent cockatiels will feed a newly hatched chick a very thin food from their own crops. If you take over from the parents with a day-one chick, be sure you use a very thin mixture of hand-feeding formula, or in a pinch buy Pedialyte (found in the baby section of your grocery store). Babies for sale and called "hand fed" are generally not removed from the parents right away, but when they are about two to three weeks old.

In addition to their breeding formula feed, I supplement the diet of adult cockatiels with newly hatched chicks by providing them with high-protein baby food cereal mixed with water, whole-wheat bread, hard-cooked egg and greens. Be sure the parents have soft food available and plenty of fresh water.

A newly hatched chick looks a little like a bumble bee, with thick yellow down. Its life should consist of eating, sleeping and pooping. If you have an active chick, chances are something is wrong. Chicks that are too cold shiver, chicks that are too warm stick their wings out to the side and pant. (This is beginning to sound like *Goldilocks!* I'll finish up.) Chicks that are just right sleep a lot and beg when they are hungry.

I usually don't handle the very young babies. Young chicks are particularly sensitive to molds, bacteria and fungus. Be sure you have clean hands if you handle them. I do peek at them, though. Generally, the chicks look like they have grown between morning and evening. Young chicks huddle together for warmth. They drape themselves over any eggs that have not yet hatched. Dad cares for the babies during the day. Mom cares for them at night.

Foods for the parents should be fresh and should be changed often. I

A ten-day-old cockatiel chick is starting to get feathers on its wings and crest. It is growing rapidly. In less than three weeks this creature will look like a bird.

American or National Cockatiel societies allows you to earn points that could lead to a championship. Each band lists the year the bird was born, the breeder's code and the bird's own number. Bands are available from band companies, and from the societies listed in the box.

To band a chick, put its three longest toes into the band. Pull the band onto its leg, using the band to bend its short toe back along the leg. Pull the short toe out of the band. I use my fingers, but you may have to use a toothpick.

I like to band my chicks at quite an early age. Sometimes then the bands fall off in the nest box and I have to search for them, but I prefer that to squeezing a band onto a bird that has grown too large. If

only leave egg, thawed frozen corn, peas or mashed beans in the cage for about fifteen minutes, allowing the parents to eat their fill without giving the food time to spoil.

It's difficult to believe how fast cockatiel chicks can grow! At one week old a chick is blind and helpless. At twelve days it can hobble

around and beg for food. It's starting to develop a personality. When chicks are about ten days old their first feathers appear. Their vocalizations change from soft peep, peep, peeps to louder and raspier cries for food.

Banding Chicks

I band my chicks about this time. A band is a method of permanent identification for a cockatiel. Closed bands are placed on ten- to fourteen-day-old chicks. The bird's foot eventually grows too large to remove the band. No matter how well we know and love our birds, cockatiels look pretty much alike. A closed band with a traceable code number on it identifies that bird positively. That is useful to future owners if their bird is ever lost or stolen. It is also a verification of the bird's age if it is ever sold or moves to a new household.

If you plan to exhibit your cockatiels, a traceable band from the

SOURCES FOR TRACEABLE BANDS

American Cockatiel Society
9527 60th Lane N.
Pinellas Park, FL 34782

National Cockatiel Society
P.O. Box 1363
Avon, CT 06001-1363

American Federation of Aviculture
P.O. Box 56218
Phoenix, AZ 85079-6218

Society of Parrot Breeders and Exhibitors
P.O. Box 369
Groton, MA 01450

Clement doesn't name his chicks, he chooses a number for them.
(David Wrobel)

IF AT FIRST YOU DON'T SUCCEED . . .

Glenn Stallard lives in Thailand, and acquired cockatiels at a weekend market on the outskirts of Bangkok. He says there are almost always cockatiels for sale at the market, though there doesn't seem to be a word for them in the Thai language. Canaries are available at the market as well, from Taiwan, Holland or Germany.

His first pair of cockatiels turned out to be two males. A younger male had not yet acquired his adult plumage with its telltale yellow head. Eventually two true pairs of cockatiels lived happily in an aviary with at least a dozen canaries. Glenn decided to breed cockatiels, and cultivated a correspondence with friendly cockatiel breeders across the globe. He made some adjustments because of his location: The cockatiels had a teak nest box, and millet grew readily in his garden.

You may have heard that cockatiels are easy to breed. After learning of Glenn's experience, you may think twice about that! Here is one letter he wrote in the midst of trying to breed cockatiels.

As my aviculturist friend pointed out, it is not unusual for the first clutch of eggs to be infertile. My experience now agrees with that. I had one pair (normal cock and lutino hen) that insisted on ignoring the nest box and using a canary nest instead. This created some problems, of course. The hen could just barely get into the nest and the cock didn't enter the nest even once. And, of course, it would have been totally impossible for both of them to be on the nest at the same time. In any case, she sat on the eggs for longer than three weeks; so I candled the eggs, found they were all four clear, and threw them out.

I then decided to move the nest box so it covered the spot where the canary nest had been. The hen *still* refused to enter it, even though the cock kept calling to her from inside. She tried to use another canary nest! Finally, I had to cut a piece of plywood to cover the entrance to *that* nest and cut a hole in it large enough for a canary but too small for her. She was furious! Nevertheless, she finally gave in and used the teakwood nest box. She laid four eggs again and began setting.

Then one day I discovered one egg smashed on the ceramic tile floor quite a distance from the nest. I still don't know how it got there. In any case, one egg hatched January ninth and a second egg hatched January tenth or eleventh. When I checked, I found the second chick dead. The third egg never hatched.

I made it a point to check at least once a day and I found the parents were feeding the single chick very well, and it was really thriving. I had a real problem with hand feeding because the parents were extremely protective and it was difficult for me to take the chick out of the nest box, even for once-a-day feedings.

In the meantime, I had put the other pair (lutino cock and pearl hen) in a large cage and fastened the other nest box to the outside of the cage. Interestingly enough, the pearl hen had always been aloof and had been pretty much ignored by both of the cocks when all four birds were free in the aviary. Still, the lutino cock, in the cage situation, began to mount her frequently.

She laid four eggs and both birds took turns nesting. Then, after about ten days or so, I noticed the cock mounting the hen again. I checked the nest box and discovered there were now five eggs. Regular checking after that showed a total of eight eggs, meaning she had laid four eggs in addition to the original four, which were still in the nest.

Just a few moments ago I discovered one egg on the floor of the cage. . . . I must say that I don't expect any chicks from *any* of these eggs, as the cock is extremely inept, even if persistent.

you have some difficulty getting the band on, you can lubricate the chick's leg with petroleum jelly.

The band number then becomes part of my permanent records. I transfer the date an egg was laid and hatched onto a record of the whole clutch. This record also includes the chick's band number, and later will include information about who the chick was sold to or what it was named.

I usually refrain from naming chicks until I'm certain I will keep them. It would be too difficult, for me anyway, to sell them if I did.

Closed, traceable bands are put on young cockatiel chicks at ten to fourteen days old. Their foot quickly grows, so the band does not slip off. These chicks are positively identified by American Cockatiel Society bands. Chicks are a normal gray and a lutino-pearl (notice the red eyes at this age).

Sometimes I name a chick before I decide, but that chick usually ends up staying.

In Chapter 15 we'll explore bringing up and selling cockatiel chicks.

A Look at Cockatiel Genetics

by

Catherine A. Toft, PhD

D r. *Catherine Toft is with the Center for Population Biology at the University of California–Davis.*

Genes carry vast amounts of information that directs the growth and development of organisms. Genes control, either directly or indirectly, all the processes essential for organisms to live and to reproduce their own kind. Genes are grouped together in units called *chromosomes*, which are normally paired, so that each individual has a duplicate set of all genetic material. This condition, which is typical of nearly all organisms, is known as *diploidy*; the organism itself is said to be *diploid* (*di-* meaning two). The cockatiel has seventy-two pairs of chromosomes.

The individual genes on the chromosomes therefore also come in pairs. The genes controlling the same trait— for example, some aspect of feather color—are in the same position on both chromosomes in a pair. The position, or location, where a specific gene is found on the chromosome is known as a *locus*.

Concepts and Terms

To understand genetics, we need to know a little about the molecular basis for genes and the information that they contain. A chromosome is actually a very large, unbroken molecule of deoxyribonucleic acid (DNA). DNA is made up of many, many repeating units known as *base pairs*. There are only four different types of base pairs; these are the "alphabet" of the genetic code. A gene is made up of many base pairs—about 1,000 base pairs, on average. The four "letters" in this alphabet can be combined in an enormous number of ways if you have 1,000 base pairs in each gene (think of the gene as a

123

word that's a thousand letters long!). A typical animal or plant has 50,000 to 100,000 genes total, on all its chromosomes.

Each gene is a particular sequence of base pairs that determines some *trait*. Sometimes something happens to change the exact sequence of base pairs. This spontaneous change is known as a *mutation*. Mutations are rare; they might occur once in a thousand or hundred thousand or even a million offspring, depending on the mutation, gene and type of organism. You can recognize a mutation because it produces a different version of that trait. So mutations are responsible for determining different feather colors, as we will see.

Different versions of the same gene at one locus, produced by mutation, are called *alleles*. There can be one, two or many alleles at a given locus. (Geneticists use the term *gene* to mean "allele" and "locus" interchangeably, but these terms are needed to understand how genetic traits are inherited and expressed.)

A Colorful Example

We can introduce more terms and principles with the example of a color-determining gene in cockatiels. In cockatiels (as in most other parrots), feather color is determined by two sets of pigments: a dark pigment called

melanin, and a yellow-red pigment (this pigment appears to be unique to parrots).

The yellow-producing gene is found at a certain locus on one chromosome. Specifically, it is found on a chromosome that does not determine the individual's sex. A chromosome not involved in sex determination is known as an *autosome*. Melanin is produced by a gene at another locus, on another chromosome, and results in the gray or black color in cockatiels and cockatoos. The gene for production of melanin is on the sex-determining pair of chromosomes in cockatiels.

In cockatiels, the normal (that is, no mutations) color of the feathers is a blending of melanin and yellow pigment producing the

soft, warm gray color, orange cheek patch and yellow face of the males. One mutation at one locus turns the yellow pigments off, which results in whiteface cockatiels.

At the locus in this example, there are just two alleles: "yellow-on" and "yellow-off." If a bird has two of the same alleles at a given locus, we say it is *homozygous* at that locus. Homozygous for yellow-on is normal for cockatiels. If a bird has one allele for "on" and one allele for "off," that individual is *heterozygous* at that locus. Aviculturists call this *split* for a given color (split to whiteface, for example).

In many genes, such as these color genes, one allele is *dominant* over the other. This means the dominant allele masks the *recessive* allele, so that only the dominant

A family of normal color cockatiels. Cockatiel colors are produced by a blending of melanin and yellow pigment. The female is Dacey, the male is Buzz and their chick can be identified because of its light-colored beak and short, upright crest.

allele is expressed. Thus, heterozygous birds have yellow pigment, just like the ones that are homozygous for the yellow-on allele. Because the yellow-off allele is recessive, to get a whiteface cockatiel, the bird needs both alleles to be yellow-off. In other words, whiteface cockatiels are *homozygous recessive* for the allele that turns yellow pigment off.

In cockatiels, a number of *loci* (the plural of *locus*) are involved in determining feather color and patterning. All cockatiel color mutations occur at different loci, with only two alleles (mutation and normal) at each locus. So in cockatiels, there can be pearl-pied-cinnamon-whiteface individuals, for example.

Not all alleles are simply dominant or recessive. Some are *partial dominants*, which means both alleles express themselves, often equally (sometimes called *no dominance* or *blending*). In cockatiels, the pied gene is not completely recessive. Birds that are heterozygous (normal split to pied) often have stray yellow feathers about their bodies and have toes that are mottled pink and gray.

The so-called "dominant" silver is actually a no-dominance allele. It might also be thought of as a *dose-dependent* allele. Two alleles (homozygous) for "dominant" silver have twice the dilution effect on melanin as does one allele (heterozygous). This allele is the only color mutation currently known in cockatiels that is not mostly or completely recessive.

With this example, we can see that knowing what an animal actually looks like is not exactly the same as knowing its genetic makeup. The appearance of an animal, or more correctly its expressed traits, is called the *phenotype*. The exact genetic makeup is called the *genotype*. We often cannot tell an animal's genotype from only looking at its phenotype. This is certainly true in cockatiels, as we shall see.

Sexual Reproduction

In sexual reproduction, two individuals (the parents) each contribute genes to their offspring. The first step in sexual reproduction is that each parent produces *gametes*, either eggs or sperm, which will combine to give the offspring its full complement of genes. Because birds (and humans, and most organisms) have all of the genetic material in duplicate, all chromosomes except the sex-determining chromosomes have a *sister chromosome*, with all the same loci on the two sister chromosomes. Therefore, when gametes are produced the number of chromosomes must be halved, or else the chromosomes in each generation would double and chaos would result. This halving process is known as *reduction division,* or *meiosis,* and that is why chromosomes conveniently come in pairs.

During meiosis, special fibers attach to a handle on the chromosomes known as a *centromere*. These fibers pull each sister chromosome in a pair apart by the centromeres, so that each gamete gets exactly one chromosome from each of the pairs. Once the gametes combine to form a new individual, the offspring also has duplicate genetic material, exactly two sister chromosomes in each pair.

At least, this is the way it is supposed to work. Sometimes mistakes are made. One mistake is particularly important in understanding cockatiel genetics: crossover, or *recombination*. During meiosis the tips of the sister chromosomes, while attached to their centromere, get very close and sometimes literally cross over. When this happens, the tips detach and reattach to the other sister chromosome, thus trading all the alleles at the loci on the exchanged part. Because this process produces new genetic combinations, it is also called *recombination.*

Determining Sex

Sex in many species of animals is determined genetically. In most, each individual has one pair of chromosomes that determine its sex; all the other chromosomes are concerned with other traits and functions.

In humans, females have two identical sex chromosomes, known as X chromosomes. Thus a human female is XX. Males have an X that they get from their mother and a Y chromosome that they get from their father. Thus the father, not the mother, determines the sex of the offspring by determining whether the sperm gets an X or a Y. We say, in humans, that males are the *heterogametic* sex, meaning that sperm comes in two types, X and Y (*hetero* means different).

Parrots have a similar sex determination, except that females are the heterogametic sex (as is true of all birds) and so determine the sex of the offspring.

In humans and in parrots, the Y chromosome is shorter than the X chromosome. As a result, it is missing all the genes that are on the corresponding part of the longer X chromosome. It is as if you took an X chromosome and just chopped off a part to get the Y chromosome, eliminating all those genes when you do that. This feature of the Y chromosome has extremely important implications for *sex-linked* traits. For example, if you have a recessive gene somewhere on the longer part of the X chromosome, it will be expressed in male humans or female parrots, even if there is only one allele, because there is no

dominant allele on the Y chromosome to mask it. An example of a sex-linked recessive gene in humans is hemophilia (boys are more likely to have hemophilia). An example of a sex-linked recessive gene in cockatiels is the lutino, or "melanin-off" gene.

Principles of Predicting Phenotypes

With these principles of sexual reproduction in mind, can we predict the exact genetic makeup of each gamete, and therefore of each offspring? Because genes come in different versions (the alleles), the answer is no. Each gamete gets only half the parent's chromosomes, and we don't know which half it got. Moreover, because of a number of reshuffling processes, such as recombination, and just the luck of the draw, we do not know exactly how the alleles at different loci are going to be combined in each gamete. That is the evolutionary purpose of sexual reproduction: to produce genetic variation among the offspring.

We can, however, predict the *probability* of certain combinations of alleles at various loci. We can only focus on a few alleles and a few loci at a time—otherwise things would very quickly get beyond our ability to predict.

Color mutations, for example, involve only a few loci with a few alleles, so we can predict the probabilities of each genotype and phenotype, much like gamblers predict the probability of a certain poker hand.

Although you cannot tell the genotypes just from looking at the phenotypes, what you can know if you understand the principles of genetics is the exact probability of an individual's genotype, given its phenotype. This is essential for breeders who want to create complicated genotypes.

Genealogy is your most valuable tool when attempting to make predictions. You may well be able

A whiteface-pied cockatiel. This cockatiel is whiteface-pied in appearance, so that is its phenotype. Its genotype cannot necessarily be determined from its appearance. *(Herschel Burgin)*

to know a particular individual's genotype for certain specific traits when you know the genealogy of this individual. Serious cockatiel breeders band birds and keep good genealogies because of the time and trouble it saves them in predicting the phenotypes of the offspring.

MENDEL AND PUNNETT

Color traits in cockatiels are regulated by single alleles at a limited number of loci. When phenotypes are determined by single alleles, inheritance follows simple rules first discovered by Gregor Mendel, the monk who worked with the color of pea flowers at the end of the nineteenth century. These are known as the rules of *Mendelian inheritance,* and traits such as cockatiel feather color are known as *Mendelian traits.* We will focus on the general principles of predicting phenotypes under rules of Mendelian inheritance.

The standard way to predict Mendelian traits is to use a *Punnett square* (named after the geneticist Reginald Punnett). The Punnett square is the best way to learn the rules of Mendelian inheritance, because it reflects the exact principles of inheritance. However, as you will see, it is cumbersome to predict phenotypes involving more than two loci with a Punnett square, and as a result, most cockatiel breeders use a T-diagram. We will go over the use of a T-diagram when we get to complicated genotypes.

Before we move to Punnett squares, there is one more set of terms to cover. A cross involving two or more alleles at one locus is known as a *monohybrid cross.* A cross involving alleles at two loci is known as a *dihybrid cross,* at three loci a *trihybrid cross,* and so on.

The Punnett Square

Let us begin with two alleles at one locus. Each parent produces two possible types of gametes: the father two possible types of sperm and the mother two possible types of ova. I say "possible" because we don't know the genotypes of these parent birds, yet. Remember that an individual has only two alleles at one locus and these alleles can be the same type (homozygous), or they can be different types (heterozygous).

When a sperm cell and an ovum combine, fertilization occurs, and the development of a baby cockatiel can begin. Half the father's sperm cells get one chromosome from a given pair during reduction division and half get the other chromosome; the same is true for the mother's ova.

Now let's begin with both parents being heterozygous, to make all the concepts as clear as possible. Sperm comes in type A and type B; ova come in type A and type B. We assume that sperm and ova combine randomly during fertilization. So there can be four possible ways that sperm and ova of two types combine. The principle is that you multiply the probability of two independent events to predict the joint outcome. The probability of a sperm being type A is 0.5 and of being type B is also 0.5. Likewise the probability of an ovum being type A is 0.5 and of being type B is also 0.5. The four possible outcomes each have a probability of 0.25, like so:

	Ovum (mother)	
Sperm (father)	Type A (½)	Type B (½)
Type A (½)	AA (¼)	AB (¼)
Type B (½)	BA (¼)	BB (¼)

This is a basic monohybrid cross with Mendelian *segregation.* Segregation is another way of referring to the rules by which alleles combine during fertilization. Thus, each of the four possible genotypes is equally possible, each with a probability of 25 percent.

However, note that two of the genotypes are really identical: AB and BA. Because we are dealing with an autosomal locus, we don't really care if an allele comes from the mother or from the father. So we can combine those two genotypes by adding their probabilities.

So the probability of getting a heterozygous baby is 0.25 plus 0.25, which equals 0.5, or 50 percent.

This outcome is a classic monohybrid cross involving two heterozygous parents: Babies are homozygous for A (AA) 25 percent of the time, heterozygous (AB) 50 percent of the time and homozygous for B (BB) 25 percent of the time (the classic Mendelian ratio of 1:2:1). Remember an important principle here: These are average probabilities. If you have only four babies, this does not mean you are sure to get one AA, one BB and two ABs! Any given brood of four babies might be all AA, all AB or any other combination.

A Common Mutation — The Pied Gene

We are now ready for some real cockatiel genetics. Let's start with a common autosomal mutation in cockatiels—the pied gene. The pied gene is an incomplete recessive but is expressed even in one dose, that is, in the heterozygous state. A normal split pied cockatiel will often have a stray yellow feather here or there and some pink toes. Cockatiel breeders call these indications of heterozygosity "split marks."

To illustrate the rules of Mendelian inheritance with the

A cockatiel that is normal split to pied, exhibiting stray yellow feathers at its nape. *(David Wrobel)*

pied gene, we can simply substitute N (normal) for the letter A and P (pied) for the letter B in the figure on the previous page. This

assumes we have two heterozygous parents.

To try something different, let's consider crossing a pure (homozygous) normal male with a split (heterozygous) female. In such a cross, 50 percent of the offspring will be homozygous normal and 50 percent will be heterozygous.

A Sex-Linked Cross — Lutino

The lutino coloration is caused by a mutation on the X chromosome that stops the production of melanin entirely.

To understand inheritance of this gene, we need to begin with one important clarification. It is tempting to refer to the "lutino gene," but this is seriously misleading. Calling this mutation the lutino gene gives the incorrect

A normal gray cockatiel that is split pied and also shows mottled foot coloring. *(David Wrobel)*

impression that the mutant allele produces yellow color. *This locus controls the production of melanin*—the dark gray color. There are two alleles: normal, or "melanin-on," and lutino, or "melanin-off." To be really precise, we should now start distinguishing the genotype from the phenotype. I will refer to the genotypes as "melanin-on" or "melanin-off" and to the phenotypes as "normal" or "lutino."

A second important point to remember is that females are the heterogametic sex in parrots. Thus, the female has a genotype of XY and the male XX. Because the melanin-controlling gene is on the X chromosome, a female has only one allele for this trait. A female then will express a recessive trait if she has only one allele, because there is no possibility of a dominant normal allele occurring on the Y chromosome to mask the recessive allele.

The most interesting monohybrid cross involving lutino is a male heterozygous for the melanin-off allele (normal-split-lutino) and a normal female. In this cross, we now have to distinguish the sex chromosomes.

The four types of gametes are: father X^N, X^L; mother X^N, Y. This cross produces the following offspring genotypes: 25 percent homozygous normal males; 25 percent heterozygous males; 25 percent normal females; and 25

percent lutino females. Thus, if two normal parents have any lutino offspring, you know the exact genotypes of both parents—the male has to be heterozygous for melanin-off and the female has only one melanin-on allele. You also know that all the lutino babies are females.

The Dihybrid Cross—Pied and Whiteface

When alleles are at two different loci and on different chromosomes, these alleles segregate *independently*. That is, the alleles at each of the two loci obey the rules of Mendelian segregation on their own, unaffected by what the alleles at the other locus are doing. So we say they are *independent* of each other. We know that all the autosomal mutations so far are on different chromosomes and that they segregate independently. In contrast, the loci on the sex chromosome are linked, because they are all on one chromosome.

In the following example, we'll be keeping track of alleles at two loci—pied and whiteface.

To begin, we start with a male who is homozygous normal at all loci and a female who is homozygous for both pied and whiteface. We can designate N to mean normal, P to mean pied and W to

mean whiteface. Thus the genotypes are:

	Locus 1 (pied)	Locus 2 (whiteface)
Male	NN	NN
Female	PP	WW

This way of writing is confusing, in that we are using N to mean normal at any locus. We should do what geneticists do and use a different letter for each locus, with the uppercase letter being dominant and the lowercase letter being recessive. Or in other words:

	Locus 1 (pied)	Locus 2 (whiteface)
Male	PP	WW
Female	pp	ww

But then we have to remember that the normal coloration is represented by different letters, depending on the locus. Which is less confusing for you? It's probably best to start with the way geneticists do it, because as you'll see, it's hard to keep track of which allele came from where.

What are the possible gametes from this cross? The father can only produce one type of sperm cell (PW) and the mother can only produce one type of ovum (pw). Predicting the outcome of this cross is easy—too easy, in fact, because you would take a shortcut and predict (correctly) that all the babies are PpWw, and not learn how to do the Punnett square for the dihybrid cross.

So, let's illustrate the Punnett square with the most complicated cross, to bring out all the principles. Similar to the monohybrid cross, the most complicated cross is when both parents are heterozygous at both loci: male (PpWw), female (PpWw). The possible gametes are:

Male: PW, Pw, pW, pw

Female: PW, Pw, pW, pw

Do you see how to do this? The alleles are segregating independently at the two loci, so two types of alleles can occur four possible ways (similar to they way we reasoned the offspring genotypes in the monohybrid cross). When reduction division occurs, sperm (or egg) cells are getting one of each of the two chromosomes in a pair. The P is on one chromosome in the pair, and the p is on the other. Likewise, the W is on one chromosome belonging to a different, independent pair and the w is on the other chromosome in that pair. Chromosome 1 in pair 1 can end up with chromosome 1 of pair 2 or with chromosome 2 of pair 2, and vice versa. There are four possible ways that two different chromosomes in two different pairs can end up together.

	Mother			
Father	PW (1/4)	Pw (1/4)	pW (1/4)	pw (1/4)
PW (1/4)	PPWW (1/16)	PpwW (1/16)	pPWW (1/16)	pPwW (1/16)
Pw (1/4)	PPWw (1/16)	Ppww (1/16)	pPWw (1/16)	pPww (1/16)
pW (1/4)	PpWW (1/16)	PpwW (1/16)	ppWW (1/16)	ppwW (1/16)
pw (1/4)	PpWw (1/16)	Ppww (1/16)	ppWw (1/16)	ppww (1/16)

The four possible types of gametes give us exciting possibilities when fertilization occurs. The four possible gametes from two parents can combine in *sixteen* different ways. Yes, sixteen! The Punnett square is above.

Note that in this Punnett square we have been as precise as we can possibly be, noting which allele came from the mother and which from the father. This precision is unnecessary and might even be confusing, because these are autosomal traits and it makes no difference whether the allele came from the mother or from the father. In other words, pP is the same as Pp. The genotype is conventionally written with the dominant allele first—Pp.

How many different genotypes are possible? Given complete or nearly complete dominance of P and W, we have fewer phenotypes than genotypes. Here are the classical ratios of *phenotypes* of a double heterozygous dihybrid cross (autosomal and segregating independently):

Phenotypes

Normal	9/16
Pied	3/16
Whiteface	3/16
Pied-whiteface	1/16

This can also be expressed as a ratio of 9:3:3:1. So now you know that if you are trying to make pied-whitefaces, you won't get very

MAKING ALBINOS

The albino is a particularly interesting dihybrid cross. Aside from being a striking phenotype, it involves one autosomal and one sex-linked mutation. The whiteface mutation shuts off the yellow-orange-red pigments, and the lutino mutation shuts off the melanin. These cockatiels have no pigment at all.

Mammalian albinos, in contrast, result from a recessive allele at a single locus. But the cockatiel albino is determined by two loci. That is, a cockatiel albino is, in reality, a whiteface-lutino.

A whiteface-cinnamon-pearl cockatiel, an example of a multihiybrid cross. *(Herschel Burgin)*

Multihybrid Crosses—The T-Diagram

Now we are ready to move into the ranks of advanced cockatiel breeders and design some fancy phenotypes using a full palette of mutations. My favorite is the cinnamon-pearl-pied-whiteface. How do we make one of those? The cinnamon-pearl-pied-whiteface phenotype is produced by homozygous mutations at four loci on three different chromosomes. Two of the loci are on autosomes (and are

many such babies if you start out with both parents heterozygous for these traits.

independent) and two are on the X chromosome (and are linked).

Using a Punnett square for such a cross is confusing, particularly when the parents are heterozygous for any of the loci. We might use the T-diagram instead. Each parent goes on one side at the top of the T. Then you are supposed to think of all the combinations of gametes in your head and write the offspring genotypes down below. For autosomal loci, where P is normal and p is pied, you make a simple list of genotypes below, like so:

Pp	Pp
PP	
Pp	
pP	
pp	

For sex-linked loci, you make more of a cross than a T, and keep the male and female offspring separate:

$x^L x^l$	$x^L Y$
$x^L x^L$	$x^L Y$
$x^l x^L$	$x^l Y$

Aren't you glad you learned the Punnett square first? You have to figure out the gametes in your head and cross them appropriately to get the offspring. It's not that hard in monohybrid crosses. But here are some dihybrid crosses:

PpWw	PpWw

PPWW
PPWw
PPwW
PPww

PpWW
PpWw
PpwW
Ppww

pPWW
pPWw
pPwW
pPww

ppWW
ppWw
ppwW
ppww

Do you see the pattern? You repeat all the possible genotypes at the whiteface locus with each possible genotype at the pied locus.

You hold one locus constant for each group of four, in this case, the double heterozygous dihybrid cross, resulting in sixteen possible combinations of four kinds of gametes from two parents.

Linkage and Crossover

Linkage was first discovered by our friend Punnett and a colleague, William Bateson, when sweet peas did not conform to the expected 9:3:3:1 ratios in certain dihybrid crosses. Figuring out what was happening took some detective work, mainly with the fruit fly *Drosophila melanogaster,* and some understanding that genes are on chromosomes and that there are a number of chromosomes. By doing hundreds of crosses with fruit flies, four linkage groups were eventually determined, and it was eventually discovered that each of these linkage groups corresponded to one of *Drosophila melanogaster*'s four chromosomes.

So, during reduction division, all the alleles at different loci on one individual chromosome go off together to form a given gamete.

In cockatiels, all the sex-linked mutations occur at loci on the sex, or X chromosome, of course. Alleles at these loci do not segregate independently, because whatever alleles are on any given X chromosome are linked together. This linkage makes it easier to predict genotypes, because there are fewer possible types of gametes when loci are linked than when they are independent.

All the autosomal mutations are apparently each on different chromosomes, because as yet no linkage groups have been detected for the other mutations.

When all the loci in a linkage group always segregate together, we say that linkage is complete. However, in most sexually reproducing species, linkage is rarely complete. That is, alleles inherited from one parent do not always stay associated in the offspring. How can this happen?

The answer is by *crossover* or *recombination* (these terms mean exactly the same thing). As I discussed at the beginning of the chapter, crossover is a simple physical phenomenon: Adjacent chromosomes exchange their distal ends (tips) when they cross over, as a result of being so close together. When they exchange distal ends, all the alleles at the loci on the exchanged segments end up on the other chromosome. Thus, the genetic material on each chromosome is recombined.

We know little about crossover in cockatiels and little about the locations of the pearl, lutino and cinnamon loci on the X chromosome. If some enterprising cockatiel breeder kept careful records for dozens of matings and many generations, then we could use that data to calculate distances between these loci on the X chromosome. However, I know of no one who has such data.

We do know that you cannot necessarily predict the genotypes of chicks, even if you know the exact genotypes of the grandparents and parents at these sex-linked loci.

For example, let's take a male with one X chromosome with a cinnamon allele that he got from his mother. He gets another X chromosome from his father, and let's assume the lutino gene is on that chromosome; we know this perhaps because his mother was lutino, for example. So, we might predict that this male will produce half cinnamon daughters and half lutino daughters, if we mate him to a pure normal hen.

$X^{Lc} X^{lC}$	$X^{LC} Y$
$X^{Lc} X^{LC}$	$X^{Lc} Y$ *
$X^{lC} X^{LC}$	$X^{lC} Y$ **

* Normal-split cinnamon son, cinnamon daughter

** Normal-split lutino son, lutino daughter

If crossover occurs, this is what we get:

Hand Feeding

I start giving chicks supplemental feedings about the time I band them, when their first pinfeathers are appearing at ten to fourteen days old. Occasionally I start earlier if the last chick is much younger than the next sibling in line or if the clutch is large. I feed the youngest first, as it is the most likely to need supplemental feedings. The chicks who have the longest necks and make the loudest noises often are the ones Mom and Dad notice most.

Hand-feeding tools should be kept sterile in disinfectant—the most handy is a bleach solution, which should be made new each time it is used. Each chick should be fed using a different syringe, or the syringe should be sterilized between uses.

Time spent hand feeding is not time spent merely nourishing the chicks. This is socialization time. Think about this chick, its future and its relationship to humanity. Just as the formative years are important in the life of a child, the weeks or even days spent with a cockatiel chick are important.

I feed the chicks one at a time, talking to them as I do so. This gets them used to human speech and associates handling with the pleasant experience of being fed. I usually place the chick in a bowl, on a towel on the table, or in my lap,

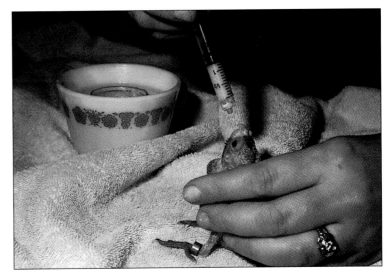

When feeding chicks, talk to them and associate being with people with being fed warm, nourishing food. *(David Wrobel)*

then hold my hand over its back. This, of course, keeps the chick in one place, but is also very important later when a full-grown bird is handled. This is not a gesture accepted by just any bird, since it is highly restrictive. I do this so that

later pet owners can pet their cockatiels down their back, can return them safely to their cages by holding their hands over the bird's back to prevent flight and can make trips to the vet easier for everyone concerned. I have had some positive

Hold older cockatiels up to your face, so they associate more of your anatomy with being fed than just the hand that feeds them.
(David Wrobel)

comments on the way my chicks accept handling, and believe this simple gesture is definitely worthwhile.

As the chicks mature and develop pinfeathers all over their body, I start holding them up to my face to get them used to that aspect of my anatomy. By this stage they beg when they see my hand enter the nest box!

Venturing Out

At about four to five weeks of age, cockatiel chicks have feathered out and they often weigh more than their parents. They don't retain that weight—it's insurance for the weight they will lose as they wean. Chicks at this age start to perch at the nest-box hole, looking out at

the world. Finally, one takes its first flight—or flop, as the case may be. Over the next three to four weeks, they will explore their enclosure and start learning to eat and drink. When a flighted chick takes off into a room, it often hovers near the ceiling, bouncing off the ceiling and walls. Apparently, landing is the hardest part of flying! Their parents still feed them, until the chicks wean.

Just before a chick is ready to leave the nestbox, I start asking it to perch on my finger as part of the hand-feeding–socialization routine. If it can perch, I get it used to scaling a ladder of fingers, one after the other. Before each attempt at perching, I make a clucking noise. It could be any noise. One friend snaps his fingers before asking his

pet, Henry, to perch. You can decide what noise to make or what word to say, as long as you are consistent. Later, when the chicks are more skittish, out of the nest and flying, they know what you want when you cluck, snap or say the appropriate word. This simple command promotes real communication between a cockatiel and its owner. The aforementioned Henry learned to fly across the room at the snap of his owner's fingers.

As a nest of cockatiel chicks matures, a few might start to bite fingers that venture into the nest box. This isn't an aggressive action, but shows that fingers mean food to them. They go right to the source, with or without a syringe. I offer spray millet in the nest box for the chicks to try their beaks on. At the point chicks become interested in other foods, some start rejecting the syringe full of hand-feeding formula. I still spend some time with these chicks, petting them down the back and having them climb up a finger ladder once or twice. Other chicks at this time hang onto their baby ways but get quite aggressive about their feedings. Some chicks climb out of their nest box and bustle towards me for feedings. They perch on the box or on a stick while I feed them and accept some caressing afterwards.

When the chicks take their first forays out of the nest box, I find that they are somewhat skittish and

Four- to five-week-old cockatiels have feathers and start to look out at the world through the nest-box hole. Finally, they start to venture out.   *(David Wrobel)*

STEPS TO RAISING TAME BABIES

Supplement feedings once a day.

Talk to the chicks while feeding them.

Hold your hand over the chick's back.

Get face to face with the chick.

Practice ladder training.

Cockatiels may become skittish and frightened as they learn new skills. If a cockatiel flies and ends up on the floor, rescue it with reassuring words. *(David Wrobel)*

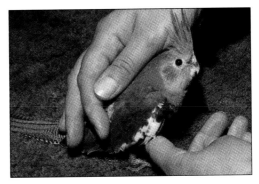

This is a good opportunity to practice the ladder, asking the cockatiel to step "up." *(David Wrobel)*

Practice "up" over and over as you raise the bird off the floor to a more comfortable level. *(David Wrobel)*

frightened. When it is time to feed these chicks I talk to them, using some of the same words I did during their earlier feeding sessions. I cluck and ask them to climb, in their slow, clumsy baby fashion, onto my finger. After a few days they accept me as the same person who got them out of the nest box. If they fly away from me, I repeatedly retrieve them and ask them to perch, by clucking and pressing against their breast, then form a ladder for them to get back to my shoulder or a perch.

Learning to eat a variety of foods at this weaning stage is important. I spread toasted oat cereal, sprouted seeds, nasturtiums, seed, frozen peas, fresh corn, hard-cooked egg, broccoli, cooked yam, seeded grasses and pellets on the bottom of the cage. I change the mixture often and vary what I offer. This is the time in a cockatiel's life when you, the breeder, are setting a pattern for what that bird will accept as food for the rest of its life. Offer variety!

People who are coming to me now for a second bird have noticed the difference in my babies since I've instituted the taming procedure I've outlined. It's not difficult. I feed baby cockatiels once in the morning. While I do so I talk to them and stroke their backs or restrain them with a hand over the back. I play the radio for my birds every day while I'm at work. When they're older we do perching exercises and they are introduced to my face. Sometimes the transition from Mom to a person is a little traumatic, but these chicks are used to being handled and adapt quickly. These chicks are everything a cockatiel can be.

Individual Differences

Despite my best efforts, cockatiels do have distinct personalities. This is often apparent even in the nest. One of my chicks absolutely refused hand feeding from the age of about two weeks on. It got the same treatment as its nestmates, but developed into a very stubborn and independent bird. Another bird was always very flighty around me, but has grown to trust its new owners—an older couple who adore the bird and give it the run of the house, a special perch and

two cages. It will run up to either new owner, but still shies from me when I visit!

The opposite is also true—some birds just like everyone. Crockotiel Dundee was the most personable baby in his clutch, always seeking affection and asking to ride around on my shoulder as I attended to the bird room in the morning. He is a tame, special bird to his new owners, too. When the breeder of my own Sunshine sold him to me, she mentioned that he was "the nice one." And so he is. More than a few visitors to my house have been smitten by his charm.

Selling Cockatiel Chicks

When baby cockatiels can eat and drink on their own and make it all the way to the top perch, they are ready for new homes. It is not as difficult to determine this as it is to trust another person with the baby you have watched grow from an ugly dinosaur into an elegant cockatiel.

Hand-fed baby cockatiels sell themselves. I usually put an ad in the newspaper to sell mine, though that does mean I receive calls at all hours and strangers come into my home.

An alternative is to offer your babies to a pet store. The advantage is that you receive all the money for them at once. You receive less

TIPS FOR PLACING A CLASSIFIED AD

Give details, including species, color and price.

Don't forget your phone number.

List appropriate hours to call.

Return calls promptly.

Be courteous.

Screen calls for genuine interest.

money (at wholesale prices), but then you don't have to bother with an ad or the hours spent with each buyer. I prefer to meet the people buying my birds, however.

While potential customers are on the phone, I assess their reason for wanting a cockatiel and how much they know about taking care of one. If they're willing to listen and learn, I don't mind if they know nothing!

I discourage people from buying cockatiels as surprise gifts. I would rather people come along and pick out their own pet.

I don't sell cockatiels to people who think birds are a money-making crop, rather than personable and intelligent pets. I don't mind if buyers breed their birds, but if their *only* motive is making a profit I do mind, especially since I know there's not much profit to be made without cutting corners on diet and veterinary bills.

Customers should leave their name, address and phone number. They will receive care information, some food, a pedigree and answers to their questions. This is Tim Berry with Bozo. (They're just modeling this step; Tim was a patient co-worker!)

When a customer comes to my house, I try to have the chicks out, away from their parents and maybe out of sight of their cage. I encourage the customer to interact with the bird and to ask questions. They usually want to know about care, life span, whether the baby's a boy or a girl and where cockatiels come from. (Not which came first, the cockatiel or the egg, but that cockatiels are native to Australia!) I show them how I clip the bird's wings and explain why I do so. I'm honest when I don't know the sex of a chick and honest about when I do. I want happy customers.

I have a buyer fill out his or her name, address and phone number in a notebook. Each page of my notebook is reserved for a clutch of cockatiels. I supply the buyer with a pedigree of the bird, including as much genetic information as I know. For example, Buzz is split to lutino and pearl; Dacey is a normal gray and wears a breeder's band.

I supply the buyer with a care sheet, an application to a cockatiel society and my local club, as well as a subscription form to my favorite avian publication. The buyer also receives a jar of the feed to which the chick is accustomed. I let the buyer know the name of a good avian vet in our area. In about two weeks I give the new owner a call. They usually have questions, and I find out the name of my baby bird.

All this attention amounts to customer service, and pays off after a few years. If you meet and exceed

your customers' needs, you will find they recommend you as a bird breeder to friends, and there will be lists for your babies so you don't need to place that classified ad. And you will have struck up the most wonderful friendships! This book would not be possible without the help of people who have bought cockatiels from me, from Carol Cottone-Kolthoff who became a cockatiel-inspired watercolorist, to Karen Gilbert who sends me welcome notes every so often about what awards "my baby" has won.

Responsibility and Potential

Cockatiels are considered easy to breed by aviculturists. That doesn't mean they are problem-free. It doesn't mean you don't have to meet their special needs. You don't just

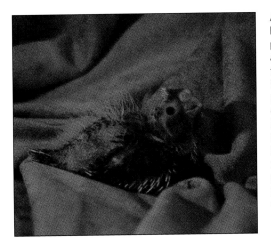

A cockatiel chick is a bundle of potential. Its pinfeathers will open and enable the bird to fly. Its breeder will socialize it to become a loving pet. Its owner will be exposed to the world of birds. The potential is being realized with each healthy chick sent out in the world. This chick grew up to be Ted, Jr. He's the spitting image of his dad!

give a pair a nest box and let them do the rest. A pair will be happy together without raising babies.

I'm glad you are learning about raising cockatiels, but I'm not the least offended if this is not for you. Cockatiels should be wanted, planned for and raised with love, and aviculture deserves responsible business people doing their best.

In this chapter I have outlined my own observations and procedures, which may vary quite a bit from what you encounter when breeding cockatiels. Our weather on California's central coast affects breeding. Procedures are different in arid areas, where birds need to be misted to be kept cool in the summer; in the basements of the Midwest, where lighting is important; and in the humid south, where food spoilage and mold are concerns.

In addition to any book on cockatiels, get to know a reputable breeder in your area who will answer your questions as you explore hobby breeding. Good places for this are the national cockatiel societies and local bird clubs, or you can ask for references from avian veterinarians and pet stores.

If you are excited about breeding cockatiels as a hobby and are ready and willing to take on all the responsibilities that accompany it, dive in! It's a wonderful experience your cockatiels will also enjoy.

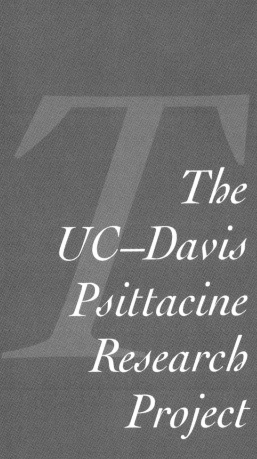

The UC–Davis Psittacine Research Project

by
Tom Roudybush, MS,
and James Millam, PhD

I n 1979 the Department of Avian Sciences at the University of California–Davis established a colony of cockatiels for research purposes. This was ground-breaking work, since this was the first project dedicated exclusively to studying the biology of psittacines (the birds in the parrot family). The faculty member most responsible for this effort was Dr. C.R. Grau, professor of nutrition. The first graduate student and the manager of the program was Tom Roudybush. In its initial stages, the project looked mainly at nutrition, management and incubation.

The program struggled for several years, but eventually established itself as a viable area of research and has stimulated the greatest student interest in the department. The project continues today with Dr. Jim Millam the professor in charge.

As with all such projects, it has yielded a number of successful experiments, but these primarily point the way for more research if we are to understand psittacines in any detail. With every answer has come many questions, and the project has focused us on what it is we need to know next.

Some of the specific material discovered in the ongoing research at UC–Davis follows. The work continues and will yield more interesting and useful results as the years pass. How useful this information is to the keeper of pet birds depends on the sophistication of the bird owner and the industry that supports pet owners. Much of the information generated has already been put to use, and without doubt much of what is generated in the future will contribute to the health and well-being of birds.

Unexpected Discoveries

Some of the successes of the project have been unexpected. For example, the work in nutrition confirmed that psittacines require the same nutrients that most other birds need, but the amounts differ in some cases and the signs of deficiency are very different. This leads us to question how representative poultry are of other birds and the usefulness of extrapolation from poultry to other birds (as is commonly done in the pet care industry).

What was once considered to be firm ground has lost some of its stability. For example, all poultry are precocial (covered with down

THE DIFFERENCE OF A FEW FEATHERS

Areas that are of no major concern in the study of precocial birds are of great concern in altricial birds. For example, water intake must be regulated by a parent or surrogate in altricial birds, while precocial birds regulate themselves from the time they hatch.

and able to move when they hatch), while the majority of birds are altricial (naked and helpless when they hatch). There may be great differences in the ways altricial and precocial birds develop as they grow, and in their nutrient requirements and the consequences of deficiencies.

A pair of cockatiels at the UC–Davis facility.

Creatures of Habit

One interesting observation about cockatiels is that they are hostages of their history. That is, they like what they are used to and respond positively to the familiar. For example, food habits are formed early and changes do not always come easily. The important issue here is that preference is not the overriding consideration in accepting a new food, but that foods outside the experience of the cockatiel are not recognized as food.

The history of the bird you purchase as a pet will determine what it needs to be fed initially. Knowing what the bird will accept and providing that food during its first days in its new home will reduce stress and ease the process of adapting to its new home.

This need for familiar things extends to breeding. When we started the Psittacine Research Project, we bred cockatiels in one-by-one-by-two-foot cages with stainless steel nest boxes. When we had relatively poor success, cockatiel breeders suggested we offer the birds more space and wood nest boxes. They reasoned that the birds needed more space and an opportunity to chew to satisfy some innate urge. We made an experiment of the change in cage size and nest-box material by setting up four groups of birds to breed. One set got large cages (one-by-two-by-four feet)

Cockatiels may not recognize a new food as something to eat. That's why it's important not to change the diet of a bird that is new to your home.

with wood nest boxes. A second group got large cages with stainless steel nest boxes, a third got small cages with wood boxes and the fourth group got small cages with stainless steel nest boxes.

The result was that the pairs of cockatiels bred best in small cages with stainless steel nest boxes. When we reviewed the experiment we found that all of the birds used in the experiment had either previously bred in small cages with stainless steel nest boxes or had been raised in small cages with stainless steel nest boxes. They bred best under familiar conditions. Again, their histories needed to be considered. This makes experimentation difficult, because it is impossible to find cockatiels that have no history to bias the experiment.

This effect of history on the behavior of cockatiels has led many breeders to make poorly supported generalizations about the behavior of cockatiels. They have correctly noted that their birds consistently act in certain ways in response to stimuli such as the availability of certain foods and the conditions of their caging during breeding. What is missing here is that the birds observed by these breeders are *their* birds, which have been raised under similar conditions, making them consistent in their responses to the conditions the breeder offers. Another bird raised by another breeder might respond differently because it is used to a different set of conditions. It is important to be aware of this phenomenon when offered advice about the behavior of

your bird. The best source of advice on your particular bird may be the breeder who raised it.

In a similar vein, there is a problem with breeding cockatiels that have been hand-raised from hatch. In one experiment with hand-raised and parent-raised cockatiels, hand-raised cockatiels had less success in breeding. This rather complex response was the result of which species the cockatiels believed raised them. For example, when the experiment began with the cockatiels being set up as pairs, the person who raised the cockatiels had to be banned from the room, because the male cockatiels he had raised courted him as a potential mate. These cockatiels imprinted on the person who raised them as the species with which they should breed. This inhibited their interactions with the female cockatiels.

The cockatiels were set up to breed twice, with an interval between the breedings. Pairs with hand-fed males showed poor success. They had low fertility, few eggs laid and few hatched. This appears to be the result of the male failing to take the aggressive lead in the pairing and nest site selection process.

As for the females, pairs with hand-fed females produced many eggs, but the outcome of this egg laying depended on the history of the male with which the hand-fed female was paired. It appears many eggs were laid by the hand-fed females because these females did not perceive the human experimenters as a threat. Pairs with parent-raised males had high fertility and more consistently laid eggs in the nest box rather than on the cage floor. Pairs with parent-raised females responded in a manner consistent with the history of the male to which the parent-raised female was paired.

During the second trial all the pairs improved their breeding performance. Pairs that were infertile became fertile and pairs that laid eggs on the cage floor laid eggs in the nest box. The fact that the rate of success improved in all pairs meant the hand-raised birds were not hopeless as breeders. They would, however, require experience to learn how to breed successfully. There is a place for hand-raised birds in a breeding program, if you are patient and allow the bird to learn the lessons needed for successful breeding.

What a Difference a Day Makes

Regardless of how cockatiels are set up for breeding, they respond quite positively to changes in day length. Day length is used by many species that live in temperate climates as a cue that spring has arrived—a change that typically signals abundant food. Although cockatiels are

considered opportunistic breeders in their native Australia, in captivity they do respond to changes in day length.

In our experiment, cockatiels were first exposed to just ten hours of light per day, or less, for several weeks. Exposure to such winterlike day lengths is important for many species to develop the ability to respond sexually to longer day lengths. Then the cockatiels were divided into two groups. All were provided with nest boxes to encourage them to breed. One group remained on short days, however, while the other group was switched to long days, generally fourteen hours or more of light per day.

The results were clear. About 90 percent of the birds with long day lengths were laying eggs within a few weeks, while in the short-day group only a small percentage laid eggs. Such photostimulation, exposing birds to short days followed by several weeks of exposure to long days, is one of the simplest prosexual environmental manipulations that can be made for birds in captivity.

Getting Eggs Off the Floor

Other research, by Scott Martin and Jim Millam, targeted how to correct a common and frustrating behavioral problem: laying eggs on

LEARNING TO NEST

We also performed the nest box preference study with sexually naive pairs.

They behaved much like the birds with histories of laying on the cage floors. Many sexually naive pairs laid first clutches in the open-sided nest boxes, then went on to lay subsequent clutches in conventional nest boxes. Again, the reverse pattern was virtually never observed.

cage floors rather than in nest boxes. In one experiment, birds with a history of laying eggs on cage floors were set up to breed with access to two types of nest boxes, one alongside the other. The nest boxes differed in only one way: The conventional box had an entrance hole two-and-a-half inches in diameter, while the open-sided nest box had a greatly enlarged entrance—essentially one entire wall was missing.

As we predicted, most birds that had histories of laying eggs on the floor now laid their eggs in the open-sided nest boxes. However, when these same pairs laid second clutches, most of them used the conventional nest boxes. The reverse pattern—first clutches laid in conventional nest boxes, second (and subsequent) clutches laid in open-sided nestboxes—was virtually never seen. Thus, the open-sided nest box served as a kind of "halfway house" for floor layers; apparently it enticed them into a nest box, and once they experienced a "partial" nest box they actually developed a preference for the conventional type.

Eggs and Incubation

Eggs from the species of birds we have examined can be stored for a period of time before incubation without any loss of viability. Optimal conditions for storage are 55°F with the highest humidity that can be maintained. Viability can also be enhanced by keeping the eggs in freezer bags and storing them at a 45-degree angle and turning them once a day. Bagging the eggs maintains their level of carbon dioxide, while turning them keeps the embryo from sticking to the shell.

Without bagging or turning, turkey eggs store for two weeks at 55°F and high humidity, chicken eggs for ten days, quail eggs for seven days and tinamou eggs for as long as six months. Cockatiel eggs store for only three days before they begin to lose viability. If cockatiel eggs are being held for artificial incubation without bagging or turning, they should be put into the incubator within three days of being laid to avoid loss of viability. Eggs that are

UC–Davis researchers have found nutrition affects both a chick's growth and its behavior. The chicks in this photo are in various stages of development, from egg to pinfeathers.

bagged and turned can be stored for six days, but the rate of hatch will decline after that.

Cockatiel eggs incubate well at 99.5°F with a wet bulb temperature of 84 to 86°F. (A wet bulb temperature is measured by a thermometer with a moist wick on the end of it. The reduction in temperature due to the water evaporation is directly related to the relative humidity in the surrounding air.) After two weeks, the dry bulb temperature should be reduced to 98.5°F and the wet bulb increased to 90°F. This change in temperature and humidity will maintain the moisture needed to lubricate the chick as it rotates within the shell during piping, thus reducing the number of chicks that stick to the shell and fail to hatch.

Nutrition and Behavior

Another series of experiments performed at UC–Davis looked at the nutritional needs of cockatiels raised by hand from hatch. In each of these experiments there were nutritional differences in what the growing birds were fed. The nutrient requirements were thus determined, but some observations were also made about the behavioral responses of chicks to dietary deficiencies.

Cockatiel chicks solicit food from their parents by begging. The behavior consists of bobbing their heads up and down and making an insistent squawking sound. The parents respond by locking beaks with the chicks and, with a pumping action, regurgitating food into

A BIRD IN THE HAND

Most parrots, including cockatiels, are either reared by their parents or by their owners, who hand feed. There are advantages to each type of rearing. Hand-reared birds are delightfully tame and make wonderful pets, but they may be sexually imprinted on humans, and hand feeding and rearing is technically difficult. In contrast, parent-reared birds are better suited for breeding purposes, but they may never be as tame as hand-reared birds.

Wendi Aengus and Lucia Arsky, working at the UC–Davis project, showed that the two methods could be fruitfully combined. Cockatiel chicks were mostly reared and exclusively fed by their parents. But during the nestling stage the chicks were removed from their nest boxes and gently handled for fifteen to thirty minutes, several times a week, after they were a few weeks old. These chicks became as tame as hand-reared chicks. And although their adult breeding performance was never determined, it is unlikely that they imprinted on humans, because they spent much less time with their human handlers than with their parents and nestmates.

the chick's mouth. When we were hand-feeding chicks that were fed a control or adequate diet in adequate amounts, begging was modest or in some cases absent. When chicks were fed a deficient diet, begging was pronounced and older chicks, two to six weeks old, constantly sought food by nibbling on anything that might be ingested.

Chicks that were fed nutrients at levels so high that their growth was inhibited rejected food. By the time they were three-and-one-half weeks old these chicks would fight being held for feeding, regurgitate the food that was fed and bite the hand that fed them.

The message here is that the adequacy of a diet fed to growing cockatiels can be approximated by the intensity of the begging response. Chicks that beg intensely are likely deficient in some nutrient or in total food intake. Should you find that you have such a feeding response, consider first whether you are feeding your birds enough total food. A chick less than three-and-a-half weeks old will often eat its body weight per day in food that is diluted to 25 percent solids and 75 percent water.

If food intake is adequate, consider whether the diet is adequate in all the nutrients we know about. For example, has the diet been used previously with good success? Does the diet contain the amounts of nutrients for which we know the requirements? Has the diet been diluted properly? Is the chick passing feces at a rate that is consistent with its size and rate of growth? If the answer is no to any of these questions, consider supplementing or changing the diet.

When to Wean?

Weaning is a misunderstood process. Studies at UC–Davis have shown that weaning is a developmental, not a learned process in cockatiels. It is inhibited by poor growth and development, but proceeds normally if the chick is provided with what it needs. We have found nutrient deficiencies during growth inhibit weaning. Other factors, such as infection, may also inhibit development and therefore weaning, but we have not documented this.

Generally, normal healthy cockatiels wean between six and seven weeks of age. If weaning occurs later, the chick is likely to have had some restricted growth. If the person hand-raising the chick waits until the developmental process is complete before offering food and water for the chick to eat on its own, weaning occurs immediately upon the presentation of food.

CHAPTER 17

Exhibiting Your Beautiful Cockatiel

You know your cockatiel is special and beautiful. Sometimes it's nice to share that beauty with a whole community of bird lovers by entering bird shows. My friends usually laugh when I tell them I go to bird shows. Maybe their mental image is the same as mine was before I knew better—birds circling a ring with their handlers, as in a dog show. Not quite!

Show birds are exhibited in special show cages, and the judge reviews their attributes on a stand with special full-spectrum lighting.

There are usually several activities held at a bird show. First there's registration, then the actual judging, then an awards banquet for exhibitors, judges and the host club. Concurrently, there is usually a sales room where you can buy birds for your own breeding program and talk to the experienced breeders who are present. Often there is some kind of raffle or drawing. Even if you don't go home with all the ribbons, you can go home with lots of prizes!

Starting Out

To start showing cockatiels, you don't need special cages, equipment or birds. You can show your pet cockatiel in the Novice division of a show, in its own cage if you want to. In the Advanced division, you must show banded cockatiels. That's for later!

It's possible to just go to a show to observe what goes on, too. If you are just going to watch, be sure to go when the judging takes place. Most judges explain why they are placing a particular cockatiel where they are, or what fault they find with the cockatiels that are not doing so well in their class. You can learn a lot about the qualities of a good show cockatiel from a good judge.

Both the American Cockatiel Society (ACS) and the National Cockatiel Society (NCS) sanction shows. They train judges, and offer a point system for a cockatiel to attain Champion or Grand Champion status over time. Their members also sell show cockatiels, and each society sells closed bands for cockatiel chicks. Either society is a good place to start when getting into exhibition with your cockatiels. Doris Wilmoth is at an ACS information booth in this photo.

Consider volunteering to help out at the show before you actually enter a bird. There's always a need for help stewarding the show (moving cages for the judges), or selling food and tickets, or cleaning up. Just jump in!

Entering the Show

When you are exhibiting cockatiels, there will be a special time to register them in the show. It may be the night before the show or early the morning of the show. You will buy show tags for each cockatiel, which should be in its own cage, and you will be given paperwork to fill out. On the tags, you include the color of the cockatiel, whether it is a male or female, its band number, the class it is in and whether it is "young" or "old." Young birds are banded with the current year's band. All other birds, whether unbanded or banded in another year, are classified as old.

You will also fill out a paper listing each bird you've brought to show. You keep one copy of this and the show secretary keeps one copy. You fasten the show tags to your cage and staple the tag shut so your name does not show (so the judges can be totally impartial).

After you have registered, you will find your section and class number in the show catalog; each section has a number corresponding to cockatiel color. Class is determined by sex and whether the bird is young or old. For example, normal gray cockatiels are shown together in one section, lutinos are shown together, cinnamons are shown together, etc. There is another separate classification for "rares," which includes many of the rare color cockatiels together.

Set up your cage in the appropriate section of the show with other cockatiels of the same color. Usually, exhibitors leave a layer of seed on the bottom of the show cage and a small water cup attached to the bars. You are going to leave your bird now for several hours.

The Judging Begins

When judging begins, several cages of cockatiels are taken up to the judge's lighted bench, and he or she evaluates them according to the written show standards. The American Cockatiel Society, the National Cockatiel Society and various parrot societies each have their own standards, and the judge uses the standards in use by the club sponsoring the show. Often the standard will be printed in the show bulletin, and it is certainly available from the national societies.

Basically, a cockatiel is judged on conformation, deportment, size and length and presentation, which

THE BEST BIRD

At some shows, but not all, there is a competition for the best bird in the show, so that the top canaries and finches and parrots and soft-bills compete with the top cockatiel for the honor of being named best bird. I never envy the judges who must make that decision, among such different and beautiful birds!

includes the cleanliness of the show cage. The judge awards a cockatiel points in each category. Judging progresses by section, and the Novices are judged separately from the Advanced exhibitors' birds. The best normal, cinnamon, pied, lutino, pearl, rare and whiteface cockatiels are chosen.

There are often awards for places within a section. For example, your cockatiel may be first in the cinnamon section, then seventh in the Novice division of a particular show, when it competes against other color birds.

The ten best Novice cockatiels are chosen as the "top bench" in that part of the show. One of the goals of showing cockatiels is to get a bird on the top bench. The ten best cockatiels are also chosen as the top bench in the Advanced division, and the top Novice bird is evaluated to see if it can be placed anywhere on the Advanced division top bench, too.

Usually the winning cockatiels are left on display for the remainder of the afternoon, with their tags now open so the owner's name is visible.

All that remains for you to do is collect your prizes, get tips from the experts for next year and enjoy the evening's banquet. The cockatiels will be allowed out of the show hall at a specific time, and your paperwork and cages will be monitored. If you placed on the top bench, your cockatiel is awarded a certain number of points towards champion or grand champion status. There are rules in each society for obtaining these titles—goals to work towards.

Finding a Show

Sound interesting? Showing birds can be a fun hobby. You can find out when a bird show will be held in your area by joining the national societies or checking show listings in a bird magazine or a bird club newsletter. Most shows are held in the fall, between September and November.

I recently interviewed a woman who has made the whole journey from pet owner to winning exhibitor, from a companion cockatiel owner to an aviary owner with seventy cockatiels. Karen Gilbert lives in the San Francisco Bay area of northern California, where she works backstage at the

long-running production of *Phantom of the Opera*. She first acquired cockatiels as pets, then became involved in exhibiting and breeding them. It could happen to you. Here's her story.

An Interview With Karen Gilbert

When did you first get interested in cockatiels?

I met my first cockatiel in 1988, while I was working for a theater company doing a production of *Gypsy*. At the time I was in my twenties. The mother of one of the little girls who was in the play thought their cockatiel Corky could be in the show; there were a number of animals in the production. Corky came to a rehearsal. It was the first time I had seen such a bird, so I had to ask what it was. Corky was not a tame bird, but when he was left in the costume room overnight, I held a mirror up to him and he said, "Hello Corky" and whistled. "What ya doin'?" was in his repertoire, too.

His owners didn't seem too interested in the bird, so I offered to take him home. They agreed, and Corky is still a member of my flock. He's about twelve years old now.

After about a month I decided to get Corky a friend. So I went to a pet store and picked out a nice lutino female, a nice bald one! At the time I didn't even know she was a female, but I was lucky and it just happened that she was. Corky and Angel are still together. They were my only cockatiels for three years, until 1991.

How were you introduced to the hobby of exhibiting birds?

I bought a whiteface cockatiel, and the woman selling the bird asked me if I would rather buy her other bird, which would be a really good show bird. Wouldn't I like to show cockatiels? I replied, "No, I don't think so!" Famous last words.

I decided I wanted one of each color cockatiel, and started purchasing them. Next I got a cinnamon white-faced and an albino. All of these were pets, too. I had a total of five cockatiels for quite a while. I became more curious about cockatiels, and joined both the National Cockatiel Society (NCS) and the American Cockatiel Society (ACS). I started to read the show reports in their bimonthly bulletins, and also enjoyed a column about showing that appeared at that time in *Bird Talk*. I already had a competitive spirit, as I used to show horses when I was a teenager.

Now I knew I wanted to show cockatiels, and decided I needed to get some better birds. I asked around about good breeders and show cockatiels. In the beginning of 1994, I purchased my first show quality cockatiels from a breeder in Florida. She sent me a cinnamon-pied male and a cinnamon-pearl-pied female. I named them Alli and Gator, since they came from Florida. I purchased a few more birds from the breeder, and I felt ready to go to my first show that fall.

That show was in October 1994 in Roseville, outside of Sacramento in California's Central Valley. I took three birds to the show, in which ninety cockatiels were entered. There were almost forty birds in the Novice division that we were in. I couldn't believe it when I placed first, second and third in Novice!

I went to the bird show banquet, where the prizes were awarded, and I got all kinds of ribbons and crystal. It was vey exciting. When I was talking to another Southern California exhibitor, she suggested coming down to San Diego for their annual bird show.

I did go to San Diego, with four cockatiels. I took the same three who had done so well in Roseville, plus a normal male, who won the Novice show. The next show was Bakersfield. This time I took six birds. My birds took the top five places in the Novice division. All this time I was collecting more ribbons and some crystal. There were plaques, as well.

In early 1995 I acquired Roudy, a gray male with show potential. At

Winning ribbons and prizes at a bird show is rewarding compensation for the time you spend caring for your cockatiels, and proof of your success. This gray hen has won a blue ribbon in her division.

my fourth bird show, he won the Novice division and moved up to the top bench. This was at a show in conjunction with America's Family Pet Show in Los Angeles. I went back to Roseville to show and this time took all ten places—the whole top bench in the Novice division. There were close to forty Novice birds.

My last show as a Novice exhibitor was in New Orleans in 1995, at the National Cage Bird Show. Exhibitors from all over the country participated. In the Novice division there were more than fifty cockatiels entered. There were almost 170 cockatiels at the show, as well as many other species. I placed second, fourth, ninth and tenth on the top Novice bench.

Where do you display your ribbons or trophies?

Most of my plaques and trophies are in the room where the babies (hopefully, future champions) are born. The plaques are on shelves of an unused bookcase. When the babies get old enough to fly, I often see them fly to the shelves and sit in front of a Best in Show plaque. They almost seem to be reading it and imagining when they will have one of their own on display.

How far do you drive to show cockatiels?

California doesn't have a lot of cockatiel shows. The farthest I've driven is Albuquerque, New Mexico, and Salt Lake City, Utah, as well as Seattle, Washington, which were all overnight trips.

How do you get the cockatiels to a show?

Usually the birds ride in their show boxes in the back of the van. I don't fly, though the birds do when the show is beyond driving distance. When I showed at the National Cage Bird Show in New Orleans, a friend flew with my birds and I took the train. They traveled in a special carrier that was sized so they couldn't hurt themselves or mess their feathers. The carrier was stowed in the overhead compartment during the flight. The plane made a stop in Dallas on the way and the compartments were opened for passengers to retrieve their belongings. Sasquatch, my silver male, saw light through the carrier and started to wolf whistle. My friend, Frank, was sitting right underneath the birds and he was given dirty looks by several women passing by to exit the plane. Frank tried to explain by exclaiming, "I've got a bird, I've got a bird!" I doubt if those women believed a bird was really wolf whistling at them.

What surprised you about showing birds—what was different than you expected?

Breeding was the big one for me. The fact that I hadn't bred the birds

Roudy and Rosebud, two of Karen Gilbert's exemplary show birds. Roudy is a normal gray male and Rosebud is a pearl hen. *(Herschel Burgin)*

I was showing was pointed out to me. At that time I still remembered showing horses, where you buy a horse, show it and breeding never enters the picture. I didn't have any idea that you couldn't just buy a bird and show it. Now there are rules that you can't buy a bird from an Advanced exhibitor and show it in the Novice division. We need to encourage more Novice exhibitors, despite the rule.

When did you start breeding cockatiels?

I started showing in the advanced division at the end of 1995. I had purchased several more cockatiels from a couple of other

A gray hen in a show cage. Show cockatiels must learn to sit on their perch and look good for a judge. They have only a few seconds to impress him! *(David Wrobel)*

breeders. The beginning of 1996, I bred my first cockatiels. Due to space limitations, I can only set up four pair at a time. That spring we had fifteen babies. I was working full time, so it was a problem to hand feed the babies. I wanted to raise hand-fed babies in order to be able to sell as pets the ones I didn't keep. I also feel that hand-fed birds are less nervous around strangers, and therefore are calmer and show better. I quickly lined up a hand-feeder through my vet's office. Later in 1996, and again in 1997, more babies were born to show.

How did your babies do in the shows?

A grey pearl hen, Lilli, one of my first babies, made the top bench at two-and-a-half months of age at the Salt Lake City show in 1996. She was my first baby on the top bench! I won my first NCS Best in Show at the same time. Lilli went on the win Best in Show at America's Family Pet Show in Los Angeles and also at the Salt Lake City show, both in 1997.

To be a Grand Champion under current NCS rules (beginning with 1996 banded birds), a bird has to have a Best in Show and seventy-five points. Those are higher standards than for pre-1996 birds, who only needed fifty points. Lilli was the first cockatiel to achieve NCS Grand Champion status under these new rules.

A few months later another of my babies, a cinnamon-pearl hen, Bayley, also became a Grand Champion with Bests in Show in Seattle and Albuquerque. I'm very proud of Lilli and Bayley. I felt bad that they had to retire. Both were only a year old when they became Grand Champions. It is an NCS rule that Grand Champions must retire, although they can still be shown at the National Cage Bird Show.

Lilli's brother, and clutch mate named Peco (a normal gray), was second in Albuquerque, Roseville and Portland, and Best in Show in San Diego.

Caiman, a cinnamon-pied male, was Best in Show in Portland. He not only won the cockatiel show, but went on to win Best in Show over every bird entered. Quite an accomplishment for a cockatiel! Caiman is the son of Alli and Gator, my first show-quality birds.

Blossom, Lilli's baby sister (hatched in July 1997), began her show career at three-and-a-half months and has made the top bench twice out of three shows.

In 1997, I showed in eightteen shows. I had nine Bests in Show, placed seventy-five birds on the top bench (at least one in each show) and made five birds Grand Champions.

What do you look for in your babies that you keep to exhibit?

I look for size and conformation when I evaluate my babies. Large heads and chests, full sweeping crests, good length, straight back line, flight feathers that don't cross—all are important in show cockatiels. I also like to know what their sex is, so I have them surgically sexed at about eight weeks of age. I try to keep female pearls, because they retain their pearls as adults.

How do you get a cockatiel ready to show?

I start by feeding a good diet all year long. A healthy bird naturally looks and acts better. A daily spray with plain water helps to condition the feathers and encourages the birds to preen.

About two months before the first show, I pull out all the tail feathers, so that they grow in fresh and beautiful. You know how cockatiel's tails can look sometimes! I don't pull flight feathers unless they are damaged.

Show box training is also important to make sure your birds are used to the box. I start by putting young birds in the show box for a short time every day, gradually increasing the time until they are comfortable spending the entire day in the box. I also practice inserting a long stick into the box (as the judge will do) to get the bird to move from perch to perch and to turn around. Some birds need a bit of time to get used to the stick, while others think it's some kind of game and play tug-of-war with the judge.

Also, some birds are naturals, standing up straight and steady for the judge, and others will do anything but stand still. I have some beautiful birds I can't show because they refuse to stay on the perch. Even the steadiest birds have days when they won't show well.

What do judges look for in show cockatiels?

Different judges seem to put importance on different things. Some like to see large, full crests, to others a straight back line is important. Most like big birds with a showy crest, and some are picky on color. One judge turned away my cinnamon with a yellow wash on his chest. You get to know what different judges are looking for and bring back cockatiels to fit their standard the next time they are judging.

What are your goals as an exhibition cockatiel breeder?

When I was a Novice exhibitor, my goals were to win ten Best Novice awards, get all ten places on the Novice bench, and win the Novice division at the National Cage Bird Show. I accomplished all but the National Show, where I placed second.

My goal as an Advanced exhibitor is to win the Kellogg's Trophy at the National Show. The Kellogg's Trophy, donated by Kellogg's feed company, is awarded to the top bird in each of fourteen divisions at the National Cage Bird Show. One of those divisions is cockatiels, and it is a highly coveted award. It means your cockatiel was the best cockatiel at a show that included exhibitors from all over the country.

Cockatiels are shown in show cages with exact standards, so that the bird and not the cage is judged. Show cages sometimes need to be painted when purchased (in standard colors), and do need to be spiffed up before each show season. *(Doris Wilmoth)*

How has your life changed since you started exhibiting cockatiels?

I've met a lot of interesting people. I've gotten to do a lot of traveling. I like to compete. It's fun to get together with everybody and talk birds. I enjoy having the babies and following their progress. I take pictures of the babies at different stages. It's hard parting with the ones I'm not keeping. I hope they all find loving homes.

This is Corky, Karen Gilbert's first pet cockatiel. She's come a long way since acquiring him, and is an accomplished exhibitor now.
(Karen Gilbert)

Has anything funny or poignant happened to you and your birds while showing?

At the end of the judging at a show in Seattle, there was a special class where everyone entered three birds that they had bred. It was called the Breeders Trio, and the birds were judged as a group. I was competing against several winning cockatiels breeders, so it was quite a thrill when my three won!

It's always great when a judge picks out one of your birds to make very positive comments about. After one of Lilli's wins, the judge commented on her perfect conformation. Another judge asked if she was for sale. It's nice to hear these things about birds you've bred.

Finding a really incredible bird where you don't expect it is nice. I went to a bird mart to purchase supplies, and saw a huge and beautiful gray-pearl hen named Rosebud. Her owner was adopting a human baby and was selling all her birds. I don't usually buy birds from a bird mart, but this bird was an exception. Rosebud went on to become a winning bird, and with her mate Roudy, she produced champion babies, including Lilli.

Since no one does these things alone, I'd like to acknowledge a couple of people who are the wind beneath our wings. Thank you to my wonderful avian veterinarian for keeping my flock in good health, and thank you to my Dad for all his help and support.

Cockatiels Enrich Our Lives

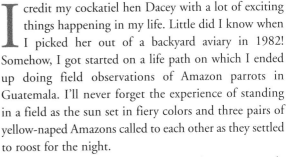

I credit my cockatiel hen Dacey with a lot of exciting things happening in my life. Little did I know when I picked her out of a backyard aviary in 1982! Somehow, I got started on a life path on which I ended up doing field observations of Amazon parrots in Guatemala. I'll never forget the experience of standing in a field as the sun set in fiery colors and three pairs of yellow-naped Amazons called to each other as they settled to roost for the night.

Sixteen years after bringing Dacey home as a study companion, I'm writing these words and she's enjoying leisure in the company of a few other cockatiels, after producing seventy chicks for me over the years. And there have been so many rich—incredibly rich—experiences in between.

I encourage you to take your interest in cockatiels as far as it will go. I will list a few of the possibilities here. You may borrow one or create your own. Your interest may involve teaching your own cockatiel tricks, including birds in your other hobbies, teaching other owners about bird care or contributing regularly to a conservation or research program.

Cockatiels in Your Neighborhood

Sharing cockatiels with your community is a rewarding experience. I have often taken cockatiels into classrooms and public libraries. I line kids up in rows and we pass a cockatiel down the row. That is often the first experience a child has with being that close to a bird. When I visited a senior center and an Alzheimer's day-care facility with

157

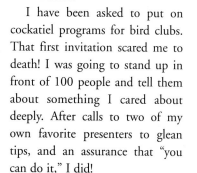

Doris Wilmoth is sharing her love of cockatiels with attendees at Bird Mart in Pomona, California. Your love of cockatiels may be so great that you choose to share it.

Consider joining a bird club in your area. It may be that more than just cockatiels will come into your life! This is Pat Fauth wearing her bird club T-shirt, with her blue and gold macaw.

my birds, I learned from participants what part their own pet birds played in their lives. It's hard to say whose experience was more rewarding after a program like that. Getting in touch with a program director or a school administrator is all it takes.

I have been asked to put on cockatiel programs for bird clubs. That first invitation scared me to death! I was going to stand up in front of 100 people and tell them about something I cared about deeply. After calls to two of my own favorite presenters to glean tips, and an assurance that "you can do it," I did!

It has led to an inner journey and several actual journeys by car and plane on the West Coast and in the Southwest. Sharing cockatiels with bird clubs has been fun. As with many things in life, teaching programs about cockatiels has inspired me to learn more, to dig up some facts and to keep an eye out for good points to share.

The Bird Community

Having companion cockatiels and participating in—or in my case, starting—a bird club means having many social experiences. In a bird club, we are brought together by our love of birds, not by our common training, economic or social level or family heritage. We are diverse, interesting and motivated.

HOBBIES

For me, including cockatiels in my other hobbies means writing and photography. I own a small business now, selling the offspring of my cockatiels from home and selling bird products at bird fairs. That's been an adventure! I have whole new sets of skills and ways to earn income. For you, an adventure including cockatiels may be designing cockatiel needlepoint, surfing the Internet or collecting bird stamps. If you love to travel, maybe you'll plan a trip to Australia. If you like to build things, perhaps you'll begin work on a new aviary out back. Maybe that aviary will be in a retirement community or new housing development, or at the local zoo. Go for it!

There's probably a club near you. If there isn't, you can start one.

Owning cockatiels has opened up the whole world of exotic birds to me. I started attending seminars and national conventions. These are great opportunities to learn more about birds and to share with others touched by the love of birds. I have developed friendships with people all over the country. At one national convention I met someone very involved in bird care and education in Virginia. It turned out my new friend was my father's Army buddy in the '50s!

Do you yearn to see cockatiels when you're on vacation? The children's zoo at the San Diego Zoo in San Diego, California, includes a roomy cockatiel exhibit.

Make a Difference

There are many ways to make a difference. Some will attract you more than others, but do go ahead and make a difference. You don't have to own an expensive, exotic bird to be involved in cockatiel or parrot rescue, to send contributions to conservation organizations, to serve a national organization or to hold an event to benefit avian medical research. Who knows where your activism will lead? When I offered my services to researchers at the cockatiel colony at the University of California–Davis, somehow I ended up in that field in Guatemala.

My point is that you did not do a small thing when you acquired your companion cockatiel. Love it, care for it and be open to what comes along. I have

two more stories for you, which show that cockatiels can make a difference in our lives at any age.

Retirement Is for the Birds

What sort of hobby would you engage in following a successful acting career? Garry Walberg, in his seventies and still auditioning

for roles, keeps aviaries of birds. You may recognize Garry as Lieutenant Monahan on the *Quincy* TV series, which ran for seven years. He subsequently was a regular in *Speed* and *The Odd Couple*, and put in a few appearances on *Gunsmoke* and *Lassie*.

After keeping horses for a while on their 1⅛-acre lot north of L.A., Garry and his wife, Flo, decided to "get a couple of birds." They found

Garry and Flo Walberg have a new hobby in retirement. They raise birds and sell their chicks at Bird Mart, along with perches that Garry designed.

BIRDS IN A MONTESSORI CLASSROOM

by Jo Miller-Cole

The little boy was overheard talking to his mother as they looked at the classroom cockatiel, Brady. "Now mother, don't stare at him or make fun of him! He's lost his toes but he can still do everything. He just can't climb real good."

Brady had been found outside in a Wisconsin winter. He lost most of his toes to frostbite, and after a series of family emergencies, his new family placed him in a Montessori classroom. Far from being the poor crippled bird, he has made a major impression on his fellow classmates.

A Montessori classroom must have nature brought into it for the child to interact with. We have in the past and continue to endanger our environment; therefore, we must educate children to respect the laws of nature. Young children in a Montessori school study botany, zoology and land forms as early as the preschool level. This is an integral part of the Montessori curriculum. They not only learn about the classifications of plants and animals, but also about the care of living things.

As a serious aviculturist, as well as a Montessori administrator--director for many years, I have been able to bring to my classes a sincere love of and respect for birds and other living things. Although we have had canaries, parakeets, finches and lovebirds, it's the cockatiels that have excited the children the most. Many of our children had never had the opportunity to come so close to birds and were surprised at the interaction they could have with them. And what a great surprise when a cockatiel said, "Ring the bell."

One cockatiel, named Squeaky, was always out of his cage watching the class. He didn't want the children to touch him, but he would edge as close to them as he could to see what they were doing. Squeaky is no longer in the classroom, however. After spending the summer months with one of our families, they couldn't bear to part with him.

Another cockatiel used to sit at the phonics table on an assistant's shoulder. The children had to be very quiet while waiting their turn, or the bird would choose to leave. When I brought a clutch of cockatiel babies to school, the children were delighted. I showed them a diagram of the digestive tract and other organs. While showing them how to hand feed the babies, you could have heard a pin drop.

Sometimes, the birds have forced me to give unplanned presentations. When Mary, our canary, laid an egg in the elementary classroom, the children were ecstatic. They thought they were going to have a baby bird. I had to explain that this was not possible, as she had no mate. Seeing how disappointed they were, I decided to get her a mate and nesting accessories. The clerk at the pet store sold me Harry. My next unplanned presentation was that everyone makes mistakes. The overflowing nest of countless eggs were laid by two females!

In trying to save face, the following year I bought another canary, this time from a breeder. Everything looked good for a while, but the eggs didn't hatch because they were infertile. A second try produced the same results. The children not only learned about patience, but about accepting disappointment. And I learned that just because I had successfully bred cockatiels, Amazons and mini-macaws, I needed to know a lot more about breeding canaries to attempt it again.

Having birds in the classroom, as well as other animals, does more than just educate children about their behavior and care. They serve as a part-time caregiver for a child who just needs a few moments of quiet time with something calming to watch, a few moments of coming closer to nature or a time-out from his or her other activities.

One student who came to us with low self-esteem and a problem with self-control has been helped by a little finch named Finchy. He changes the water, food and paper daily. He beams with pride every morning after his job is finished. He feels good about himself, and a child who feels good about himself will meet with success. He is on the road to becoming one with the universe. This bond between child and living creature has given him a mission in life.

Before putting birds in a classroom, there needs to be serious thought and preparation. A cage can't be placed just anywhere. It is the responsibility of the teacher to be sure the cage is in a safe area away from drafts and windows that could be opened or perhaps let in too much sunlight. It's best to place the cage in a quiet area and in a space where the staff can always observe it. Also, plants in the classroom have to be checked to be sure they are safe for birds.

If you have a bird that will be allowed out of the cage, be sure there are no electrical wires that can be chewed on or any sharp objects, or a sink or a fish aquarium nearby that the bird could fly or fall into.

Before introducing the bird to the classroom, the children should be advised as to what they can and cannot do around the bird. Although a lot depends on the particular bird, children have to be warned of the dangers that poking pencils, fingers or other objects in the cage can incur. After getting the bird, be sure to keep its wings clipped so it doesn't escape if someone is careless and leaves a door or window open.

Unlike fish in aquariums, birds need to be taken care of over weekends and breaks. Be sure there is someone who is willing to do this or to take the bird home. If having a bird as a permanent resident is not feasible, there are bird enthusiasts who would be glad to bring a bird or birds for show and tell.

Birds make a delightful addition to a classroom. I can't imagine a class without one. They are a wonderful teaching tool. Children learn to respect and appreciate life. And, of course, as with any living thing, sometimes we learn about death. We live in a real world, so we must expose a real world to our children. Nature is education.

out about a breeder selling all his English budgie stock and equipment, so for $1,000 they bought a complete setup. When they purchased a Rottweiler puppy from someone who also bred birds, cockatiels and lovebirds were added to their collection.

The horse barn was available, so Garry, who is quite handy, converted it into aviaries. Aviary wire was used to enclose the stalls, and appropriate feeders and feeder stations were fashioned. During the course of designing the aviaries, Garry came up with many innovations and paid special attention to cleanliness. Water bottles have a sloping roof over them so they do not become contaminated by droppings. A sponge to clean dishes is a designated bird sponge. Garry devised a wire holder for cuttlebone and special oak perches to hang on the walls of his aviaries.

So that he is sure he has serviced every aviary, Garry has a system of placing a nail connected to a string into a hole to mark it as finished. With so many aviaries to service, and the importance of daily care, that seemed like a good idea.

When it was time to expand, Garry also converted a former paddock into an aviary, using materials

Garry houses his cockatiels in aviaries converted from a former horse barn.

Garry Walberg with Squeaky.

two hours with his charges, Garry developed a special bond with Squeaky, a gray male. Squeaky's beak was slightly deformed, but he was able to eat and definitely had a winning personality.

Although he lives in an aviary with many other cockatiels, he still flies to Garry and they enjoy a special relationship. For a while Squeaky was a free-flying pet, coming home to roost. Neighbors pointed out the presence of hawks in the area, however, so Squeaky is safely confined to his aviary now.

at hand. It is a handsome structure, with one wall that folds up or down to shield the birds inside from wind. There is a central service aisle, skylights and an entry containing a brick floor and plants. The emphasis is on convenience rather than frills. An old frying pan hanging on the wall of the service isle is marked "bird bath." A radio plays soothing music.

Garry's aviary duties start at twenty minutes to eight every morning, and chores last until 1 P.M. Did anyone say retirement? Garry admits he could putter

around all day in the aviaries! He enjoys watching the birds and their habits. He knows most of them by their parenting abilities, their lineage or special characteristics. One top-producing cockatiel hen has especially large babies in a variety of color mutations. The birds are colony bred in large aviaries with several pairs. Two males are caring for the babies of one hen in the largest cockatiel flight.

Garry became a hand feeder during his first breeding season when some cockatiel chicks were not being fed properly. Up every

A cockatiel chick. This is the end, but it is also the beginning of your own story. Enjoy!   (Nancy Kasten)

Appendix A

(Nancy Kasten)

Resources for Learning More About Birds

As far as birds are concerned, it's very appropriate to say, "You've come a long way, baby!" There has been tremendous advancement in aviculture, avian medicine, bird-keeping and conservation awareness over the last fifteen years. We benefit from that progress daily. Our birds receive better care and better diets, and we receive better support from the veterinary and avicultural communities. This has been accomplished, for the most part, through the personal dedication of leaders in the bird world, private funds and support from the avian community.

Some current avian issues deal with technology in our changing world. Such innovations as DNA research and the popularization of the World Wide Web have affected how we keep and breed exotic birds in this country, and the ways in which we interact with each other.

I can't resist looking forward. It would be hard to guess what amazing technological advances will influence us in the next century. With computers operated by voice commands, what will we find out about parrot intelligence? What mischief will our birds get into?! Will there be laser surgery for birds? What will we learn about care and diet as our birds get older? Will the cage become obsolete as we set up *habitats* and *environments* for birds?

My guess is we will hear more about birds in the media—radio and TV programmers will acknowledge they are the third most popular pet. There will be more attention paid to arrangements for caring for birds that need to be placed because their owners can no longer keep them. Education about bird care and the love of birds will extend to our youngest and oldest citizens, with educational programs in schools and senior centers.

I think there will also be more support out there for bird owners, through care and behavior resources in local communities. Birds in our care and in the wild will continue to be influenced by what people do, from legislation to development to population size to our care of the environment and the world's resources.

What else? That's probably up to you—the people who love birds and support the organizations and programs *creating* the future!!

Accommodations

Pets are not welcome everywhere, but Motel 6 will usually be able to accommodate both you and your avian companion. For reservations and information, call (800) 4MOTEL6.

Check ahead when traveling to major amusement parks for on-site boarding facilities.

Adoption Centers/Programs

It isn't only cute, cuddly baby birds who need homes. Sometimes circumstances prevent people from keeping pet birds. There are an increasing number of adoption programs where you can adopt a bird in need, or where you can donate a bird you can no longer keep. In your area, ask local veterinarians and club members for a referral. Requirements vary, and programs range from privately run centers to services offered by a bird club.

CALIFORNIA

Bird Adoption Center (Sacramento area)
(530) 295-1052

Bird Adoption Center (Livermore area)
Vivian Daoust at (510) 443-6802
Avivian@aol.com

Capitol City Bird Society Adopt a Bird Committee
(916) 722-4604

EarthAngel Parrot Sanctuary
1300 Midvale Ave. #409
Los Angeles, CA 90024
(310) 477-3116 or (310) 823-2600

Mickaboo Cockatiel Rescue, (MCR)
P.O. Box 1631
Pacifica, CA 94044
(415) 869-4049
jellin419@aol.com

Parrot Education & Adoption Center
P.O. Box 34501
San Diego, CA 92163
(619) 232-2409 (phone and fax)

West Los Angeles Bird Club Adoption Committee
(310) 820-4717

COLORADO

Rocky Mountain Society of Aviculture
(303) 237-2011

FLORIDA

Feathered Friends Adoption Program
4751 Ecstasy Circle
Cocoa, FL 32926
(407) 633-0483 or (407) 725-8703

ILLINOIS

Greater Chicago Cage Bird Club
(847) 305-9609

MASSACHUSETTS

Boston Cockatiel Society, Inc.
(617) 734-6258

MICHIGAN

Bird Sanctuary (Detroit)
(313) 291-5793

NEBRASKA

Greater Omaha Cage Bird Society
(402) 496-4130 or (402) 339-0054
costantinou@delphi.com

NEVADA

Reno Area Avian Enthusiasts (RAAVE)
P.O. Box 10393
Reno, NV 89510-0303
(702) 825-2770

NEW JERSEY

Nancy's Parrot Sanctuary
37 Broadway
Belle Mead, NJ 08502
(908) 359-9940 (phone and fax)

NEW YORK

Big Apple Bird Association
(212) 714-7793

Greater Rochester Hookbill Association
Placement Committee
(716) 328-7725

Long Island Feather Enthusiasts
Adoption Committee
(516) 543-2017

Long Island Parrot Society
(516) 957-1100

PENNSYLVANIA

Adopt-A-Bird (Doylestown)
(215) 348-7423

York Area Pet Bird Club of Pennsylvania
(717) 993-2888

TEXAS

Dallas Cage Bird Society Project
HAVEN Committee
(214) 323-1074

UTAH

Best Friends Animal Sanctuary
Kanab, UT 84741
(801) 644-2001

Wasatch Avian Education Society (WAES)
P.O. Box 540753
North Salt Lake, UT 84054
(801) 825-5497

Avian Research

The Alex Foundation
Department of Ecology & Evolutionary Biology
University of Arizona
Tucson, AZ 85721

International Avian Research
Foundation, Inc. (IARF)
480 East Broad Street, Suite 113
Athens, GA 30603
(706) 353-7898 or fax (706) 613-0117

Psittacine Research Project
Department of Animal Sciences
University of California
Davis, CA 95616

Aviaries

Kaytee Avian Education Center
585 Clay Street
Chilton, WI 53014

Loro Parque
38400 Puerto de la Cruz
Tenerife, Canary Islands
Spain

National Aviary
Allegheny Commons West
Pittsburgh, PA 15212

Tracy Aviary
589 East 1300 South
Salt Lake City, UT 84105

Certification Programs

Birdkeeping is a popular agricultural practice on small farms, in basements, spare rooms and garages all over the country. In the last few years, certification programs have been developed that set certain standards of care and professionalism. An aviary can be certified through the Model Aviculture Program (MAP). You can be assured of a certain level of husbandry and professionalism by buying birds from a MAP-certified facility. There are some zoos that recognize the program and work only with MAP-certified facilities. For more information, write MAP, P.O. Box 1657, Martinez, CA 94553.

Bird breeders and retailers have been able to take certification courses offered by the Pet Industry Joint Advisory Council (PIJAC). These courses deal with the care, handling and health of birds, and are offered in conjunction with pet industry trade shows and at bird conventions all over the country. People who have passed the course are called Certified Avian Specialists (CAS). You may purchase the workbooks from this course through PIJAC. For more information, call (202) 452-1525 or (800) 553-7387. Or write to PIJAC, 1220 19th Street, N.W., Suite #400, Washington, D.C. 20036.

Bird Behaviorists

Right up there with the most important advancements over the past few years is the recognition of bird behaviorists, the accessibility of behaviorists in more areas of the country and new information about bird behavior. Some of the species we keep have only been available as pets within this decade, so we are learning how to live with them. Birds are adapted to different lifestyles than our canine and feline pets, and having resources for dealing with this is important.

Understanding behavior is also important so that a bird and owner can develop a long-term, satisfying relationship. Many birds are given up because owners did not take the time to work out problems or understand their pet's behavior. If you think about it, it's quite an accomplishment to live with an animal designed to forage for food, broadcast seed on the forest floor, fly miles daily, have complex social interactions and specific breeding behaviors that include chewing wood and regurgitating to the object of their affection! It is understandable to seek help with these matters and I encourage you to find a behaviorist, join a bird club or attend a seminar for exposure to the basics of bird behavior. You may also subscribe to a publication devoted to bird behavior, the *Pet Bird Report*, 2236 Mariner Square Drive, #35, Alameda, CA 94501, or call (510) 523-5303.

Conservation

Often bird ownership opens up a whole new world. As you explore resources about your bird, you might become aware of the conditions of its wild cousins and take an interest in bird conservation. Many (but not all) of our birds come from developing countries in the tropics. Other species might be rare in aviculture in the United States, but are abundant in their native lands and considered pests. The opposite is also true. Aviculturists in this country raise a stable population of scarlet-chested parakeets and Gouldian finches, both of which are endangered in their homelands.

Birds in their native habitat are only a part of a whole ecosystem, and often require it all to thrive. They also require the support of local people and government recognition of the value of conserving habitats and/or species. Some birds are native to countries where their human neighbors have concerns such as minimal wages, their children's health and schooling and even the stability of the government. Bird conservation is not a simple issue!

The great thing about birds is their flashy color and personality. Often they are a flagship species for conservation in a region. Conservation takes many forms. Some conservation organizations concentrate on saving habitat. RARE Center mounts successful educational campaigns in island countries to promote pride in native species and to involve the government in legislation and creation of reserves. They are also willing to tackle some of the social issues, creating the opportunity for jobs and encouraging social responsibility through family planning.

Conservation in native habitats often starts with assessing a bird's current status. Field biologists specialize in this discipline. We often don't know much about the wild populations of species kept as pets. Various measures, from supplying nest boxes to educational campaigns, are often next steps after the factors affecting population are actually recorded.

Conservation sometimes takes the form of release back to the wild. This has been a dream, with many complications to its success with parrots, who need to be taught about predators and food sources.

In the United States, conservation consists of conserving species through captive breeding. What is involved is studbooks, national associations and individual, motivated aviculturists taking responsibility for the future of certain species.

Any part you take in conservation will be appreciated. You might fly somewhere exotic to count birds, financially support a conservation organization, or take up responsible breeding of an endangered species. Whatever you choose to do, it will enrich your life and offer a whole new world to the next generation of bird owners.

Center for the Study of Tropical Birds, Inc.
218 Conway Dr.
San Antonio, TX 78209-1716
(800) 858-CSTB or fax (210) 828-9732

Loro Parque Fundacion
38400 Puerto de la Cruz
Tenerife, Canary Islands
Spain
34-22-374081 or fax 34-22-375021

RARE Center for Tropical Conservation (a nonprofit, volunteer organization dedicated to the conservation of endangered tropical wildlife and its habitats)
1616 Walnut Street, Suite 911
Philadelphia, PA 19103
(215) 735-3510 or fax (215) 735-3515

World Parrot Trust
USA Active Members Group
P.O. Box 341141
Memphis, TN 38184
(901) 873-3616 (phone and fax)
cwebb@wspl.wspice.com

World Parrot Trust
Glanmor House
Hayle, Cornwall,
TR27 4HY, United Kingdom
01736 753365 or fax 01736 756438

Dining

Can you imagine anything nicer than dining while beautiful birds swoop overhead?
www.rainforestcafe.com

Disaster Preparedness

There is a thirty-page brochure for pet owners listing thirty-five resource agencies. It is available for five dollars, which includes shipping. Make your check or money order payable to Diana Guerrero. Send to: Ark Animals, P.O. Box 1154, Escondido, CA 92033-1154; (800) 818-7387.

Educational Opportunities

American Federation of Aviculture
P.O. Box 56218
Phoenix, AZ 85079-6218
(602) 484-0931 or fax (602) 484-0109

Association of Avian Veterinarians
Avicultural Conferences
AAV Conference Office
2121 South Oneida St., Suite 325
Denver, CO 80224
(303) 756-8380

Bird Seminars
P.O. Box 51247
Pacific Grove, CA 93950

Canadian Parrot Symposium
108 Meadowvale Rd.
West Hill, Ontario
M1C 1S1, Canada
(416) 282-7375 or fax (416) 282-8995

International Aviculturist's Society
P.O. Box 2232
LaBelle, FL 33975
(941) 674-0321 or fax (941) 675-8824

Mardi Gras Avicultural Conference
Dr. Greg Rich
3610 West Esplanade
Metairie, LA 70002

Parrot Education and Adoption Center
Call Bonnie Kenk at (619) 232-2409

The Training Center offers a correspondence course in professional bird training techniques
647 West Harvard St.
Glendale, CA 91204.

Lost Pets

To enroll with AKC Companion Animal Recovery (yes—this is for birds, too) there is a one-time fee of nine dollars per pet. For appropriate forms, or to report a lost or found pet, contact AKC Companion Animal Recovery, (800) 252-7894, fax (919) 233-1290 or e-mail found@akc.org. Write to: Companion Animal Recovery, 5580 Centerview Drive, Suite 250, Raleigh, NC 27606-3394.

National/International Bird Societies

American Cockatiel Society
9527 60th Lane North
Pinellas Park, FL 34666
http://www.acstiels.com

American Federation of Aviculture
P.O. Box 56218
Phoenix, AZ 85079-6218
(602) 484-0931 or fax (602) 484-0109

International Aviculturist's Society
P.O. Box 2232
LaBelle, FL 33975
(941) 674-0321 or fax (941) 675-8824

National Cockatiel Society
P.O. Box 1363
Avon, CT 06001-1363

Rainforest Action Network
or the Protect-an-Acre Program
450 Sansome St., #700
San Francisco, CA 94111
(415) 398-4404 or fax (415) 398-2732
AMAZONIA@ran.org or http://www.ran.org/ran/

World Parrot Trust
USA Active Members Group
P.O. Box 341141
Memphis, TN 38184
(901) 873-3616 (phone and fax)
cwebb@wspl.wspice.com

World Parrot Trust
Glanmor House
Hayle, Cornwall
TR27 4HY, United Kingdom
01736 753365 or fax 01736 756438

Pet Loss Support Hotlines

Companion Animal Association of
Arizona
(24 hours)
(602) 995-5885

Delta Society Pet Grief Support Program
in Seattle, Washington
(512) 227-4357

Grief Recovery Institute
(800) 445-4808
University of California–Davis
(M–F 6:30–9:30 P.M. PST)
(916) 752-4200

Tufts University Pet Loss Support Hot Line
(Tuesday and Thursday, 6:00–9:00 P.M. EST)
(508) 839-7966

University of Florida
(904) 392-4700, ext. 4080

Pet Sitters

National Association of Professional Pet Sitters
1200 G Street, NW, Suite 760
Washington, D.C. 20005
(800) 296-PETS or fax (202) 393-0336
http://www.petsitters.org

Pet Sitters International
418 East King Street
King NC 27021
(910) 983-9222
Pet sitter referrals: (800) 268-7487

Poison Control Center

ASPCA/National Animal Poison Control Center,
1717 Philo Rd., Suite 36
Urbana, IL 61801
(800) 548-2423 or (900) 680-0000

Posters

The poster Cockatiel Embryonic Development shows fifteen stages of cockatiel embryonic development, an embryonic mortality curve and information on optimal incubation conditions. Request by title and number 21504 from ANC Publications, University of California, 6701 San Pablo Ave., Oakland, CA 94608-1239.

Radio Programs

PetTalk America
P.O. Box 9786
Bakersfield, CA 93389

Therapy and Assistance Animals

The Delta Society recognizes that the presence of animals in the lives of people who are ill or troubled helps to improve healing. Their Pet Partners Program trains volunteers and screens their pets for visiting animal programs. These kinds of programs are standard practice in many nursing homes and a growing number of hospitals, helping both children and adults. Animal-assisted therapy is incorporated as part of the treatment program for depression, attention deficit hyperactivity disorders, head injuries, speech disorders and many other conditions.

There are twenty-five birds currently registered as pet partners. Some of the participants are an African grey parrot owned by Ken McCort in Ohio, a former fighting cock named Elvis and a cockatiel owned by Claudette Greenwall of Mississippi.

If you are interested in participating in Pet Partners with your pet bird, a training course is required. This can be either a one-and-a-half-day workshop and pet test or through home study. A newsletter keeps participants up to date. Your pet would be evaluated by a local trainer for suitability for the program. Areas important to bird partners are being comfortable traveling, interest in jewelry, tolerating strange behavior and large groups (the claustrophobia quotient) and a willingness to be passed from person to person.

Training for health care professionals and educators offers guidance on the applications of animal-assisted therapy to ensure safe and effective programs, accurate documentation and evaluation, and successful risk management and infection control. For more information, call the Delta Society at (800) 869-6898 or write 289 Perimeter Road East, Renton, WA 98055-7329; (206) 226-7357 or fax (206) 235-1076.

Television

The Pet Department
fX Studios
212 Fifth Avenue
New York, NY 10010
(212) 802-4000

Travel (Ecotours)

Explorations, Inc.
27655 Kent Road
Bonita Springs, FL 34135
(800) 446-9660 or (941) 992-9660

Holbrook Travel
3540 NW 13th Street
Gainesville, FL 32609
(800) 451-7111 or fax (904) 371-3710

Water

If you cannot trust your water supply after a disaster, there is a way to treat the water. Chlorinate a gallon of tap water by adding six to ten drops of bleach. Shake it up and let it sit for one hour. Then add 500 milligrams of a vitamin C tablet that you have crushed up. Make sure it dissolves. This will dechlorinate the water.

For more information about drinking water, contact Dr. William Cooper, Drinking Water Research Center, Florida International University, Miami, FL 33199; (305) 348-2826 or fax (305) 348-3894.

Videos

Pet AVision, Steve and Linda Malarkey
P.O. Box 102
Morgantown, WV 26507-0102
(800) 521-7898

Video on Alex, the African Grey Parrot
Avian Publications
P.O. Box 120607
St. Paul, MN 55112
(612) 571-8902

Bibliography

Books

Avian Medicine: Principles and Application, Ritchie, Harrison and Harrison, Wingers Publishing, 1994.

Cockatiel Handbook, Allen, Dr. Gerald, and Allen, Connie, TFH Publications, 1978 and 1981.

Cockatiels: A Complete Introduction, Radford, Elaine, TFH Publications, 1987.

The Complete Bird Owner's Handbook, Gallerstein, DVM, Gary A., Howell Book House, 1994.

The Complete Cockatiel, Vriends, Dr. Matthew M., Howell Book House, 1983.

Encyclopedia of Cockatiels, Smith, George A., TFH Publications, 1978.

Experiences With My Cockatiels, Moon, Mrs. E.L., TFH Publications, 1980.

Guide to a Well-Behaved Parrot, Athan, Mattie Sue, Barron's Educational Series, 1993.

Molecular Systematics and Biogeography of the Cockatoos (Psttauformes: Cacatuinae), Brown, David M., Master's Thesis, University of California–Davis, 1997.

My Parrot, My Friend, Doane, Bonnie Munro, Howell Book House, 1994.

Parrot Incubation Procedures, Jordan, Rick, Silvio Mattacchione and Co., 1989.

Parrots of the World, Forshaw, Joseph M., Illustrated by William T. Cooper, TFH Publications, 1977.

Parrot Training Handbook, Warshaw, Jennifer, Parrot Press, 1996.

Magazines

Greeson, Linda, "Show Cockatiels," *Bird Talk,* Fancy
  Publications, April 1997.

Thompson, Dale R., "Mutations," *The AFA
  WATCHBIRD*, September 1982.

Index